FINANCIAL FREEDOM

FINANCIAL FREEDOM

A Proven Path to All the Money You Will Ever Need

GRANT SABATIER

Foreword by Vicki Robin

Avery

AVERY

an imprint of Penguin Random House LLC
375 Hudson Street
New York, New York 10014

Text copyright: © 2019 by Millennial Money LLC

Most Avery books are available at special quantity discounts for bulk purchase for sales promotions, premiums, fund-raising, and educational needs. Special books or book excerpts also can be created to fit specific needs. For details, write SpecialMarkets@penguinrandomhouse.com.

Library of Congress Cataloging-in-Publication Data
[Insert CIP TK]

Printed in the United States of America
1   3   5   7   9   10   8   6   4   2

This publication is designed to provide accurate and authoritative information in regard to the subject matter covered. It is sold with the understanding that the publisher is not engaged in rendering legal, accounting, or other professional services. If you require legal, financial advice or other expert assistance, you should seek the services of a competent professional.

Dedication TK

For things to reveal themselves to us, we need to be ready to abandon our views about them.

—Thich Nhat Hanh

Live for today, remember yesterday, plan for tomorrow.

—fortune cookie

CONTENTS

FOREWORD BY VICKI ROBIN   1

1. MONEY IS FREEDOM
How I Went from $2.26 to $1 Million in Five Years   5

2. TIME IS MORE VALUABLE THAN MONEY
Why You Can and Should "Retire" Early   19

3. WHAT IS YOUR NUMBER?
(It's Probably Less Than You Think)   36

4. WHERE ARE YOU NOW?
Getting Clarity on Your Finances   78

5. NEXT-LEVEL MONEY
How to Build Wealth Quickly   95

6. IS IT WORTH IT?
11 Ways to Think About Money Before You Buy Anything   122

7. THE ONLY BUDGET YOU'LL EVER NEED
How to Live for Free and Increase Your Savings Rate at Least 25%   142

8. HACK YOUR 9-TO-5
Use Your Full-Time Job as a Launching Pad to Freedom   157

9. MORE MONEY IN LESS TIME
How to Start a Profitable Side Hustle   179

10. **THE SEVEN-STEP FAST TRACK INVESTMENT STRATEGY**
Accelerate Your Moneymaking Money!   210

11. **REAL ESTATE INVESTING**
How to Turn $10,000 into Millions Using Other People's Money   263

12. **MORE THAN ENOUGH**
How to Live Off Your Investments for the Rest of Your Life   287

13. **THE FUTURE OPTIMIZATION FRAMEWORK**
Daily, Weekly, Monthly, Quarterly, and Annual Habits   300

14. **LIVING A RICHER LIFE**
A Path to Financial Independence   311

Acknowledgments   319

Glossary   321

Notes   329

Index   333

FOREWORD

What do you do for a living?"

Before the Industrial Revolution, most people raised or foraged food, fiber, and fodder from the land. Farmers had to be jacks and jills of all trades, masters of all the technologies needed to survive, and they worked in clans and tribes to thrive together.

Since the Industrial Revolution, we have answered the above question with our jobs—from mining to management. We said, "I am a miner, a secretary, a teacher, a factory worker, a CEO." Our jobs were our identities and our workplaces, our tribes. The union movement provided a balance of power to the corporation's focus on the bottom line, and our jobs also became our retirement planning and healthcare. Stultifying perhaps, but secure.

In the last decade, though, major forces have exerted pressure on the building blocks of this middle-class existence, and the promise of half a century—that every generation will be better off than the last—has landed somewhere in the rubble.

"What do you do for a living?"

You can no longer answer with a profession or a role. To make it, you'll need every tool in this book's toolbox for piecing together a work life that is lucrative as well as balanced.

Grant Sabatier was out of money and living back with his parents when he woke up to the fact that "Job Charming" wasn't coming to save him. He was drifting and knew he would drown if he didn't change direction.

Enlightenment can come from a cold hard look at reality. In today's vernacular, Grant got "woke."

He figured out how to make money through all the legal and ethical opportunities in front of him, and with each step he saw more ways to make money until he went, step by step, from broke to millionaire to financially independent in a little over five years.

Grant's genius is on full display in the entrepreneurial attitudes and strategies in this practical, fiercely focused book. You may be attracted to the glitter of getting a lot richer a lot faster than you ever thought possible, but I invite you to consider that it's not so much about the money you will make in the next year or two following Grant's approach, but rather about the capacity to make money for the rest of your life no matter what the economic, financial, or investment landscape offers you. We don't know if robots will clean your house or your version of Alexa (whatever that becomes) not only orders groceries but beats you at poker and sympathizes with you after a tough day. We do know that every human will need to capture the emerging opportunities to get what they need. We will all need this alert relationship with making money.

You can regard the contingent or gig or on-demand nature of jobs as a blessing or curse, but on a practical level you will need to adapt.

Grant's bigger point, though, is that making a lot of money isn't the point. Time is. Time for love, for learning, for caring, for playing, for contributing to others—that's what you are buying through becoming an effective and efficient earning machine. You can weight your big earning years, as he did, into your twenties and invest as much as possible into moneymaking assets—from the stock market to real estate—so you liberate the rest of your life for your larger dreams. He makes a convincing case that money invested early in your life, through the magic of compounding, grows on its own, making you wealthier by the year.

You don't have to use these tools to go Grant's route, though. You can use them to make efficient use of every earning hour and opportunity to simply give yourself more non-earning hours throughout your life for your passionate causes or raising a family or your solo hike on the Pacific Crest Trail.

In *Your Money or Your Life*, the book I wrote with Joe Dominguez that's now become a venerable personal finance classic, we suggest that you maximize your income without sacrificing your integrity or your health in service to the promise of financial independence. We put no attention on *how to maximize your income.* We ourselves had not been working for money for two decades! In chapter 6 of *Your Money or Your Life,* "The American Dream—on a Shoestring," we offered hundreds of ideas for saving money—some common sense, some radical—but chapter 7 on work and income had one job: to bust the assumption that work = earning money. Work is what we do for love, curiosity, contribution, learning, service, self-development, conviviality, homemaking and home maintenance, shouldering responsibilities for the common good. Most of the world's work has nothing to do with money. We were making the case that readers could exit wage slavery (being compelled to work by the need for money) and join the owners of wealth whose money works for them. In this sense, Grant's book fills a major gap in *Your Money or Your Life* that I didn't even realize was there. Thank you!

Grant and I stand on solid common ground. We believe there is more to life than money, that mastering our relationship with earning, spending, saving, and investing liberates our time for the real work of becoming better human beings and making the world a better place. We also share a passion for the possibility that establishing a solid financial foundation from which to do this more important work should be available to everyone. Our books are one way we are trying to give this gift of freedom to others, but our partnership is about challenging the collective assumptions that blind us to how financial security for everyone could be possible. Just because a just and equitable society where everyone has a chance to develop and give their gifts has been an elusive dream for generations, it doesn't mean that we should not dream it.

It's like the flight attendant's instruction to put your oxygen mask (which flows money rather than air) on first and then assist others around you to put on theirs. This book is your oxygen mask. Put it on. Make money efficiently and effectively and buy your freedom. Then join us in making sure everyone can breathe free.

VICKI ROBIN
Author of *Your Money or Your Life,*
New York Times bestseller and personal finance classic

CHAPTER 1

MONEY IS FREEDOM

How I Went from $2.26 to $1 Million in Five Years

G rant, wake up!" my mom yelled to me from the bottom of the stairs. It was eleven A.M., and I'd slept in—again. Waking up in my childhood bedroom, I felt like I was back in middle school, but I was actually twenty-four years old, unemployed, and living with my parents—a situation all too familiar to millennials like me.

It was August 2010. I'd moved back home two months earlier after being laid off from my job as a researcher at a newspaper. My parents had told me I could crash at home but that I needed to be out in three months and they weren't going to give me a dime. Every night at dinner, they asked how my job search was going, looking at me skeptically as I tried to avoid eye contact.

The truth is, I'd recently stopped applying to jobs. I'd sent out over two hundred résumés in the past month alone and hadn't gotten a single call back. You can send only so many résumés into the abyss before it starts crushing your soul.

As I rolled over in bed that August morning, I tried to think about anything other than my current financial situation. In any case, I had an even more primal desire: I was craving a Chipotle burrito. I knew I was getting low on funds, so reluctantly I checked my account balance on my phone. The savings account I'd labeled DO NOT TOUCH right after I'd lost my job had $0.01 in it. My checking account balance was scarcely better: $2.26, barely enough to afford a side of guacamole, let alone a whole burrito. I took a screenshot of my account to remember this feeling and serve as motivation for the future. Eventually I hung the picture in my closet as a daily reminder, and I still see it every morning.

Defeated but still hungry, I made myself a turkey sandwich and headed outside to the backyard. It was an unseasonably cool summer day in the D.C. suburbs, the sounds of lawn mowers and neighborhood kids enjoying the last week of summer vacation filling the air.

I threw myself down on the grass, just as I'd done so many times as a kid. As I looked up into the clear blue sky, pierced only by the occasional plane headed to Washington National Airport, I contemplated how I'd arrived at this point. I'd always done what I was "supposed" to do. I'd gone to a top university, worked hard, gotten good grades, and even managed to get a job offer before I graduated. After graduation, I started working for an analytics company and assumed I was now on the path to building wealth and becoming a successful adult. But, as it turned out, I was making a huge trade-off.

My first job was located in a sterile office park two hours away from where I lived. The windows in my building didn't open, and the office manager couldn't be bothered to replace the air filters, so the air was always stale. I sat in a four-foot-wide half cubicle under fluorescent lights so bright they were almost blinding. I was so worried about doing a good job and making sure my boss liked me that, by the time I got home, I was too wiped out to do anything fun. I'd zone out in front of the TV and overeat out of boredom. I gained twenty pounds, and even though I was tired all the time, I had trouble sleeping because I was too anxious about the next day. At 4:50 A.M., the alarm would go off, and I'd crawl out of bed to repeat the routine once again. As the day wore on, I'd watch the minutes of my life tick by on my computer clock.

"You'll get used to it," my dad told me by way of encouragement when I called to complain. "Welcome to the real world."

I tried to convince myself that this would all be worth it, that every minute I spent behind that desk and every dollar I earned was one minute and one dollar closer to some distant dream future in which I could live the life I wanted to live. But in reality, I was actually just trading my time for enough money to pay my bills. I got paid twice a month and was living paycheck to paycheck. The first check went directly to rent, while the second went to paying off my credit card balance, which always seemed to keep going up. I told myself I would save money at the end of the month, but I actually ended up spending more than I was making. I worked hard all week, so I went out and spent recklessly on the weekend. Work hard, play hard, right? I assured myself I would save money next month. That I would save money when I was making more money. That I would save money when I was older.

Then, just six months after I started my job, I got fired because I wasn't making the company enough money. I later did the math and realized that in those six months, I'd traded 1,400 hours of my life for $15,500 after taxes. And not only did I have nothing left, I owed $12,000 in credit card debt.

Over the next two years I bounced between unemployment and a few other jobs, but I still never managed to save anything. I was so worried about money that I started suffering from debilitating anxiety attacks so powerful that my heart felt like it would stop beating and I literally thought I was going to die. I was letting the best hours of my life during the best years of my life burn out with each biweekly paycheck.

It sucked, but I was far from alone in my plight. According to Gallup's annual survey of the American Workforce in 2017, 70 percent of employees in the United States are disengaged at work. Meanwhile, 69 percent of Americans have less than $1,000 in savings and live one disaster away from poverty, bankruptcy, or crippling debt.

When the Great Recession hit, I lost my job again. By the time I showed up back on my parents' doorstep, after three years in the working world, I had traded 4,700 hours of my life for $87,000 after taxes. And besides that $2.26, I had absolutely nothing to show for it. I didn't even have my prized Volkswagen camper van anymore because I'd sold it six months before just to make ends meet.

As I lay there in the backyard, my thoughts of the past turned to thoughts of the future. As I considered my options, I saw the next forty years—the best years of my life—stretched out before me. I imagined myself stuck in another bleak office, in another nondescript office park, in another stifling cubicle. If I somehow managed to save enough of my salary after all of my bills were paid, I *might* be able to retire in my sixties.

Given the trends of my generation, however, even that dismal prospect seemed unlikely. Among the 83 million millennials in the United States, the average income is $35,592 per year, less than half of what our parents made at our age when adjusted for inflation. With an average of $36,000 in student loan debt, most of us don't get out of debt for years, let alone start to save any real money.

If we look closely at these numbers, it's no wonder we aren't saving enough to retire in even three to four decades. While investment guides generally recommend you sock away 10 to 15 percent of your income (even though, as I'd later learn, that definitely isn't enough), millennials under twenty-five are saving only 3.9 percent of their income for retirement, while older millennials, those aged twenty-five to thirty-four, are saving 5.35 percent. This will make it impossible for most of us to ever retire. Literally impossible!

In case that doesn't scare you enough, who knows how decisions by our government and shifts in the economy will affect our futures? Will social security even be around in forty years? Will we be able to afford healthcare as costs go up and as our need for it becomes greater? Inflation isn't slowing down anytime soon, meaning our paltry savings will end up being worth even *less* than it is today. What are we supposed to do? Work until we fall down dead at our desks? We are on our own.

I realized that doing everything I was "supposed" to do wouldn't guarantee anything, even retirement in forty plus years. What kind of life is that? I didn't want to spend my days in a job I hated just so I could get by. I wanted to feel passionate about my work and love my life.

I didn't want to worry about money all the time or depend on a boss who might decide to fire me at any minute, just so I could pay my rent. I wanted to be in control of my own income and time. I didn't want to put off traveling the world because I couldn't afford it or I was allowed only ten days of vacation a year. I wanted to be able to have enough time to really explore the world. I didn't want to spend the most precious moments of my future kids' lives in an office. I wanted to be there to watch them grow and help them figure out how to realize their own dreams.

And I didn't want to wake up at sixty-five and realize that I'd traded more than seventy thousand hours of my life working a nine-to-five for . . . what?

I realized that if I wanted something different, I was going to have to *do* something different. So that day, lying in the grass, I set two seemingly unrealistic goals: to save $1 million and to "retire" as quickly as possible.

I didn't know how I was going to do it—or even *if* I was going to be able to do it—but I spent the next five years doing everything I could to make it happen. I read every personal finance book and investing guide I could get my hands on. I worked a nine-to-five job for benefits and connections, but then launched two companies and started several side hustles to earn extra income. I saved 25 percent, then 40 percent, then up to 80 percent of my income some months and put that money to work in the stock market so it could grow. And I figured out how I could optimize my lifestyle to maximize my income and savings, and have a lot of fun along the way.

Fast-forward five years later to 2015, and I had a net worth of over $1 million. I didn't win the lottery or come into some surprise inheritance. I didn't strike it rich on some hot new app that I sold to Google for a billion dollars. I didn't hustle for the mob or rob any banks. I simply learned everything I could, questioned all of the popular advice about money I came across, and maximized the value of my time through a combination of personal finance, entrepreneurship, and investing—three things absolutely anyone, even someone with $2.26 in the bank and a lack of marketable skills, can learn to do on their own.

I'll admit it wasn't easy. In fact, it was the hardest thing I've ever done in my life. But not for the reasons you may think. The strategies I used require some effort and discipline, but they aren't complicated. What made my journey difficult was that it required me to step outside my comfort zone, take some calculated risks, and do things that no one else around me was doing, that no one I knew had done. A lot of people thought I was crazy, and even my girlfriend wouldn't come over to visit my crappy but inexpensive apartment. I definitely made decisions that many people wouldn't even consider. I was living on the edge, but I had a mission and that kept me motivated. I also learned an insane amount about how almost anyone can find ways to save and make more money.

One of the most profound lessons I've learned along the way is that most of the "accepted wisdom" about money, work, and retirement is either incorrect, incomplete, or so old-school it's obsolete. We've accepted this version of the "real world" because it's what others have done for generations, but it just doesn't work anymore—unless you *maybe* want to retire in thirty to forty years. Things have changed, and despite all the pessimism surrounding the financial prospects for so many people today, it's actually never been easier to make more money, manage your own money, and live a life free from the typical nine-to-five. The challenge is in opening yourself up to the opportunity, questioning the advice and example of others, and learning to do things differently even if people think you're crazy.

Most of what's in this book wasn't even possible ten years ago. None of it is taught in schools, and most people you know aren't even aware that it's possible. I learned it only because I made it my mission to do so and dedicated thousands and thousands of hours to learning everything I could, testing it for myself, and making mistakes from which I could learn. Once I realized how much knowledge I had gained, I knew I needed to share it with the world.

In 2015, soon after I reached my goal of making $1 million, I started

MillennialMoney.com to build a community and share my strategies, habits, and hacks to build wealth as quickly as possible. Over the past three years more than 10 million people have visited Millennial Money or listened to my podcast, and tens of thousands have reached out to me directly to ask questions and share their own financial successes. I recently heard from Victor, who was able to get a $60,000 raise; Mia, who sold her first $20,000 side-hustle engagement; Eric, who increased his savings rate from 3 percent to 40 percent in two months; and Melissa, who lives for free in million-dollar mansions thanks to information she learned on the site.

Many more have been able to launch profitable side hustles, start investing, negotiate life-changing work remote opportunities, leave their full-time jobs to pursue their passions. Many have fast-tracked their financial freedom and are now on pace to retire in ten years or less, decades earlier than they otherwise would have been if they hadn't implemented these strategies. While the site has proved a great resource, I still get asked all the time "How, *exactly*, did you do it?" The answer to that question is much too long to be explained in a single blog post, which is why I decided to write this book.

The strategies in this book are designed to help you make as much money in as little time as possible. In the chapters that follow, I'll lay out the exact framework and each step I used to go from $2.26 to over $1.25 million and financial independence in just five years. I'll show you why you don't really need a budget, why you can keep buying that small-batch coffee even though it costs $20 a pound, and why you should definitely still go out with your friends or take that last-minute trip to Yosemite.

I'll show you how you can literally live rent free or, even better, buy a home and make money on it each month. I'll show you why spending just five minutes a day managing your own money instead of handing it over to a money manager will help you earn hundreds of thousands of dollars more over the long term. I'll show you how saving just an additional 1 percent of your income can help you to reach financial independence up to two years earlier. And I'll show you how to increase your savings rate so you can "retire" in as little as five years. Most important, I'll show you how to make enough money so you never have to work again—unless, of course, you want to.

If you're thinking that this all sounds too good to be true or that you have to be some sort of financial genius to pull it off, don't worry—you don't. I've never taken a business or finance class in my life. Unfortunately, one of the most damaging and popular myths about money is that it's complicated. In large part, this is the work of the financial industry and money managers, who use fancy words, confusing equations, and abstract acronyms to make it seem complicated so you'll pay them a lot of money to take care of it for you. And forget about early retirement—most banks and money managers make money off you only when you're making money and investing it. I've never, ever seen—and I've been looking—any bank or advisor who recommends you save 25 percent or more of your income so you can retire earlier.

Most of the concepts in this book are actually pretty simple, and any math you'll need you learned in elementary school. I certainly intend to cover a lot of ground, but my goal is not simply to give you a laundry list of advice you need to follow. This is a strategy, a blueprint, a philosophy, and I want to help you understand the mechanics behind money so you understand why and how the advice works, and how you can get results quickly.

The more ideas you can implement from this book, the faster you will build wealth, change your life, and reach financial freedom. If you want to be able to walk away from corporate America in five years like I did, the surest way to do so is to follow my example step by step. If you're not quite that crazy, you can pick the ideas that work best for you and still achieve amazing results. Because the strategy employs so many different techniques, it is customizable, scalable, and one you can use indefinitely.

This plan is broken down into seven steps that I will walk you through closely and teach you how to use. This plan works because it's designed to maximize all areas of your financial life. Each of the steps build on the others and the sum of the steps is much greater than each one on its own. If you follow the plan and stick with it, I promise you will end up with more money than you ever thought possible.

Step 1: Figure out *your number*. While my number was the amount I would need to reach financial independence so I never have to work again in my life, financial freedom might mean something different to you than it did to me. *Your number* is how much money you need to reach your financial freedom. Maybe it's how much money you need to get out of debt, save six months of expenses, have enough money so you can take two years off to travel the world, or have enough money to live the rest of your life without ever having to work again. No matter what financial freedom means to you, the first step is to figure out how much money you need to need to get there. I'll walk you through the exact process and show you how to get there faster.

Step 2: **Calculate where you are today.** After you figure out how much money you need, I'll walk you through how to analyze where you are today and explain why your net worth is the most important number in your financial life. I'll also share a simple strategy for how to think about and handle any debt you have.

Step 3: **Radically shift how you think about money.** If you keep thinking about money the same way you always have, then you won't make as much money as possible. How you were taught to think about money is probably holding you back in some way, so I'll share the ten different ways I think about money and teach you how to use them to save and make more.

Step 4: **Stop budgeting and focus on what has the biggest impact on your savings.** While it's important to track what you spend, it's not where you should spend most of your time. Budgets actually reinforce a scarcity mindset and hold most people back from saving and making more money. I'll show you how to calculate and increase your savings rate in order to fast-track your financial independence without sacrificing the things you love. There is a much simpler way to budget to maximize your return on your time.

Step 5: Hack your nine-to-five. Whether you love your full-time job or can't wait to get out, you should use it strategically to make more money today and as a launching pad to make a lot more money in the future. I'll show you how to calculate your market value, your value to your company, and negotiate a raise to ensure you're making as much money as possible. I'll also show you how to maximize your benefits, including the best remote-work options possible, increase your skills, find a higher-paying job, and maximize the opportunities to use your nine-to-five to reach financial freedom as quickly as possible.

Step 6: Start a profitable side hustle and diversify your income streams. It's never been easier to start a profitable side hustle and make extra money, but the problem is most people don't do it right. They spend their time side hustling for someone else instead of themselves, which means they aren't earning as much money as possible. Or they spend their time trying to grow a side hustle that was doomed from the beginning. I'll show you how to pick, launch, and grow a profitable side hustle so you can make more money in less time and seek out the moneymaker's holy grail—passive income streams that make enough money to cover your living expenses and then some!

Step 7: Invest as much money as early and often as you can. When you invest money, your money makes money and you don't need to trade much, if any, of your own time. While there are an infinite number of ways to invest, the investment strategy in this book is designed to help you achieve financial freedom as quickly as possible by focusing on investments and an investment strategy designed to generate the highest returns with the least amount of risk.

The path in this book and these steps are designed so you can revisit them as often as you need to recalibrate your own numbers as your lifestyle and goals change. At first the path might feel unfamiliar, exciting, and maybe a bit daunting, but as you follow it, your relationship with money will change. You'll discover new things about yourself and your life. You'll also start seeing moneymaking opportunities everywhere.

But this book is ultimately about more than saving a specific amount of money or retiring at a certain age. More than anything it's about freedom. When you have *enough* money, you more space and time to explore the world, to connect, to reflect, to grow, and to feel alive. You have the freedom to create the life you want. A life where you have more time for the people and things that make you happy. A life with less stress and more options.

A life you love.

Financial Freedom, of course, means different things to different people, and as I'll explain, different people need vastly different amounts of money to feel free. I recently met a young couple with two kids living in New York City who think they need $5 million to be free, but the traveler I met in the Flagstaff, Arizona, train station feels free making only $5,000 per year. Maybe financial freedom to you means being debt-free, or having more time to spend with your family, or being able to quit corporate America, or having $5,000 a month in passive income, or making enough money to work from your laptop anywhere in the world, or having enough money so you never have to work another day in your life. Some monks feel free without any money, choosing instead to live within a self-sustaining community.

Ultimately, the amount you need comes down to the life you want to live, where you want to live it, what you value, and what brings you joy. Joy is defined as a feeling of great pleasure and happiness caused by something exceptionally good, satisfying, or delightful. Aka "The Good Life."

While it might sound impossible to figure out how much money you need to live a life you love or how to "maximize your happiness per dollar," each step in this book is designed to get you there. Once you take the time to figure this out, you will likely find that you need a lot less money to reach financial freedom than you think and that you can reach it faster than you've ever thought possible.

While you can determine what financial freedom mean to you and set that as you goal, I wanted to break down financial freedom into seven levels that each have a profound impact on most people's lives when they reach them.

Seven Levels of Financial Freedom

1. Clarity, about where you are and where you are going
2. Self-sufficiency, when you earn enough money to cover your expenses on your own
3. Breathing room, when you escape living paycheck to paycheck
4. Stability, when you have six months of living expenses saved and debt repaid
5. Flexibility, when you have at least two years of living expenses invested
6. Financial independence, when you can live off investments forever so work becomes optional
7. Abundant wealth, when you have more money than you'll ever need

Shout-out to a great writer, and friend, J. D. Roth of Get Rich Slowly, whose levels inspired these.

As you reach each level of financial freedom you'll feel more empowered and in control, and likely less stress around money. You'll also have access to more options and opportunities. You can take more risks that make you more money and your life richer.

Money is no longer some abstract confusing thing that you want, it's something you have and know how to get. Once you know how money works and you've mastered it, you can let it go and come to it on your own terms. Instead of a worry, it becomes an opportunity. Instead of it controlling you, you control it. You have freedom through money.

I worked really hard to get to each level as quickly as possible. The more time you dedicate to the strategies in the book, the faster you will reach the next level of financial freedom. Once I reached one of my goals, my next goal was almost always to double my money. So when I had $1,000, my next goal was $2,000, and when I had $2,000, my next goal was $4,000. This made it easier for me to set a goal that was tough but achievable. If $1 million had been my only goal, I wouldn't have made it. Set smaller goals along the way and push as quickly as you can to them. Celebrate each success in a small way to mark the milestone. No matter how long it takes, just keep at it. Trust me, it gets easier over time and you'll build momentum because of the habits and strategies you used to get to your previous goal. Your first $1,000, $10,000, and $100,000 are the toughest to save.

You can get to level 5 (when you have at least two years of living expenses invested) in a few years with a lot of hustle, but the biggest distance is between levels 5 and 6 (when you can live off your investments forever). This is when you just have to go all out and make, then save, then invest as much money as you can. You just have to keep at it. The extra time and energy you invest now will expand into freedom.

If you really commit and are willing to make the trade-offs, you can realistically reach financial independence in ten years or less. If you really hustle and get lucky, you might even be able to do it in five years or less. I'll be the first to admit that it was lucky I started investing before a big bull market, but if I hadn't made and invested as much money as I could, then I wouldn't have been able to take advantage of it. While you can't rely on luck, you can rely on the proven path in this book to help you whether luck comes along or not. No matter what, reaching financial independence in ten, fifteen, or twenty years is a lot faster than forty years—or never! That's a ton of extra time to do whatever you want.

For me, financial freedom meant reaching financial independence at the age of thirty so I didn't have to work in a cubicle for the rest of my life. Before I had money, I spent so much of my time anxious and worrying about it that I felt trapped. Pretty much every choice I made was driven by money. Not only was I trapped by what I could or could not afford, but my time was also controlled by my need to make money. I went to bed and woke up at certain time so I could arrive at the office by a certain hour so I didn't piss off my boss, who could fire me at any moment. I loved to travel, but even if I could have afforded a trip abroad, I could go to only so many places with ten days of vacation a year. Money—or my lack of it— was all I thought about.

Once I reached financial independence and had enough to walk away from work forever—even though I have chosen not to—I completely stopped worrying about money. Over time my anxiety started to disappear, which, based on what I've heard from others who've reached financial independence, is common. I'm more present, calm, and grateful, and happier. I feel more in control and connected with the world and my relationships. I have more time to do the things I love to do, like traveling, writing, playing guitar, and teaching, and because I don't *have* to work, I can choose to do work that I find fulfilling and meaningful instead of just what will pay the bills.

Financial freedom, financial independence, early retirement, whatever you call it—it feels big, open, limitless, just like those summer days when you were a kid lying in the grass and feeling like the whole world was open and anything was possible.

What does financial freedom mean to you? What would you do tomorrow if you didn't need to work for money? Only you can answer these questions.

I'm here only to teach you how to get there.

Hit me up!

What does financial freedom mean to you? Use the hashtag #financialfreedombook or hit me up on Twitter @sabatier or @millennialmoney, Instagram @millennialmoneycom, email me at grant@millennialmoney.com, or share at financialfreedombook.com. I'd love to hear from you.

CHAPTER 2

TIME IS MORE VALUABLE THAN MONEY

Why You Can and Should "Retire" Early

I f some ninety-year-old rich dude offered you $100 million to trade places with him, would you do it? Of course not. Why? Because time is more valuable than money.

The average person has approximately 25,000 days to live in their adult life. If you're reading this book, you likely need to trade your time for money in order to live a life that is safe, healthy, and happy. But if you didn't have to work to make money, you'd be able to spend that time however you want. No one cares about your time as much as you do. People will try to take your time and fill it up with meetings and calls and more meetings. But it's your time. Your only time. This book is designed to help you make the most of it.

The goal of this book is to help you retire as early as possible. When I say *retire*, I don't mean that you will never work again, only that you have enough money so that you never *have* to work again. This is complete financial freedom—the ability to do whatever you want with your time.

I don't ever plan to retire in the traditional sense of the word, but you could say that I'm "retired" now because I have enough money and freedom to spend my time doing whatever I want. I no longer have to work for money, but I still enjoy making money and it's attached to many of the things I enjoy doing. I love working and challenging myself and hopefully always will, so checking out to a life of leisure just isn't my vibe.

If you want to "retire" sooner rather than later, you need to rethink everything you've been taught about retirement and probably most of what you've been taught about money. As a society, we have collectively adopted one approach to retiring: get a job, set aside a certain portion of your income in a 401(k) or other retirement account, and in forty plus years you'll have enough money saved that you can stop working for good. This approach is designed to get you to retire in your sixties or seventies, which explains why pretty much every advertisement about retirement shows silver-haired grandmas and grandpas (typically on a golf course or walking along the beach).

There are three major problems with this approach:

1. It doesn't work for most people.
2. You end up spending the most valuable years of your life working for money.
3. It's not designed to help you "retire" as quickly as possible.

We'll start with the first problem. To illustrate why traditional retirement advice doesn't work, I'd like to introduce you to Travis. Travis is an old friend of my parents, so I've known him for a long time. Back in 2012, when I was already well into my quest to become a millionaire by thirty, I ran into Travis at a holiday party thrown by another family friend. While schmoozing with the other guests and snacking on Virginia honey ham in my festive holiday jacket, I struck up a conversation with Travis, who had heard (via my parents) that I was thinking of starting a business. Travis and I typically see each other only once a year at this holiday party, so he had no idea that I'd made almost $300,000 in the past year by pursuing a whole bunch of opportunities: building websites, running ad campaigns, flipping domain names, selling mopeds, and various other things.

"So you want to be an entrepreneur?" Travis said. "Pretty cool, man. But it's going to be pretty tough at first. It always is for entrepreneurs. You've got to make sure to save some money. I've been saving five percent of my income for retirement since I started working, and I'm planning to retire in the next ten years."

Travis was about forty-five at this time and had been working for twenty years. I asked him how he had decided to save 5 percent of his income for retirement back in his twenties.

"Oh, back when I first started out," he said, "a coworker of mine told me I should start saving that much, so I did."

I was speechless. By this point I had read hundreds of books about investing and personal finance, and I knew that, despite his confidence, Travis was probably *never* going to be able to retire, let alone in the next ten years.

I don't have access to Travis's financial statements, so it's possible he has some savings, income, or assets that I don't know about, but let's assume all he has is his income and whatever he's set aside for retirement since he entered the workforce. Travis is a project manager at an energy consulting company. I don't know what he takes home, but according to websites like PayScale and Glassdoor, he probably makes about $60,000 a year.

Even though I don't know his exact salary, I know a lot about what Travis spends his money on because my parents have known him for a long time. In the past three years, he has bought a new house (for at least $500,000), redid the kitchen *and* put an addition on the new house (for at least another $150,000), and bought not one, but two new cars. By outward appearances, the dude is living like a king, but based on what he's likely earning, he's probably living on an insane amount of credit to afford this lifestyle, even when you factor in his wife's income. She works in a similar role and likely makes about the same amount of money as Travis. Neither Travis nor his wife come from money, so a big inheritance to offset their spending is unlikely.

Let's take a quick look at the numbers. If Travis has been saving 5 percent of a $60,000 annual salary, that means he's saving about $3,000 per year. Even if he's been making $60,000 a year since he was in his mid-twenties (which is unlikely, since incomes usually rise over time), he would have set aside only $60,000 total by now ($3,000 × 20 years = $60,000). If he's invested that money in his company's 401(k) and his company has matched the standard 3 percent of his contribution over that period, he'd have an additional $36,000 saved, for a total of $96,000 (3 percent of $60,000 = $1,800 × 20 years = $36,000).

Thanks to the magic of compounding (see the box below), any contributions he's made will have grown for as long as they've been invested. We can't know exactly how much his 401(k) would be worth without knowing what specific assets (i.e., stocks or bonds) he has invested in, but we can be fairly certain that it's worth more than his original investment.

Compounding accelerates money growth and will make you richer.

There is a reason Einstein is said to have called compounding "the eighth wonder of the world," because it's so amazing. Compounding exponentially increases the value of your money over time, even if you don't increase your investments, because your interest grows interest (aka your money keeps making more money).

The key to fast-tracking financial freedom is to speed up compounding by making and investing as much money as early and frequently as you can.

Here's how it works. As a stock goes up, the value of any money invested in that stock increases by a certain percentage. The growth is known as interest. If the stock keeps going up, then both your original contribution and the past interest keeps growing. Over time, the more money you invest and the more the interest grows, the faster your money compounds. It looks like a curve, as you'll see below.

Of course, the earnings (or losses) of the stock market can vary wildly from month to month and from year to year, but over the long term, many economists have found that the real dollar returns (meaning returns adjusted to account for inflation and stock dividends) of the U.S. stock market average between 7 and 9 percent per year. However, when it comes to estimating potential stock market returns, it's better to be a bit more conservative, so for this reason, I'll be using 7 percent as the estimated stock market rate of return throughout the course of this book.

For the sake of simplicity to illustrate the impact of compounding, let's say the market grows by 10 percent in a given year. If you invest $100 and it grows by 10 percent, you will have $110 at the end of the year (10 percent of $100 = $10; $100 + $10 = $110). If the market grows by another 10 percent the following year, you will earn 10 percent not only on your original $100 investment but also on the $10 return you earned the previous year. This means that at the end of the second year, you would have earned an additional $11 (10 percent of $110 = $11) for a total of $121.

This is the one of the craziest thing about money and compounding: $1 or 1 percent might not seem like a lot, but it can have a massive impact on how much money you have over time thanks to compounding. To illustrate, let's look at what happens to that $100 if we keep it invested at 10 percent annual growth for forty years, without adding any more money to it.

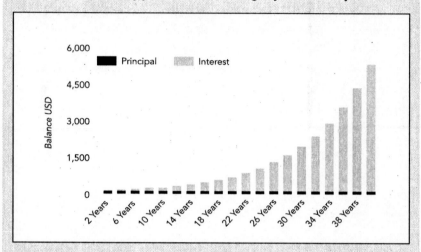

Yes, that's right. That original $100 investment (aka your principal) will be worth $5,370 in forty years, and you didn't even contribute any additional money to it! That's a 5,270 percent increase! If you continue to add to your principal (which is what you typically do when investing for retirement, since you invest more at least every month) that money will be worth even more. Even if you add only $1 per month to your original $100 contribution, you'd have deposited a total of $480 over 40 years, but it would be worth $11,694! Awesome!

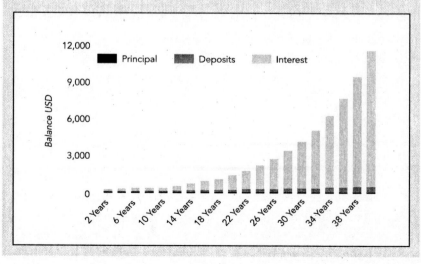

If Travis has been saving $3,000 per year, and that money has been growing at the average 7 percent annual rate (see box), he would have $142,348 after saving for twenty years. This is certainly a lot of money, but it's not enough to live on if he plans to retire by fifty and live into his seventies or eighties. And this assumes he was smart and put his money in a total stock market index fund, which tracks the performance of the entire stock market and is therefore most likely to generate the average 7 percent return over time. If he didn't, he would most likely have even less saved.

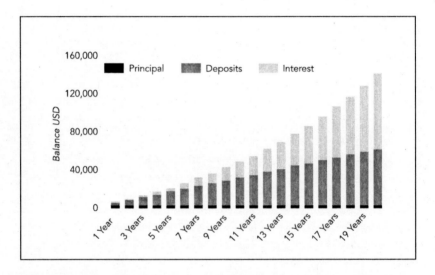

I don't mean to pick on Travis. In fact, most Americans approach retirement the same way he does. As of 2016, the median household income in the United States is $57,617, and the average American is saving only 3.6 percent of their income per year. That means the average American household is saving $2,074 per year—even less than what we assumed Travis is saving. As mentioned in the last chapter, the average millennial is saving between 3 and 5 percent of his or her income, which, based on the average millennial income of $35,592, equals about $1,067—$1,776 per year. For simplicity's sake, let's round that up to $2,000 a year. Saving $2,000 per year growing 7 percent per year equals $470,967 in forty years. While $470,967 is a lot of money, keep in mind that due to inflation, which is unpredictable, $470,967 likely won't have the same purchasing power in forty years that it does today.

Inflation increases or decreases what you can buy with money.

Due to inflation, the value of money decreases over time, so if you need only $1 to buy something today, you will need more than $1 to buy the same thing in the future. This is why you could buy a cup of coffee for 15¢ in 1920, but it costs over $2 today. Inflation is generally caused by supply, demand, production costs, and tax policies. It is country specific, so it can vary dramatically by the strength of a country's currency and its purchasing power. This is why it's more affordable to live in certain countries if you currently live in the United States, where the dollar is strong compared to other currencies. You can use that strong dollar to live in many places in the world for less than you would spend living in the United States. For example, it's currently a lot cheaper to live in Bali, Thailand, or many South American countries.

In the United States, inflation causes prices to increase between 2 and 4 percent every year on average, which means any money saved today will buy less in the future. However, this is just the average, and some years—for example, in the 1980s—inflation was over 10 percent! Of course, not everything rises in price, and in fact some things actually get cheaper over time. But as a whole, the staples of life, like housing, transportation, food, energy, and clothes, will be more expensive in ten years than they are today. However, there are ways (some of which we'll explore later in the book) to insulate yourself from inflation. Just because prices will be a lot higher in the future doesn't necessarily mean your money won't go as far; you just have to be creative, buy less, and be more self-sufficient.

Kristy and Bryce, who retired in their early thirties, have created what's known as an *inflation shield*, where they've essentially minimized the impact of inflation on their savings by living in countries with lower inflation than their home country of Canada. Depending on where you live and the strength of your home currency, you may be able to get a lot more for your money living in another country or utilizing cheaper services outside of your country, like healthcare, which is significantly cheaper outside the United States and even free in some countries.

Also, if you invest your money in the stock market, you will still end up with more money than you started with because the average 7 percent annual return of the stock market has already been adjusted for inflation and dividends, so 7 percent is the "real" average annual return.

Even so, you should always pay attention to ways you can minimize the effects of inflation on your money as much as possible, so you have more money to invest and keep invested!

Over the past decade, inflation has been at historic lows and the stock market returns have effectively insulated investors from inflation, but it's realistic to estimate that inflation will increase over the coming decades, and even a small 2 to 3 percent average increase per year would significantly reduce the purchasing power of your savings in the future.

For example, adjusted for 2 to 3 percent inflation, that $470,967 the average American saving 5 percent could have after forty years would have the purchasing power of only approximately $144,378 in today's dollars. Given that the average life expectancy in America is roughly seventy-nine years (and going up), you would have to make that $144,378 last for roughly fourteen years if you retired at sixty-five. Not factoring in any social security benefits you may receive (since we don't know what state social security will be in in forty years), that leaves you $10,312 in 2019 purchasing power to live on *per year*! No matter how you slice it, we are way behind.

If you're reading this book, you're probably interested in being in a position to "retire" as quickly as possible. Let's assume you work for a pretty sweet company that will match any contribution you make to your 401(k) up to 4 percent (many companies provide a dollar-for-dollar match on retirement contributions up to a certain percentage), and you're already saving 10 percent of your income in your 401(k), so you're effectively saving 14 percent of your annual income (10 percent from you + 4 percent from your employer). If you do have a 401(k) with an employer match and you're not contributing any money or not contributing enough money to max out the match, then put this book down right now, log into your 401(k) account, and start contributing at least enough to receive your employer match. It's completely free money! A 100 percent return! Do it!

If you are already saving more than 10 percent, first, congratulations! You are saving more than 99 percent of the United States population! But don't break out the champagne just yet; you still might not be able to retire. Let's say you make $50,000 a year. If you started saving 14 percent of your salary ($7,000 per year) at age twenty-five and your savings grew at 7 percent annually, you'd have about $1,117,589 at the age of sixty-five. Not bad for forty years of saving, but it's still *forty years* of saving, and while $1,117,589 might sound like a lot, let's say inflation increases just an extra

2.5 percent per year. Then your savings amount to only $416,224 in 2019 purchasing power.

That's still not bad, but because you've been investing in a 401(k), you haven't paid taxes on that money until you withdraw it. If we factor in taxes, that $416,224 could be worth between 15 and 35 percent less depending on what tax bracket you are in when you start to withdraw the money.

All right, enough of that depressing news. You get the point: the first major problem with traditional retirement advice is that even if you follow it perfectly (and most people usually don't), you still might not have enough to live on when you are in your sixties. When I did this calculation, it blew me away—clearly the popular advice to save 5 to 10 percent of your income is not enough. While I'll help you calculate your target savings rate later in the book, you should be saving as much money as early and often as you can.

If you want to be sure you will be able to retire at sixty-five, you need to start (and keep) saving at least 20 percent of your income from the age of thirty. Here's how big a difference it makes. If you are making an average of $50,000 over this thirty-five-year period and saving 20 percent, or approximately $10,000, you'd have deposited $349,860 by the time you retire. Factoring in the 7 percent growth rate adjusted for inflation, that

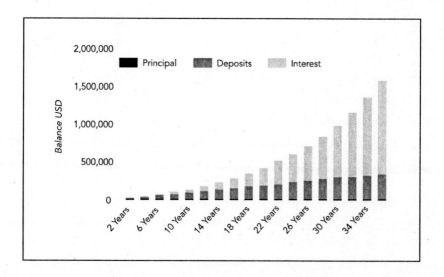

investment would be worth $1,615,340. And this is assuming that your salary never increases, which it very likely would over time, so you will have even more money.

REWRITING RETIREMENT

Saving 20 percent of your income will significantly increase the chance that you can retire after forty years. But this brings us to the second and third major problems with traditional money advice: it is not designed to help you "retire" early and requires you to work full time between your twenties and your sixties.

There is nothing inherently wrong with this, and people can live perfectly happy lives working for forty years and then enjoying the fruits of their labor when they're older. But it requires a huge trade-off—basing forty years of your life around earning money—and the payoff is not guaranteed.

Unless you go the extra mile, the only information you're usually given about saving for the long haul is to invest a certain portion of your annual salary into a retirement account like a 401(k) (if your company provides one) or an IRA (individual retirement account). And because most of us aren't taught any more than that, we don't know enough to question this advice. We assume if everyone else is doing it, and everyone else *seems* to be chugging along just fine, then it's good enough for us.

All my life, I had grown up around people who worked and hoped they could retire one day. Neither of my parents come from money, and I knew growing up that we didn't have a lot of money. We weren't poor by any stretch, but given that we lived outside of Washington, D.C., surrounded by some of the wealthiest suburbs in America, my parents lived a frugal lifestyle. My parents bought used cars, we took an annual beach vacation, and we drove twelve hours each way to spend holidays in Indiana.

Despite our East Coast address, my parents retained their Midwestern values. I was consistently exposed to the classic American work ethic: get a job, pay your dues, save wisely, and if you play your cards right, you can retire some time in your golden years. Everyone I knew worked well into their sixties, if not longer. My grandparents worked well into their seventies because they couldn't afford to retire earlier than that.

As of this writing, both of my parents are in their sixties and still working. They probably have enough money to retire, but they worry it might not be enough in the long run. They also both wonder what they would do with their time if they did retire. When you spend almost your entire life working for a paycheck, what happens when you break that routine? What happens when your identity is wrapped up in your title and job responsibilities? What happens when you're now too tired to pursue your dreams, or maybe it's been so long that you lost your dreams along the way?

My dad recently told me about a few of his neighbors who had retired after forty years in the workforce. "They spend a lot of their time in their yards picking up sticks," he said. I don't know these people, but I can't imagine this is what they hoped they'd be doing in the twilight of their lives.

This illustrates a common problem with the typical approach to retirement that few people consider: Despite the fact that they work so hard to be able to retire, 48 percent of Americans over fifty-five haven't even thought about what they want to do when/if they retire. I don't know about you, but this makes me pretty sad because it means many Americans are choosing to work for several decades of their lives without giving any thought to what they're working toward. They have collectively adopted the traditional retirement narrative—work until your sixties or seventies—without pausing to question whether this is what they really want out of life or if there's a better way.

Until I started questioning this narrative on my own, I was doing exactly the same thing. No one ever told me I *couldn't* "retire" in my twenties or thirties; the idea was simply so unusual that it never came up. The only person I knew growing up who retired "early" was Jim, another family friend, who retired at the age of forty-nine after saving and inheriting enough money to do so. This stuck in my mind at an early age after hearing my parents talking about it.

The blind acceptance of this narrative has created a society full of people who are living lives that they didn't really choose and deferring their dreams—sometimes forever—because they assume they have to work to make money. In her deeply moving book *The Top Five Regrets of the Dying*, nurse Bronnie Ware says the top two regrets of those facing the end of their lives are "I wish I'd had the courage to live a life true to myself, not the life others expected of me," and "I wish I hadn't worked so hard."

She goes on to say that the vast majority of her patients never accomplished at least half of their dreams, often because of their choice to keep working instead of following them. These people pushed on, saved, and worked only to look back and wonder what it was all for. Is this what you want? Do you want to defer your dreams until sometime in the far-off future when you might not have the energy or drive to do anything but pick up sticks all day?

It was only after I started my quest to earn $1 million as quickly as possible that I started to notice the limits to typical financial advice and the traditional retirement narrative. As I learned more about how to earn, save, and invest money, I realized that making money quickly is not nearly as complicated as it's made out to be. In fact, given the efficiencies of the internet, it's easier to do than ever before. What is difficult is letting go of the assumption that there is only one surefire path to retirement—earning a steady paycheck for several decades and saving a portion of it for later—and that any other path is reserved for the lucky few.

It's important to note that there are some limits, and being able to "retire" early is definitely a privilege that not everyone has or will have. There are millions of people in the United States who are simply trying to keep a roof over their heads and buy food to feed their families. If you are making less than $25,000 per year, then it will be a lot harder to retire early because you simply won't be able to save as much as someone earning a higher income. Unless of course you can live on $7,000 a year, like the happy wanderer I met in Flagstaff, Arizona. I'm not saying it isn't possible; it will just require a lot of creativity and sacrifice.

That being said, one of the cornerstones of my own financial freedom strategy was figuring out ways to earn more money rather than simply focusing on ways to save it. Instead of spending all of my time pinching pennies, I spent it looking for ways to make more money. If you are making $25,000, then I want to help you make $50,000, or if you are making $50,000, I want to help you make $100,000. And so on. The more money you make, the more money you can invest, and the faster you will reach financial freedom.

TIME IS MORE VALUABLE THAN MONEY

Trust me, the hardest part about becoming financially independent isn't actually doing it. Once you learn the basic concepts of earning, saving, and investing, executing the strategy is relatively simple and you will start seeing results immediately. That's not to say it's easy—it requires an incredible amount of persistence and discipline—but it's certainly not rocket science.

The hardest part of fast-tracking financial freedom is learning to look at the world differently, to accept that even though you may not know a single person who has done it, it is possible to earn enough so that within just a few years, you will never have to worry about money again. When you're just starting out, it can be incredibly difficult and intimidating to ignore all of the "experts" and "gurus" and other people in your life— people like Travis—who keep telling you the "surest" and "best" routes to retirement or making money. Or to ignore your friends, family, or coworkers when they laugh and tell you there's no way you can actually make a lot of money and "retire" early. But if you want to live life on your terms, you need to manage money on your own terms as well, and that requires a new perspective.

TIME VERSUS MONEY

One of the main reasons traditional retirement and personal finance advice is so limiting is because it is based on the false assumption that money is limited. The vast majority of personal finance advice out there is focused on cutting back and spending less and doesn't acknowledge the simple truth that money is limited only if you don't try to make more of it.

Money is inherently infinite. It's a human invention, and as long as people are helping the economy grow by working, spending, and investing, governments can print more money to keep up. Yes, there is and always has been a massive gap between those who have a lot of money and those who don't, and billions of people live in places where they don't have the moneymaking opportunities that those of us in democratic, capitalist societies have. But in theory, there is enough money in the world for everyone to have all the money they need.

The problem is, many people don't take advantage of these

opportunities and instead accept whatever money they are given—generally whatever their bosses are willing to pay—without considering other ways to make more money. They say they want to make more money but spend all of their free time binging on Netflix, gaming, or just wasting time.

This is too bad because when we believe that money is scarce, we end up sacrificing a great deal of time in order to make and save it. And unlike money, time *is* inherently limited. In one of my favorite books, *Your Money or Your Life*, author Vicki Robin asks us to ponder a simple but transcendent question: What are the hours of your life worth? What are you willing to trade them for? How much money are you willing to trade for your time?

If we believe money is scarce, we will spend precious time trying to save it when we actually don't have to. We'll spend hours clipping coupons, driving an extra mile to save three cents a gallon on gas, or hunting for a deal online just to shave a few bucks off our bill. I once spent over four hours looking for the best deal on a new TV. It was only later that I considered the money I'd saved hardly made up for the time I'd wasted—time that I will never get back.

The same goes for earning money: every minute we spend trying to make money is a minute we can't use to do something else—it's gone forever. Most people work between 70,000 and 80,000 hours over the course of their careers, but even that doesn't account for all of the time they spend *because* they have to work. The average American commutes fifty-two minutes to and from work each day. That's about 8,700 hours over the course of a typical career. All told, you're spending more than a year of your life doing something you wouldn't have to do if you didn't have to earn money to survive.

Even these stark numbers don't tell the whole story. The average American works 34.4 hours a week. If we add in time for commuting, that's about 38.7 hours. There are 168 hours in a week, so after you subtract about 56 hours for sleeping, that leaves 73.3 hours. That sounds like a lot—more than double what you spend working in a week—but consider that not all hours are created equal. Studies have shown that we are most alert and energetic early in the day, but that's the time we're usually working. By the time we get off the clock, we're usually so tired or run-down from working all day and commuting that we don't want to do anything except sit on the couch. This is why the average American watches 5.4 hours of TV a day.

Sure, we have weekends, but how often do you spend those running around trying to catch up on all the errands and chores you didn't get to during the week? The point is, you are trading the best hours of your week and your life for a paycheck. I'm not anti-work; in fact I like working. Humans need to work to be happy. But like time, not all work is created equal. There is a huge difference between working at a job you hate, being stuck at a desk or on the clock for forty or more hours a week, and doing work you love and are passionate about, on your own time, and having the freedom to do something else if you want to.

The same trade-off occurs when you look at your life as a whole. You typically have more energy and are healthier in your twenties, thirties, and forties than you are later in life, but if you have to spend those decades working for money, then you're not taking full advantage of this time. You are wasting time.

From a financial standpoint, if you gradually save a small percentage of your income over the course of forty plus years, you are also wasting time that your money could use to grow. When you invest money in the stock market, it grows in value over time because (on average over the long term) it earns returns every year. If you're saving only 5 to 10 percent of your annual income each year over the course of several decades, you're not giving your money nearly as much opportunity to compound as you would if you invested more earlier in your life. You are wasting time.

Don't waste time. You are in control. Remember it's your time. If you take advantage of opportunities to make more and make the most of your money, you can save a lot more money and correspondingly even more time. Every $1 invested today is worth hours, if not days, of your freedom in the future. The more you save today, the more of your time you buy in the future.

If you want to fast-track financial freedom, you need to earn and/or grow as much money in as little time as possible. The earlier you start and the more you save, the sooner you will reach financial independence. This is at the heart of my strategy, and it will rapidly decrease the number of years and the amount of money you need to reach financial independence.

Remember: *The key to fast-tracking financial freedom is to make and invest as much money as early and frequently as you can.*

Fortunately, the relationship between money and time is not strictly linear: If you want to make more money, you don't necessarily need to sacrifice more time to do so. You don't have to be limited by your own hours or even the hours in the day. You don't have to look far to find examples of people who can work half as many hours to earn twice as much money as someone else, and it's not always because they are smarter or more experienced, or work in a more lucrative field. You can even find people who make money by trading very little, if any, of their own time because they've invested a lot of time up-front to build consistent long-term income streams.

Likewise, people who invest their money spend minimal time (other than what it takes to set up and manage their accounts) trying to make that money grow because as long as their money stays invested in the stock market, it will grow automatically over time. This is known as *passive income* because you don't have to actively do anything to earn it, and it is the ultimate moneymaking strategy. What's better than being able to make money doing literally nothing?

Once you reach the point where you no longer *have* to trade your time for money, you can choose to spend that time however you please. When you have enough (or even just close to enough!), you can quit the higher-paying job you hate to take a lower-paying one that is meaningful to you. You can explore, grow, give back, follow your passions, and find new passions. You can travel the world, pick up a new hobby, learn a new skill, volunteer—the possibilities are infinite.

Anita retired at thirty-three so she could sleep in every day and travel the world without having to negotiate vacation days with her boss or worry about missing an important email. Sarah retired at thirty-two so she could learn to play the violin and start a band. Michelle did it at twenty-eight so she could live in an RV, travel the country, and blog full time. Justin did it so he could sit in a hammock at eleven A.M. on a Tuesday and read a good book. Kristy and Bryce did it at thirty-one and thirty-two respectively so they could travel the world on a whim. J.P. did it so she could walk her dog in the middle of the day, discover new passions, and raise a family. Brandon retired at thirty-four so he could spend his time making music and exploring new passions. I did it because I didn't want to spend the best years of my life working in a poorly lit cubicle at a stressful job I didn't particularly enjoy. And because I did it, I have the time to write this book and teach others how to escape the rat race.

So how do you make enough money to "retire" in as little time as possible? The first step is to know how much money you need.

RECAP

1. **Money is unlimited.** Time is not. Don't waste time.
2. **The traditional approach to retirement has three major problems**
   I. It doesn't work for most people.
   II. You end up spending the most valuable years of your life working for money.
   III. It's not designed to help you retire as quickly as possible.
3. **Compounding exponentially increases the value of your money over time, and the earlier and more you invest the faster your money will grow.** The key to fast-tracking financial freedom is making and investing as much money as early and frequently as you can.
4. **Inflation causes price to go up every year for most staples like housing, transportation, and food, but there are ways to minimize the impact of inflation so you will need less money and you can let your investments keep growing**
5. **Don't defer your dreams into the future.** The top two regrets of those facing the end of their lives are "I wish I'd had the courage to live a life true to myself, not the life others expected of me," and "I wish I hadn't worked so hard."
6. **The vast majority of personal finance advice out there is focused on helping you maximize whatever limited money you already have.** It's focused on frugality, scarcity, cutting back, and spending less and doesn't acknowledge that money is limited only if you don't try to make more.
7. **The relationship between money and time is not strictly linear: If you want to make more money, you don't necessarily need to sacrifice more time to do so.**

CHAPTER 3

WHAT IS YOUR NUMBER?

(It's Probably Less Than You Think)

Only when you know your destination can you figure out the best route to get there. You need to figure out *your number*—which is how much money you need to reach your *financial freedom*. What financial freedom means to you might be different than what it means to me or someone else. Maybe *your number* is how much you need to get out of debt, escape living paycheck to paycheck, have two years of expenses saved so you can travel full time for a while, or have enough money so you can work part time and spend more time with your kids. No matter what financial freedom means to you, the strategies in this book are designed to get you there as quickly as possible.

For me, financial freedom meant reaching financial independence, the moment when I had enough money so I could live off my investments and never have to work again. While I *could* keep working, I would no longer have to work to make money to live. My number is the point at which I would reach level 6 of financial freedom (financial independence), or my FI number. In this chapter I'm going to show you how to calculate your own FI number, or as I'll refer to it throughout the book, *your number*. No matter which level of financial freedom you are currently at, the process to calculate your level 5 number will also help you learn the steps to calculate how much you need for levels 2, 3, 4, and 5, which I'll highlight throughout the chapter.

This is by no means an exact science, since several variables—your lifestyle, where you live, whether you have kids, stock market returns, when you want to "retire," and the impact of inflation, just to name a few—will affect how much money you need in the future.

Although you will be able to calculate your number by working through the advice in this chapter, it's not realistic to come up with a perfect number today because your dreams, value, and the things you love might be different in the future. Unless you already have a ton of money invested and are earning a relatively high salary of which you save a significant portion, it's likely going to take you at least five to ten years before you have enough money to make work optional.

You aren't the same person you were five years ago, and you won't be the same person five, ten, or twenty years from now. This is why your number will, and should, change as you change. But taking the time to estimate your number now will allow you to better plan and execute the strategy you need to reach it and adjust it over time. I recommend revisiting your number at least once a year to see if it's still accurate. Trust me, you'll get better at calculating it over time.

How much money you need each year to live today and in the future is directly related to the lifestyle you want for yourself today and in the future. The more expensive your lifestyle, the higher your expenses and the more money you'll need to hit your number, which means the longer you'll likely need to work. Whether you are willing to make the trade-off is up to you. But if you look closely at what really makes you happy, what's really important to you, you can start to deconstruct how much money you need.

What does the great day, month, and year look like to you? What are you doing? Who are you with? Where are you? Are you having a barbecue with your friends? Playing in the yard with your kids? Traveling to some exotic land? Hiking the John Muir Trail? Playing music in a local bar? Dancing late into the night? Golfing on a nice Sunday? Reading in a hammock? Cooking with your partner? Take a few minutes to write down what a great day looks like for you. Why is it so great? Why does it bring you joy?

Then think hard about how much money you need to live this life. When many of us make more money, we reward ourselves with new and nicer things—a bigger house, a nicer car, better clothes. But that's an old-school consumer mindset you need to push against if you want to hit your number faster. I'm not hating on nice things, it's just that a lot of people end up spending money on them without thinking about what they actually want or need. Sometimes we spend money on things because it's how we grew up, or it's what our families or friends do because it's what we think we're supposed to do, or even because we're bored. If you really look at what you love doing and what makes you happiest, you might need a lot less money to live a life you love than you think you do. Be honest with yourself: what do you really value most in your life?

The more money I've made in my own life, the less money I spend and the less I feel like I need to do what I love. It's a feeling I never expected, but once I realized I had enough money to buy pretty much anything I wanted, then I no longer wanted to buy it. Just having the ability to buy something was enough.

When you see the true value of money, you naturally spend less. Many of the richest and most successful people I know are the most frugal. But this doesn't mean they're cheap. Frugality is not about not spending, it's about not wasting—your money, your time, and your resources. It's about buying and using only what you need. Needs are different than wants. While our needs used to just be food, shelter, and clothing, they now also can include things essential to your mental, physical, emotional, and spiritual survival and well-being. I'm not here to tell what to buy or not to buy, but there is definitely a fine line between wants and needs. Only you can know what you truly need. Just asking yourself that question before you buy anything is one way to find out, and the more often you do it, the less you realize you actually need.

If you really want something, wait thirty, sixty, or even ninety days before buying it, and you might not even want it anymore. Impulse is an enemy of financial freedom. Or the next time you think about buying something, ask yourself, Is this worth trading my freedom for?

As you read through this book, keep this in the back of your mind. The less money you need, the sooner you can reach financial independence. You need a lot of money to retire, but you probably need less than you think. That's because—and this is something you won't read in any traditional personal finance or retirement book:

The younger you are, the less money you need to have saved before you can "retire" as long as you follow a few simple rules.

You can "retire" with less money at thirty than you'll need at sixty and not have to work for that extra thirty years! It sounds crazy, but because of how the market works and the magic of compounding, it's true. Here's why:

Even though the younger you are, the longer you need your money to last, your money has more time to grow—in this case, an additional thirty years of compounding. Even if you take 3 or 4 percent withdrawals adjusted for inflation from your investment portfolio, your money is still likely to grow at least 3 to 4 times by the time you're sixty. So if you save $1 million by thirty and can live off 3 or 4 percent, then you can live off that money for thirty years and your balance will have grown to $3 or $4 million, or even more. And you can even adjust your withdrawal for inflation and spend more money over time. This isn't unrealistic if you want it.

The younger you are, the more time and likely energy you'll have, so you can always go back to work or supplement your investment withdrawals (by doing something you love doing). Or if you can build some side or passive income streams, or work part time, then you can "retire" from the job you don't like and work on one you do, even if it pays a lot less money.

Even if you do save up enough to reach financial independence at the age of thirty you might take a few years to chill or travel, but you'll probably want to work again at some point. If you're the type of person who is going to hustle to hit your number (I know you are!), then you're the type of person who is likely going to make money doing something in the future.

Trust me, no matter how old you are when you reach financial independence, you'll be so pumped up you'll eventually want to dive into other projects that excite you in which you'll end up making money. This extra money you might make in the future will give you more security and reduce how much money (if any) you need to withdraw from your investments.

Let's dig a little deeper so you can see how to make your money last forever. Typical retirement advice suggests that you should save at least 25 times your *expected* annual expenses (i.e., the amount of money you plan to spend each year in retirement) before you retire. This calculation became standard advice thanks to a popular academic paper known as the Trinity study. I won't get into too many of the specifics of this study, but here are the basics. The authors analyzed how long an investment portfolio would last based on the performance of the U.S. stock market between

1926 and 1997 depending on two variables that you'll learn a lot about in this book:

1. asset allocation (the percentage of stocks versus bonds, which determines the level of risk/reward in the portfolio)
2. withdrawal rate (the amount of money one withdraws from an investment portfolio each month to live on)

The authors analyzed how likely it was that your money would last thirty years based on your asset allocation and withdrawal rate. Thirty years was chosen because the average person in the United States was retiring between sixty-two and sixty-five at the time of the study, so based on average life expectancy, thirty years was pretty much as long as they would need the money to last.

The study showed there was at least a 98 percent success rate of the money lasting thirty years if you withdrew 4 percent the first year, then 4 percent plus inflation (6–7 percent) each subsequent year, and you kept the portfolio invested in either 100 percent stocks or 75 percent stocks and 25 percent bonds. The success rate ultimately depended on the asset allocation and withdrawal rate. Here's the chart from the study that shows the projected success rate of a target asset allocation based on the expected withdrawal rate. Note that these numbers are adjusted for inflation (so the impact of inflation has been factored in).

Based on the Trinity study, your asset allocation percentage and withdrawal rate ultimately determine the amount of money you need to have saved to last for the rest of your life. If you want to withdraw 4 percent each year adjusted for inflation, then you want to have 25 times your expected annual expenses saved (100/expected withdrawal rate = 25 times), with a target asset allocation of at least 75 percent stocks and 25 percent bonds, in order for your money to last thirty years.

But the Trinity study looked at the success rate only over a thirty-year period, which means that if your bank account reached $0 in year 31, it was still a success. The study was based on withdrawing both your investment gains and your principal (the amount you contributed). But this isn't really that helpful if you retire at thirty years old and need your money to last

WHAT IS YOUR NUMBER?

Portfolio Success Rate with Inflation-Adjusted Monthly Withdrawals: 1926 to 1997
(Percent of all past payout periods supported by the portfolio)

Payout Period	Annualized Withdrawal Rate as a % of Initial Portfolio Value									
	3%	4%	5%	6%	7%	8%	9%	10%	11%	12%
100% Stocks										
20 years	100	100	91	77	66	57	42	32	28	19
25 years	100	100	85	69	56	42	33	29	25	15
30 years	100	98	81	65	56	44	33	33	19	7
75% Stock/25% Bonds										
20 years	100	100	94	77	66	51	38	19	17	6
25 years	100	100	85	65	50	33	25	13	4	0
30 years	100	100	86	63	47	35	14	7	0	0
50% Stocks/50% Bonds										
20 years	100	100	92	75	55	30	17	9	2	0
25 years	100	100	79	52	31	15	4	0	0	0
30 years	100	95	70	51	19	9	0	0	0	0
25% Stocks/75% Bonds										
20 years	100	100	89	51	28	15	9	4	0	0
25 years	100	96	48	19	17	6	0	0	0	0
30 years	100	74	26	19	7	0	0	0	0	0
100% Bonds										
20 years	100	96	57	23	15	13	9	0	0	0
25 years	100	52	19	15	10	0	0	0	0	0
30 years	79	19	16	12	0	0	0	0	0	0

20 years = 53 overlapping periods; 25 years = 48 overlapping periods; 30 years = 43 overlapping periods
Results for 15 years are available from the authors.
SOURCE: Philip L. Cooley, Carl M. Hubbard, and Daniel T. Walz, "Sustainable Withdrawal Rates from Your Retirement Portfolio," *Journal of Financial Counseling and Planning* 10, no. 1 (1999), http://afepe.org/assets/pdf/vol1014.pdf.

another sixty years. The study is also based on historical data, and future stock market performance might not be as strong or could be stronger—we just don't know.

But other studies since the Trinity study have shown that even in the worst down markets, a 3 to 4 percent (plus inflation adjustments) investment withdrawal rate has an extremely high rate of success over a period of fifty plus years. While the first ten years of stock market returns after you "retire" are important, over a long period the stock market has always recovered and kept growing. Also keep in mind that if your investments grow 40 percent over a period of a few years and you're living off, say, 4 percent plus 2 percent for inflation = 6 percent, then your net increase is going to be 34 percent, which will continue to grow over time. Your $1,000,000 would now be worth $1,340,000 after withdrawals.

So if your expenses stay relatively the same over a five-year period, but your portfolio is way up over that same period, then the withdrawal percentage needed to cover your expenses would actually go down. Over time this gap will likely widen even more, meaning the longer and more your money grows, the likelier it is you can actually increase your expenses and withdrawals and still never run out of money. And as I previously mentioned, it's very realistic that your investment portfolio could be double, triple, or quadruple in size over any thirty-plus-year period as long as you withdraw the standard 3 to 4 percent plus increases for inflation.

To increase the percentage chance of your money lasting for the rest of your life (or even way beyond), you should be prepared to do a few things a little differently than the Trinity study recommends. In essence, you should strategically minimize your investment withdrawals so that you can leave as much of your money invested and growing over time. While we will elaborate on this idea later in the book, it's important to get the gist of it in order to set some context.

Here's how you can "retire" a lot faster with less money and increase the potential that your money will last for the rest of your life (and even way beyond).

1. **You can save more than 25 times your expected annual expenses.** Other early retirees use 30 times or more. It's up to you to decide what you are comfortable with. I personally use the 25 times as my multiplier and feel very comfortable with it because I have an additional full year of living expenses in cash as a buffer that I can use, multiple side income streams,

and skills that I know I can use to make money if needed in the future. And I'm still making money.

2. **You should defer taking your investment gains as long as possible.** If you do decide to actually retire and have a side hustle or passive income stream that is either offsetting or perhaps completely covering your monthly expenses, then you need less of your invested money and you can let your investments keep compounding and growing without withdrawing any of the money. A good example of this is investing in real estate and using your rental income to cover your living expenses while letting your stock investments keep growing. Also, as we've already discussed, just because you have the freedom to retire, it doesn't mean that you need to or will. Trust me, the last thing you will want to do if you retire at thirty is never work again; just because you no longer have to make money doesn't mean you won't or you won't want to. So later in life when you do make money you can live off it instead of pulling from your investment gains.

3. **As you get closer to retiring, you should start increasing your six-month emergency fund to cover a full year of living expenses.** You never know what's going to come up in the future, so having an emergency fund of one year of expenses will give you more flexibility. You won't need to withdraw money from your investments to cover emergency expenses, or to take withdrawals if the stock market is really down one year. The emergency fund also gives you the ability to spend more money if you want to without having to withdraw from your investments. Having a "bonus cash" buffer gives you more flexibility. You don't actually have to keep it in cash, since you would be losing money to inflation, but putting it in CD (certificate of deposit) accounts is a wise decision.

4. **When you do start taking out investing gains, live on as little of the money as possible, even when the market is way up.** For example, if the stock market is up 23 percent over the past year, but you withdraw only 3 percent of your investment growth, then you can keep 20 percent of the gains in the market to keep compounding into the future. Doing this over time will create a much larger investment surplus than you will need and give you the opportunity in the future to withdraw more money. If the market is down, then consider using your cash or starting a side hustle so you have to withdraw as little money as possible.

5. **Last, try and preserve your investment principal (the money that you originally contributed), because your principal is the largest balance driving your investment growth.** The Trinity study was built around withdrawing both your investment gains and your principal balance, but if you preserve your principal and most of your investment gains, the chances of your money lasting well beyond thirty years increase exponentially.

And remember this is by no means an exact science, but it gives us enough information to more accurately calculate *your number*. Which we'll do next.

HOW MUCH MONEY DO YOU ACTUALLY NEED?

To help you figure out how much you might need to retire, almost every bank that sells retirement products offers a retirement calculator. Retirement calculators are pretty easy to use: go to the bank's website and plug in a bunch of numbers (e.g., how much money you currently have saved for retirement, how much you plan to contribute to your retirement plan each year, the amount of money you expect to need each year after you retire, when you plan to retire, etc.); the calculator then presents you with the amount it figures you need to retire.

When I first started on my own financial freedom journey, I set a goal of earning $1 million in five years. That was a nice big number and it would definitely put me in a great financial position, but would it be enough for me to "retire" at thirty? I started playing around with some online calculators, but they always told me I needed to save a ridiculous amount of money—something like $3.5 million* by the time I was sixty-five based on expected annual expenses of $50,000. Even if I was saving the maximum amount in my 401(k) (which as of this writing is $18,500 per year) growing at 7 percent per year, I'd end up with only $1,891,751 after thirty years—a little more than half of what I would supposedly need. Was this some sort of joke? How can anyone outside of the 1 percent ever save enough to retire?

To make things even more complicated, I wasn't trying to figure out what I'd need in forty years, but what I'd need in five. If I needed $3.5 million when I was sixty-five and would likely live only another twenty-five to thirty years, wouldn't I need to have more saved up if I wanted to make that money last sixty to seventy years?

It wasn't until I really dug into the numbers that I realized the answer was no. This is yet another problem with the standard approach to retirement. Because financial services companies assume you're planning to retire in your sixties or seventies, their calculators do not account for all the variables that can change if you plan to retire earlier.

For one thing, they assume each dollar you have saved will be worth much less in terms of purchasing power in the future (which it undoubtedly will because of inflation), but prices don't go up for *everything* and you can actively find ways to live outside of inflation, since it impacts only what you buy—not what you already own or grow or make. For example, prices on homes go up, but if you already own your home, inflation won't impact you beyond taxes. Living outside of inflation isn't factored into the fancy retirement calculators, so the numbers they provide look a lot higher than they actually are. But if you want to reach financial independence in the next five to ten years, the money you save today will have depreciated

---

* This number did not account for any Social Security benefits I might receive in retirement, which would reduce the amount I'd need to save. Most calculators allow you to factor this number in, but I chose not to, since I hoped to retire more than thirty years before I was old enough to get social security.

far less by the time you're ready to retire, so you don't need to have as much saved to make work optional.

The other problem with these calculators—and this is true no matter what age you plan to retire at—is that they assume the amount you have when you retire is all you'll have to live on for the rest of your life. In other words, once you start living on your investments, you will be drawing from a fixed amount that won't continue to grow and earn returns as it did up until that point. Following this logic, if you retire at sixty-five with $3.5 million saved, you'd need to make that $3.5 million last for as long as you needed it.

But this isn't how investing works. If you're living off a retirement or other investment account, it's highly unlikely you'll withdraw all of the money at once. Instead, you'd take out only what you needed for a certain period of time while keeping the rest invested in the market. The longer you keep money invested, the longer it will have to compound and the more your initial investment will grow. BOOM! If you retire at thirty, then you have an additional fifty plus years of compounding if you live until eighty. Whereas if you retire at sixty, you'll have only twenty years of compounding until you are eighty. Sure, at sixty you need less money for the rest of your life than you do at thirty, but it has less time to grow. Remember the key to compounding is the earlier and more you invest, the faster your money will grow. Yet another reason compounding is so awesome!

For the sake of illustration, imagine you have $1 million invested and your investment grows 7 percent (adjusted for dividends and inflation, that's $70,000) over the course of a year. You now have $1,070,000 invested. Let's say you're no longer earning an income and are able to live on $40,000 (4 percent of your initial investment) per year after taxes. If your money is in a taxable investment account, you can withdraw $40,000 and still have $1,030,000 left over. You haven't even touched the original $1 million, and the balance (the original $1 million plus the $30,000 leftover returns) will continue to earn returns as long as it remains invested. The key is to never touch your investment principal and withdraw only as little of your investment growth as you need to live on, but never all of it. If you can continue this pattern of withdrawing less than your returns year after year, then not only will you be living off your investment growth, but the total value of your investments could also easily double, triple, or quadruple over the following years.

And even if the money is in a tax-advantaged account, which typically has penalties for early withdrawals, there are ways you can eliminate the penalties by getting creative, as I'll show you below. This is why you actually need *less* money to retire in your twenties or thirties than you do in your sixties or seventies. Thanks to the magic of investing, your number is at the point at which you can live entirely off the returns your investments are making, and that number is likely a lot less than you think.

Compounding makes this strategy even more powerful because, in addition to your initial investment, your *returns* will continue to earn returns. Continuing the scenario described above, let's say the $1,030,000 you keep invested earns another annual return of 7 percent. By the end of that year, you'd have gained $72,100 instead of $70,000. If you up your annual withdrawal rate to 4 percent (instead of a flat $40,000), your money will continue to compound at 3 percent per year (assuming an average 7 percent return over time), and even if you never contribute money to that account again, you will end up with—wait for it—$3,262,037 at the age of sixty-five! Not only would you have not had to work during those forty years, but your portfolio balance would have grown by over $2 million, almost tripling in total value. Look at this!

Once again, time is on your side here, because the more money you have invested sooner, the more it will grow over time. Look again at the chart above. If you don't have $1 million saved until age forty-five, your money will have only twenty years to grow until you reach sixty-five and would be worth only $1,820,020—and you would have been working an additional twenty years!

Of course, this is a hypothetical scenario, but it illustrates the point that because of compounding, you do in fact need less money to retire the younger you are—as long as you keep some of your investment gains compounding. Anita retired in 2015 at age thirty-three and withdrew 3 percent of her approximately $800,0000 portfolio to live on for the next two years. The total stock market grew 11 percent during that time, so 8 percent of the gains in her portfolio continued compounding. Kristy and Bryce retired at thirty-two with $1 million and live off 4 percent of their interest, but

Annual Investment Gains on $1-Million Assuming 3% Average Return After Withdraw and No Additional Annual Deposits

Year	Begin Year Balance	Yearly Gains	Year End Balance
1	$1,030,000	$31,328.44	$1,061,328.44
2	$1,061,328.44	$32,281.32	$1,093,609.76
3	$1,093,609.76	$33,263.19	$1,126,872.95
4	$1,126,872.95	$34,274.92	$1,161,147.87
5	$1,161,147.87	$35,317.42	$1,196,465.29
6	$1,196,465.29	$36,391.64	$1,232,856.93
7	$1,232,856.93	$37,498.52	$1,270,355.45
8	$1,270,355.45	$38,639.08	$1,308,994.53
9	$1,308,994.53	$39,814.32	$1,348,808.85
10	$1,348,808.85	$41,025.31	$1,389,834.16
11	$1,389,834.16	$42,273.14	$1,432,107.30
12	$1,432,107.30	$43,558.91	$1,475,666.21
13	$1,475,666.21	$44,883.80	$1,520,550.01
14	$1,520,550.01	$46,248.98	$1,566,798.99
15	$1,566,798.99	$47,655.69	$1,614,454.68
16	$1,614,454.68	$49,105.18	$1,663,559.86
17	$1,663,559.86	$50,598.77	$1,714,158.63
18	$1,714,158.63	$52,137.77	$1,766,296.40
19	$1,766,296.40	$53,723.60	$1,820,020.00
20	$1,820,020.00	$55,357.65	$1,875,377.65
21	$1,875,377.65	$57,041.41	$1,932,419.06
22	$1,932,419.06	$58,776.37	$1,991,195.43
23	$1,991,195.43	$60,564.11	$2,051,759.54
24	$2,051,759.54	$62,406.23	$2,114,165.77
25	$2,114,165.77	$64,304.37	$2,178,470.14
26	$2,178,470.14	$66,260.25	$2,244,730.39
27	$2,244,730.39	$68,275.62	$2,313,006.01
28	$2,313,006.01	$70,352.29	$2,383,358.30
29	$2,383,358.30	$72,492.12	$2,455,850.42
30	$2,455,850.42	$74,697.04	$2,530,547.46
31	$2,530,547.46	$76,969.02	$2,607,516.48
32	$2,607,516.48	$79,310.11	$2,686,826.59
33	$2,686,826.59	$81,722.40	$2,768,548.99
34	$2,768,548.99	$84,208.07	$2,852,757.06
35	$2,852,757.06	$86,769.34	$2,939,526.40
36	$2,939,526.40	$89,408.51	$3,028,934.91
37	$3,028,934.91	$92,127.95	$3,121,062.86
38	$3,121,062.86	$94,930.11	$3,215,992.97
39	$3,215,992.97	$97,817.50	$3,313,810.47
40	$3,313,810.47	$100,792.72	$3,414,603.19

their investments grew 13 percent over the past year. Steve retired with $800,000, but only a year later, his investment portfolio is now over $1 million, reducing the percentage he needs to withdraw next year to cover his living expenses.

One word of caution: Stock market gains are not predictable or guaranteed, so you should consider market conditions when you start to withdraw. Although over the long term the stock market tends to experience average annual gains of 6 to 7 percent, it can fluctuate greatly from year to year—up 20 percent one year and down 11 percent the next.

Fortunately, the longer you keep your money invested, the less you have to worry about short-term market fluctuations, even in a downturn. If you can get through the first ten years with your investment principal intact and if you can live on a 4 percent withdrawal rate, your chance of success should be closer to 100 percent, since after that ten-year period, your investments should have compounded enough that you can live off your returns forever. Of course, a major economic collapse could decrease your chance of success slightly, so you should pay attention to the market and start to withdraw only once you've reached the point that you can do so without diminishing your principal*.

Another benefit of allowing a portion of your investment gains to continue growing is that at some point in the future, you'll be able to start taking larger withdrawals when/if you need them without the risk of running out of money. Buying that $500,000 lake home when you're thirty could wipe out a huge portion of your savings. But if you wait until you're fifty and have been allowing your returns to compound for twenty years, you will be able to afford that same house—even if it costs more due to inflation.

CALCULATE YOUR NUMBER

Knowing all of this, you can calculate your number much more accurately than any retirement calculator can. You just need to figure out how much money you'd need to have invested before you can live solely off a portion

---

* FYI: The IRS will start forcing you to take withdrawals from some of your tax-deferred accounts after you are seventy and a half, so you can start using some of your hard-earned investing gains to throw some great parties.

of your returns while keeping some of your returns invested so they can continue to grow.

While the most accurate way to calculate your number is to determine how much money you will need to live on each year for the rest of your life once you decide to retire (aka your expected annual expenses), it's nearly impossible to do because you don't know how your goals, desires, wants, and needs are going to change over the next ten, twenty, thirty, forty or more years. This is where the retirement calculators and financial planners fall short—they expect you to know how much money you will want to spend in the future and then base their calculation off that number.

But for even the best planners, coming up with an exact target for your expected annual expenses in the future is unrealistic. The finance industry often sells a level of precision with investing and retirement planning that's really just guessing. They also don't focus on helping you determine how much money it would take to live a life you love, because you're the only one who can really do that. This is why I recommend you approach this more holistically, finding the amount of money you need to live today and adjusting it once a year as you change and grow.

With that in mind, I recommend using your current annual expenses to calculate your number for two reasons:

1. If you plan to retire in the next few years, your recurring expenses likely won't change that much.
2. It's much easier to figure out how much you currently spend than what you'll be spending twenty, thirty, or forty years down the road.

Also, no matter where you are today, you can also use your current expenses to determine how much you need to reach the next level of financial freedom, since levels 2 through 5 are based on your current expenses.

1. Self-sufficiency, when you earn enough money to cover your expenses on your own = 1 times your monthly expenses
2. Breathing room, when you escape living paycheck to paycheck = 3 to 5 times your monthly expenses

3. Stability, when you have six months of living expenses saved and debt repaid = 6 times your monthly expenses
4. Flexibility, when you have two years of living expenses invested = 24 times your monthly expenses

The easiest way to calculate what you spend in a year is to look at how much you've spent each month over the past twelve months in the categories outlined below. You can do this pretty easily by looking at your bank and credit card statements over the past year and calculating your average monthly spending in each category.

Check out the simple tool at https://financialfreedombook.com/tools you can use to make this really easy by pulling your spending directly from your accounts. You can also download this spreadsheet to customize yourself. It also might be worth it to do the calculation manually so you can see how the numbers work. Each quarter, I update a manual spreadsheet that looks like the one below, which includes a breakdown of how much the average American household spends in these categories each year. How do your numbers compare?

Once you've figured out your expected annual expenses, you can calculate your base number. To do this, you'll need to draw on some of your sixth-grade math skills to determine the amount of money you need to have invested before you can withdraw enough to cover your annual expenses. Written as a formula, the calculation looks like this:

Withdrawal rate percentage × your number = annual expenses

Let's say you spend about $50,000 a year. Assuming you'll be withdrawing at the recommended rate of 4 percent a year, your calculation would look like this.

.04 × Your Number = $50,000
$50,000/.04 = $1,250,000
or written another way $50,000 × 25x = $1,250,000

FINANCIAL FREEDOM

Expense	Avg. US Household Annual (2016)	You Monthly	You Annual
Housing			
Mortgage/Rent			
Property Taxes			
Maintenance and Cleaning			
Home/Renter's Insurance			
Electricity			
Oil/Gas			
Water/Garbage/Sewer			
Phone			
Cable/Internet			
Other (Including vacation and hotels)			
Total Housing	$18,886		
Transportation			
Car Payment			
Maintenance/Repairs			
Gas/Oil			
License/Registration			
Insurance			
Bus/Train Fare			
Flights (including vacation)			
Taxis/Ridesharing			
Total Transportation	$9,049		
Food			
Groceries / Eat at Home			
Eating Out			
Total Food	$7,203		
Apparel & Services			
Clothing and Shoes			
Jewelry			
Dry Cleaning/Laundry			
Total Apparel and Services	$1,803		
Cash Contributions			
Donations			
Other			
Total Cash Contributions	$2,081		

WHAT IS YOUR NUMBER?

Expense	Avg. US Household (2016)	You Monthly	You Annual
Healthcare			
Health Insurance			
Long-Term Care Insurance			
Disability Insurance			
Medical Expenses			
Dental Expenses			
Other			
Total Healthcare	$4,612		
Insurance and Pensions			
Life and Personal Insurance			
Pension and Social Security			
Total Insurance	$6,831		
Entertainment			
Events			
Memberships			
Lessons / Hobbies			
Pets			
Total Entertainment	$2,913		
All Other Expenditures			
Tuition			
Books/Newspapers			
Personal Care			
Legal/Accounting Fees			
Total Other	$3,933		
Taxes (Depend On Income)			
Federal			
State			
Local			
Total Taxes			
Total Expenditures	$57,311		

SOURCE: Bureau of Labor Statistics https://www.bls.gov/news.release/cesan.htm

While I personally used the 25 times rule, if you want to be a little more conservative, then I recommend using a 3.5 percent withdrawal percentage to provide a little cushion.

For 3.5 percent: $50,000/0.035 = $1,428,571

If you plug $50,000 into an online retirement calculator, it will tell you that you need to save between $3 million and $4 million if you want to retire in your sixties. But based on a simple calculation, you find you need less than half of that to reach financial independence more than thirty years earlier.

Obviously, though, if your expenses increase or decrease, your number will, too. Perhaps you currently don't make a lot of money and are living on $20,000, but you eventually hope to move out of the apartment you currently share with three roommates and intend to have kids one day, which will of course increase your expenses. Or maybe you have dreams of traveling or being able to buy that sweet vintage car. The higher your expenses, the higher your number, but even cutting back on a few expenses can reduce the amount of money you'll need.

THE IMPACT OF A SINGLE RECURRING EXPENSE ON YOUR NUMBER

Throughout the book we will dive deeper into how you can specifically save money on your three biggest expenses—housing, transportation, and food—but one simple way to reduce your expenses, and thus your number, is to calculate the impact each recurring expense has on your number by using the following simple equation: your monthly expenses × 12 months × 25x annual expense multiplier = the impact of that recurring expense on your number).

For example, I spent over $350 a month in takeout food in 2017, so if that expensive habit continues, I will need: $350 month × 12 months = $4,200 per year × 25x = $105,000. In other words, I'll need $105,000 saved to support this habit for the rest of my life. If I could just cut this figure down to $200 per month, then I would need: $200 month × 12 months = $2,400 per year × 25x = $60,000, or $45,000 less. Any type of recurring expense increases your number. Keep this in mind as you read through the book and work to reduce your expenses.

ADJUSTING YOUR NUMBER FOR ONETIME FUTURE EXPENSES

While the 25 times multiplier helps you estimate how much you'll need for your living expenses, it doesn't factor in future onetime expenses that might increase the amount of money you'll need to withdraw. Most retirement calculators also aren't designed for you to estimate future onetime expenses. But you should estimate how much money you might need at different stages of your life and for onetime big expenses like a kid's college education or a big vacation home. If you have some big onetime expenses in mind, you will want to build them into your number either today or the next time you adjust your calculation.

Here's how. If you estimate you will need $80,000 for your child's state college tuition, room, and board, you don't need to add $80,000 to your number, since you won't be paying that $80,000 in monthly installments for the rest of your life (or hopefully not!). The way you add it is by estimating when you will need the money and determining how much you need to invest for it to grow to be $80,000 when you need it. For example, if your child is three years old today, you won't need that $80,000 college tuition money for the next fifteen years, so you need to calculate how much you need to save today at 7 percent expected annual compounding rate so it will be worth $80,000 in fifteen years.

Using a really simple calculation (and one of the most valuable in personal finance) known as the *present value formula*, which measures the time value of money, you can measure how much you need to invest today to get the $80,000 over the next fifteen years:

PV (present value) = amount of money you need to invest to get to your goal (e.g. = ?)

$$PV = FV \, \frac{1}{(1+r)^n}$$

FV (future value) = how much money you need for college tuition
(e.g., $80,000)

r = investment growth rate adjusted for inflation (e.g. = 7 percent
expressed as 1.07)

n = number of years for the money to grow (e.g. = 15 years)

So for this example it's PV = $80,000*(1/(1.07)^15), so PV = $28,995.68.

You need to save $28,995 today for it to be worth $80,000 at 7 percent compounding growth over the next fifteen years. You should add this to your number. Then after fifteen years you can withdraw the money to use for college tuition at once or over time and let the money keep growing. You should use this same formula to adjust your number for any big one-time expenses in the future.

Another factor that's a pretty big wild card is the future cost of health-care, which is not only getting more expensive in the United States but will also likely increase as you get older and need more care. This is why it's so important to plan and regularly revisit your number quarterly, or at least once a year to make adjustments. Don't worry; you'll be a pro at this in no time.

No matter how big your number is, you might be thinking, *Whoa, how can I save that much money?* While $1,250,000 was a lot less than the $3.5 million the retirement calculators were telling me, I initially felt over-whelmed. That's a lot of money to save when you are broke. I started wondering if I really needed that much money.

Ultimately how much money you need depends on one big variable . . .

THE LIFESTYLE FACTOR

While you are calculating your number and analyzing your expenses, it's the perfect time to take a hard look at your current spending and evaluate whether or not you need to spend that much to live the life you want. Obviously, the lower your expenses, the less money you'll need. Also, the lower your expenses, the more you can save and invest, and the more you invest, the quicker it will grow and the faster you can reach financial independence. Could there be a way to spend less money and still live a life you love? Cut back to the essentials, those things that regularly give you joy, meaning, purpose, and fulfillment.

Money matters only if it helps you live a life that you love, but we rarely consider what we *really* need. As a result, we often spend money on things that aren't really important to us—sometimes at the expense of what makes us happy. We get caught up in what others are spending their money on and tend to adopt a lifestyle similar to that of those around us, even if we don't really want what they have. Or we spend money because today it makes us feel powerful, when in reality the money will be worth more and give us more power tomorrow than today.

We also tend to spend more money as we make more money, a trend known as *lifestyle inflation*—which explains why a pop star or an athlete can earn millions of dollars per year and still end up deep in debt. This also explains why so many people who make $100,000 or more are still living paycheck to paycheck or are deep in debt; they're spending more than they need to and living a lifestyle they can't afford. They consume first and pay themselves last, if at all. It's always best to pay yourself first through investing.

We often think about spending money so we can get something, but in reality, whenever we spend money instead of investing it, we are actually taking from ourselves—we are taking both the time we spent to make the money and the future freedom it can buy.

In the United States, we are taught from a young age to buy anything we need or anything we want because "I work hard and I deserve it." We are also taught to solve our problems by buying something—especially when it comes to our basic needs.

When we get hungry, we buy or order food, instead of trying to grow our own or trade with people who do. Or we order out instead of eating what we have. This is why it's so easy to spend $60 on takeout on a Wednesday night or why I spent over $2,000 one year on Mexican food. This is one of the areas where I struggle, but I'm working at it.

When we need a place to stay, we rent the most expensive apartment or buy the biggest house we can get a mortgage on. We rent expensive hotel rooms instead of looking for opportunities to house-sit, rent a room, camp, or crash with a friend. Now, don't get me wrong—I enjoy staying in really nice hotels around the world, so I spend my money on it. But I can't stand spending $500 on some overpriced corporate chain hotel in Pittsburgh.

When we need to get to our jobs or we get a promotion, it's easy to justify buying a new car even if our old car is fine. I fell victim to this trap when I bought a $20,000 Mini Cooper just after getting my first job out of college, ensuring that for years at least $400 per month would need to go to a car payment. I should have bought a car for less than $1,000, which I eventually did instead.

When our kids are upset or just to make them happy, we buy too many overpriced toys they don't need. When we get sick, we head to the store to buy cough syrups and vaporizers, or to the doctor to get medications that mask our symptoms, but don't solve the root cause. We medicate so we can keep moving, instead of resting—which ends up causing more health issues and being more expensive over time.

When you do need something, searching for free alternatives, asking your friends or family for help for help, or bartering can you save money. There is almost always a cheaper—or in many cases, even a free—way if you get creative. It just comes down to how much you really want to save. For example, if you need a dress for a party, you can borrow one from a friend for free, rent one, or buy a used dress instead of buying it new. I recently bartered with my dog boarder for an entire week of dog boarding (a $400 value) by helping her with her Facebook ad campaign; it took me only about thirty minutes. I built a simple website for my barber in a few hours in exchange for free haircuts ($240 value). It's a win-win.

If you actually step back and ask yourself what you *really* need, what *really* brings joy to your life, you'll be better able to spend money mindfully and with intention. This doesn't mean you shouldn't buy a beautiful vintage Mercedes, stay in five-star hotels, or splurge on designer shoes if those things bring you joy; it just means you will spend less money in other areas that aren't as important to you and that you will need to account for these things when calculating your annual expenses. If you're making $30 per hour after taxes and want to buy a $60,000 car, you're going to be trading 2,000 of the premium hours of your life for that vehicle. If you work forty hours a week, that's fifty weeks—an entire *year*—you need to work to buy that car. If that car is worth a year of your life, then great; just realize the trade-off you are making.

Also realize that the $60,000 car actually costs more than $60,000 because you lose the opportunity to invest that money for your future self. At 7 percent compounding, that $60,000 would be worth $120,579 in ten years, $242,324 in twenty years, and $486,989 in thirty years! Is that $60,000 car today worth having to save $486,989 more to hit your number? *That $60,000 vintage car is actually costing you $486,989 in the future.* So you are actually trading 2,000 hours of your life AND over $400,000 in growth potential. I would rather have the money in the future, but your choice is up to you.

Double your money with the Rule of 72

A simple way to estimate how much something will be worth at 7 percent compounding is to use the rule of 72, in which you divide 72 by your expected compounding rate (7 percent) to determine how many years it would take for your money to double. At 7 percent compounding, 72/7 percent = 10.2 years, so at that compounding rate, your money will double every ten years. Thus, if you invested the $60,000 instead of buying the new car, your money would be worth $120,000 in ten years, $240,000 in twenty years, and so on.

If you're like most people, though, you'll find that experiences—travel, going out with friends, hanging out with your family in the park, getting lost in a music festival, camping, meeting new people, etc.—might bring more joy to your life than possessions. These might still require some money, but it will likely be a lot less.

Financial freedom comes down to being honest with yourself about what really brings you joy and what's important to you. Spend money on what you really value and save on what you don't. Everything else—what your friends do, or your neighbors buy, or your parents say, or your co-workers splurge on—is just noise. There will always be some shiny new thing to buy (our entire economy depends on our buying stuff!), but if you spend money only on what's important to you, you'll spend less and reach financial independence faster.

Living a happy life or a life you love might seem like a really foreign concept right now, or you might be saying, "I don't really know what makes me happy." Don't worry, you're not alone. Many people don't know what makes them happy—they just want more time, space, and freedom to figure it out. Or they want to get out of the rat race as quickly as possible, and that's cool, too. This is a journey, and as you explore new ways to save and make money, you'll be surprised to uncover new things that bring you joy, bring you peace, give your life meaning, and make it more fun.

Over time as you consider how much you need to spend each year in order to actually be happy, you'll likely find your number is a lot smaller than you think. For example, Steve never felt fulfilled by his full-time IT job, so a few years ago he decided he wanted to retire early and knew that would require him saving a significant amount of money. He started by carefully analyzing his spending and evaluating how much money he needed each year to be happy. He figured he could live on $40,000 or less per year and support his lifestyle by living in an Airstream with his wife and not having to be burdened by homeownership.

Sure, Steve could have made more money by staying at his job, and he knew that retiring early would mean he'd have to live a little leaner to make it work. But he also knew that time is more valuable than money or the things money can buy, so he retired at the age of thirty-five with $890,000 invested. By taking stock of what made him happy and how much money he'd need to maintain a fulfilling lifestyle, he was able to retire much earlier than he thought he'd be able to and live off his investment gains while still keeping his investments growing! Over time Steve may decide to live on more than $40,000 per year, and if he allows his money to compound long enough, he'll be able to do so without a problem. He's also already picked up a few small side hustles he can do on his own time, like blogging to supplement and reduce his investment withdrawals.

You might even be able to "retire" already

You might be in a really stressful job making $120,000 a year, but you need only $40,000 to cover your expenses, so if you already have a decent amount of money saved, you could quit your stressful job and take a less stressful job that covers your monthly expenses and be happier. Or if you want more time with your kids, you could switch to a part-time job. Far too many people stay in jobs they hate simply because:

1. They don't feel like they have a choice or
2. They don't realize they don't really need more money or
3. They don't realize they could live on less money and actually cover their expenses doing a job they love.

I've talked with so many people who tell me "I'm stuck at my job and I hate it," but they've never taken a close look at their expenses to see how much money they really need or they aren't willing to make a change in their lifestyle so they can actually be happier. Life's too short to not enjoy it.

> The big thing was finding a spending level that made me happy. I found this out by buying as little as possible and then started adding back in the things that were really important to me. I tested my lower spending threshold and determined it was too low and led to deprivation. And then I pushed my upper threshold. I've found the balance. We actually realized we don't want to travel and eat out as much as we thought we previously wanted. Figure out what's important to you and what spending makes you happy. It gets easier when you test your limits a bit.
> —Brandon, who reached FI at thirty-two and retired at thirty-four

After a few years of monitoring my own spending and reducing my expenses, I was able to determine that I can live a life I really love spending $50,000 per year in a city like Chicago.

2016		
Average Annual Expenditures	Avg. American Household	Me and Wife
Food	$7,203	$6,000
Housing	$18,886	$24,000
Apparel and services	$1,803	$1,000
Transportation	$9,049	$2,000
Healthcare	$4,612	$7,000
Entertainment	$2,913	$3,000
Personal insurance and pensions	$6,831	$2,000
All other expenditures	$3,933	$4,000
Cash contributions	$2,081	$1,000
Total	$57,311	$50,000

This is my sweet spot—when I spend more, it doesn't make me any happier or make my life much richer. But let me also be clear that while $50,000 is my target, I'm not perfect, and after spending less than $50,000 every year from 2010 through 2015 and reaching financial independence, in 2016 I fell victim to the dreaded lifestyle inflation and spent over $200,000, which included many frivolous purchases that I regretted soon after I made them. Spending $200,000 actually made me less happy than spending $50,000. I made a lot of money mistakes in 2016 and it threw off a lot of my calculations. I needed to recalibrate and recommit to my path, which I did. If you make money mistakes, don't let them derail you. Just recommit to the path.

But now at thirty-two, as I'm writing this, I know that what makes me happy and what I value will continue to change over time. I will likely move a few more times and might want to change my lifestyle, so I revisit my annual expense target and factor it into any adjustments to my number at least once a year.

As you get more comfortable and develop a deeper relationship with money, you'll get better at understanding the trade-offs you can make today with your time, your money, and your expenses in order to live a life you love today and for the rest of your life.

LOCATION, LOCATION, LOCATION

Housing is by far the biggest expense for Americans. Where you live will have the most profound impact on how much money you need. If you want a mansion in the Hamptons and an apartment in Manhattan, you are going to need millions of extra dollars, which means you will likely need to make some huge trade-offs in your life while you are trying to save that money.

However, if you told me you wanted this lifestyle and you'd be willing to sacrifice in order to get it, I'd urge you to consider what specifically appeals to you about these locations before you move forward. Maybe you want to live in the Hamptons because you love the ocean. But do you need to *own* a place in the Hamptons, considering it's too cold to enjoy the beach there six months out of the year? Could you get just as much pleasure from renting a place there for a few weeks during the summer (perhaps splitting the cost with friends)? Even better, could you house-sit for someone who already owns a home there and stay in the Hamptons for a few weeks for free? If you really have to own a place by the ocean, what about moving somewhere more affordable like Wilmington, North Carolina, where the average home costs 10 percent of what one in the Hamptons does!

Just before finishing this book, my wife and I decided to move to New York City, where we don't plan to live forever, but if we did, I would likely need at least 2 times the $1,250,000 I saved by age thirty. The more affordable the place you live is, the less money you need to have saved to reach financial independence. And if you couple a low cost of living with high income opportunities, as in Minnesota, where there are many large companies with high-paying salaries but the cost of living is low, you can reach financial independence even faster.

New York City is another animal entirely; you are going to pay a significant premium to live there. But the cost of living still varies widely within New York City. For example, if you buy an apartment in Queens,

The Ten Most and Least Expensive Urban Areas in the Cost of Living Index (COLI)
Second Quarter 2017
National Average for 253 Urban Areas = 100

Most Expensive			Least Expensive		
		COL			COL
Ranking	Urban Areas	Index	Ranking	Urban Areas	Index
1	New York (Manhattan) NY	235.0	1	McAllen TX	76.0
2	San Francisco CA	192.3	2	Conway AR	77.8
3	Honolulu HI	186.0	3	Harlingen TX	78.5
4	New York (Brooklyn) NY	180.2	4	Richmond IN	78.7
5	Washington DC	153.4	5	Tupelo MS	79.2
6	Orange County CA	152.4	6	Kalamazoo MI	80.5
7	Oakland CA	150.4	7	Wichita Falls TX	80.5
8	San Diego CA	146.9	8	Knoxville TN	82.2
9	Seattle WA	146.9	9	Martinsville-Henry County VA	82.4
10	Hilo HI	146.8	10	Memphis TN	82.3

The *Cost of Living Index* measures regional differences in the cost of consumer goods and services, excluding taxes and non-consumer expenditures, for professional and managerial households in the top income quintile. It is based on more than 90,000 prices covering almost 60 different items for which prices are collected three times a year by chambers of commerce, economic development organizations or university applied economic centers in each participating urban area. Small differences in the index numbers should not be interpreted as significant.
The composite index is based on six components: housing, utilities, grocery items, transportation, health care, and miscellaneous goods and services.
SOURCE: Cost of Living Index published by C2ER (*coli.org*). http://coli.org/quarter-2-2017
-cost-of-living-index-release.

you will still have access to all that Manhattan has to offer without the huge price tag.

Here is a sample of the most expensive and least expensive places to live in the United States. This data is provided by the Council for Community and Economic Research and is updated quarterly on their website http:// coli.org.

One way to estimate the financial impact of living in one place over another is by using a location-specific multiplier to compare two places. For example, while writing this book I am living in Chicago, which has an average cost of living as determined by the cost-of-living index (COLI), but when the book is published, I will be living in Manhattan, so I could multiply my current expenses by 2.35 (the multiplier for New York City). Below is a chart comparing my current expenses (about $50,000 a year) to what I'd have to spend to live in New York City.

If you have a vision of where you want to be in the future, then you can make more granular projections by digging into each specific expense category. If you want to compare the cost of living between two particular cities, you can find a really detailed breakdown for a small fee at https://store.coli.org/compare.asp. You can use a free cost of living calculator (Bankrate has a good one), and also do your own searching to get specific estimates based on the lifestyle you want. For example, the cost of living index or calculator will tell you what the average price of a home in a specific market is or how much more or less expensive a home is in two different cities, but the data is based on medians and averages—not on your lifestyle. Maybe you want to live in a more expensive house than the average or spend

	Avg. American Household	Me and Wife	Adjustment For City Multiple
Average annual expenditures	2016		2.35 (New York City)
Food	$7,203	$6,000	$14,100
Housing	$18,886	$24,000	$56,400
Apparel and services	$1,803	$1,000	$2,350
Transportation	$9,049	$2,000	$4,700
Healthcare	$4,612	$7,000	$16,450
Entertainment	$2,913	$3,000	$7,050
Personal insurance and pensions	$6,831	$2,000	$4,700
All other expenditures	$3,933	$4,000	$9,400
Cash contributions	$2,081	$1,000	$2,350
Total	$57,311	$50,000	$117,500

less money on food than the average family, both of which you can project by putting them into more granular expense projections.

The best way to make these projections is by revisiting your expense sheet and filling in as much detail as possible about your vision. If you want to see how much a certain lifestyle would cost in a specific place, you can search for more detailed projections based on that location and start adjusting them.

For example, you can easily look up a home similar to one you'd like to live in on Zillow or Trulia or another home search website and look up how much the mortgage on that home and property taxes would be. Using this information, you can get a more accurate projection, for example, of what it would cost to live in your dream home on a lake in Michigan. You can also do similar searches for the cost of gas in that area and other transportation-related expenses. While this might be too much detail for you at this point, it's an approach you can use in the future as you adjust your number to be as accurate as you want. It's also an effective way to understand the trade-offs you can make (maybe you will decide to live in a smaller house so you can travel more). You can use the same chart you used to analyze your current expenses to project expenses in another location or use the online version at https://financialfreedombook.com/tools.

Once you calculate your expected annual expenses based on your current and/or future expenses, you can calculate your new number. In my case, if I wanted to live in New York City for the rest of my life, my number would be:

Withdrawal rate percentage × your number = expected annual expenses

$.04 ×$ number $= \$117,500$

$\$117,500/.04 = \$2,937,500$

That is $1,687,500 *more* than what I'd need to save ($1,250,000) if my expenses stayed at $50,000 a year. That is an *insane* premium to live in New York City.

Using the same strategy, you could also calculate how much money you could save by moving to a less expensive city. If you wanted to move from Chicago to Memphis, let's say, it would cost you only 82.8 percent of what you currently spend, meaning if you currently live on $50,000 a year, you could conceivably live on $41,400 a year, if not less. Or you could continue to spend $50,000 but be able to live in a nicer neighborhood or in a nicer house. In the former case, your number would be:

$$\$41,400/.04 = \$1,035,000$$

Of course, these are simply rough estimates to use for planning purposes, and you can certainly find places to live in in New York City that cost less than $56,400 a year. Regardless, it's a useful exercise to help you calculate your number.

As you've already learned, if you're even more adventurous and want to live abroad, there are several great places where you can live on much less than you can in the United States. In fact, because inflation is country specific (since different countries have different currencies and economies, the value of money changes differently over time from place to place), things tend to get more expensive in the United States than they do in other parts of the world. Under certain circumstances, the value of money can actually decrease (a process known as deflation), so certain places may become *less* expensive over time.

My friends Kristy and Bryce use inflation rates to their advantage when determining where they want to live at any given time. They use the term *geographic arbitrage* to describe their process of figuring out to where to live based on inflation rates in different countries. At present, they live in Canada and have calculated that they can live on $40,000 a year. If inflation rates get too high at home, they can simply move to another country. "If shit hits the fan," Bryce says, "we're going to Thailand." Thailand is incredibly affordable because prices there haven't really increased in twenty years. As of this writing, the twelve most affordable developed countries to live in are Ukraine, Thailand, Taiwan, Vietnam, Mexico, Hungary, Ecuador, the Czech Republic, the Philippines, Poland, Malta, and Spain.

FINANCIAL FREEDOM

Expense	Avg. US Household Annual (2016)	You Monthly	You Annual
Housing			
Mortgage/Rent			
Property Taxes			
Maintenance & Cleaning			
Home/Renter's Insurance			
Electricity			
Oil/Gas			
Water/Garbage/Sewer			
Phone			
Cable/Internet			
Other (including vacation and hotels)			
Total Housing	$18,886		
Transportation			
Car Payment			
Maintenance/Repairs			
Gas/Oil			
License/Registration			
Insurance			
Bus/Train Fare			
Flights (including vacation)			
Taxis/Ridesharing			
Total Transportation	$9,049		
Food			
Groceries / Eat at Home			
Eating Out			
Total Food	$7,203		
Apparel & Services			
Clothing & Shoes			
Jewelry			
Dry Cleaning/Laundry			
Total Apparel & Services	$1,803		
Cash Contributions			
Donations			
Other			
Total Cash Contributions	$2,081		

WHAT IS YOUR NUMBER?

Expense	Avg. US Household (2016)	You Monthly	You Annual
Healthcare			
Health Insurance			
Long-Term Care Insurance			
Disability Insurance			
Medical Expenses			
Dental Expenses			
Other			
Total Healthcare	$4,612		
Insurance & Pensions			
Life And Personal Insurance			
Pension And Social Security			
Total Insurance	$6,831		
Entertainment			
Events			
Memberships			
Lessons / Hobbies			
Pets			
Total Entertainment	$2,913		
All Other Expenditures			
Tuition			
Books/Newspapers			
Personal Care			
Legal/Accounting Fees			
Total Other	$3,933		
Taxes (Depend On Income)			
Federal			
State			
Local			
Total Taxes			
Total Expenditures	$57,311		

Data Source: Bureau of Labor Statistics https://www.bls.gov/news.release/cesan.htm

THE POWER OF RECURRING INCOME
TO REDUCE YOUR NUMBER

As you calculate and adjust your number over time, one variable that can significantly reduce the amount of money you need is how much income you are generating either actively or passively. You might be thinking, *If I'm earning income, then I haven't really retired*, which is true based on the traditional definition of the word, but I prefer to think that you're retired once you no longer have to work for money and can do whatever you want. Remember your number represents the amount of money that you can live on for the rest of your life without *having* to work. If you keep working or earning money in some way, then you will need less money. There is a big difference between working at a job because you have to earn money and working a job because you enjoy the extra income from doing something you like and the chance to stay busy and engaged.

If you're able to generate any additional income (through rental income, an online business, or a business that someone else runs), then you'll need less money saved and your number will be lower. In fact, your additional income will give you more freedom; it might even be enough consistent income to offset (or completely cover) your monthly expenses, effectively reducing the amount of money your need to withdraw from your investments to live on. Plus if you're not relying on your investments to support you financially, you can let the money in your portfolio grow, which will make it compound even faster.

To measure the impact of consistent, expected additional (active or passive) income, you can subtract your average annual income from your target investment withdrawal amount. For example, say you are able to make $2,000 a month in after-tax side income from rental property or blogging. That's $24,000 less you would need to withdraw from your investments each year.

To calculate the impact this will have on your number, simply subtract your side income from your annual expense target (the amount of money you need to live on). If your expected annual expenses are $50,000 per year and you're earning $24,000 in side income, then you would need to withdraw only $26,000 from your investments, which is 48 percent less than what you otherwise would have.

Since you need only $26,000 instead of $50,000, you can use this number as your new adjusted expense withdrawal target and adjust your number by multiplying this $26,000 by 25 times (the multiplier you used above). That gives you a new number of $26,000 × 25 = $650,000! That's $600,000 less than you originally calculated for your number! That's a ton less that you need to save, all because you've developed a consistent income stream of $2,000 a month.

Let's say you're making $75,000 per year after taxes and saving 33 percent of your income ($25,000) in addition to your $2,000 a month in side income, then you can reach financial independence about twenty to twenty-five years sooner, depending on the performance of your investments! Of course, if you can earn a steady income and/or increase the amount you save each year, you can hit your number even faster. Any amount of reliable consistent monthly income will have an impact over time and reduce the amount of money you need to reach financial independence. Even $200 a month is $2,400 a year, or $2,400 × 25 = $60,000 less that you need in your number.

Check out how much even a small amount of recurring income per month and year reduces your number in the chart below.

Keep in mind that you should use this to offset your number only if the income is actually consistent and you expect it to continue. Rental income is likely going to be reliable (and probably will go up over time), whereas side-hustle income for an online business might fluctuate from month to month. This is why it's important to recalculate your number at least once a year as your income sources or the reliability of your income sources change.

Another benefit of side income is that it provides a hedge against your investment performance and can give you more security that your money will last for the rest of your life. For example, Brandon had enough money to retire at thirty-two but kept working until thirty-four before he did, and because his blog generates side income, he has the option of spending more money each year if he wants and doesn't have to worry about

Monthly Side Income	Annual Side Income	25x multiplier (reduces your number)	30x multiplier (reduces your number)
$250	$3,000	$75,000	$90,000
$500	$6,000	$150,000	$180,000
$1,000	$12,000	$300,000	$360,000
$1,500	$18,000	$450,000	$540,000
$2,000	$24,000	$600,000	$720,000
$2,500	$30,000	$750,000	$900,000
$3,000	$36,000	$900,000	$1,080,000
$4,000	$48,000	$1,200,000	$1,440,000
$5,000	$60,000	$1,500,000	$1,800,000
$6,000	$72,000	$1,800,000	$2,160,000
$7,000	$84,000	$2,100,000	$2,520,000
$8,000	$96,000	$2,400,000	$2,880,000

needing to draw as much from his investments. Just blogging on the side allowed him to reclaim his time faster and also gave him more security. He also loves blogging, so it was a win-win. The same is true for Steve, Justin, and Michelle, who all "retired" before they were thirty-five and blog to offset their monthly expenses.

BREAK IT DOWN

While your number might feel really large and impossible to attain, it will be much easier to reach if you break it down into smaller goals. Since it's difficult for humans to comprehend large numbers and also difficult for us to think about the future, breaking your number down into more accessible goals really helps. I recommend breaking down your number into yearly, monthly, weekly, and daily savings goals.

Years to Reach	Your Number	Yearly Goal	Monthly Goal	Weekly Goal	Daily Goal
1	$1,250,000	$1,250,000	$104,166.67	$24,038.46	$3,424.66
2	$1,250,000	$625,000	$52,083.33	$12,019.23	$1,712.33
3	$1,250,000	$416,667	$34,722.22	$8,012.82	$1,141.55
4	$1,250,000	$312,500	$26,041.67	$6,009.62	$856.16
5	$1,250,000	$250,000	$20,833.33	$4,807.69	$684.93
6	$1,250,000	$208,333	$17,361.11	$4,006.41	$570.78
7	$1,250,000	$178,571	$14,880.95	$3,434.07	$489.24
8	$1,250,000	$156,250	$13,020.83	$3,004.81	$428.08
9	$1,250,000	$138,889	$11,574.07	$2,670.94	$380.52
10	$1,250,000	$125,000	$10,416.67	$2,403.85	$342.47
11	$1,250,000	$113,636	$9,469.70	$2,185.31	$311.33
12	$1,250,000	$104,167	$8,680.56	$2,003.21	$285.39
13	$1,250,000	$96,154	$8,012.82	$1,849.11	$263.44
14	$1,250,000	$89,286	$7,440.48	$1,717.03	$244.62
15	$1,250,000	$83,333	$6,944.44	$1,602.56	$228.31
16	$1,250,000	$78,125	$6,510.42	$1,502.40	$214.04
17	$1,250,000	$73,529	$6,127.45	$1,414.03	$201.45
18	$1,250,000	$69,444	$5,787.04	$1,335.47	$190.26
19	$1,250,000	$65,789	$5,482.46	$1,265.18	$180.25
20	$1,250,000	$62,500	$5,208.33	$1,201.92	$171.23
21	$1,250,000	$59,524	$4,960.32	$1,144.69	$163.08
22	$1,250,000	$56,818	$4,734.85	$1,092.66	$155.67
23	$1,250,000	$54,348	$4,528.99	$1,045.15	$148.90
24	$1,250,000	$52,083	$4,340.28	$1,001.60	$142.69
25	$1,250,000	$50,000	$4,166.67	$961.54	$136.99
26	$1,250,000	$48,077	$4,006.41	$924.56	$131.72
27	$1,250,000	$46,296	$3,858.02	$890.31	$126.84
28	$1,250,000	$44,643	$3,720.24	$858.52	$122.31
29	$1,250,000	$43,103	$3,591.95	$828.91	$118.09
30	$1,250,000	$41,667	$3,472.22	$801.28	$114.16
31	$1,250,000	$40,323	$3,360.22	$775.43	$110.47
32	$1,250,000	$39,063	$3,255.21	$751.20	$107.02
33	$1,250,000	$37,879	$3,156.57	$728.44	$103.78
34	$1,250,000	$36,765	$3,063.73	$707.01	$100.73
35	$1,250,000	$35,714	$2,976.19	$686.81	$97.85

Let's say you need to save $1,250,000 (which was my number when I first did this calculation). Depending on how soon you want to reach financial independence, you can easily break this down by dividing it by the number of years, months, weeks, and days until you reach that point. Although any money you invest will be compounding as soon as you put it in the market, it's best to leave out the expected return rate for the purposes of this first calculation. Just know that, depending on how the market is growing, you could conceivably reach this number much sooner.

The chart below shows how much money you would need to save, starting from nothing, each year, month, or day depending on when you want to retire. To figure this out using your number, you can use the simple calculator I created at https://financialfreedombook.com/tools/.

If you want, you can also factor in the expected 7 percent annual return rate to adjust the numbers based on compounding. This calculation is a little more challenging but easy enough to do in Excel or using the online calculator I built for you. To do it manually, use the following equation: $S = (Y - A\,(1 + r)^n) / (((1 + r)^n - 1)/r)$

S = how much you need to save each year to hit your number by the time you want to retire

Y = your number

A = amount you already have invested (aka your principal)

r = annual compounding rate (as a decimal—i.e., 7 percent = 0.07)

n = number of years to retirement

So using my number of $1,250,000:

Y = $1,250,000
A= $0 as the amount already invested
r = 7 percent (.07)
n = 5 year
$(($1,250,000 - \$0)/((1 + 0.07)^5)) / (((1 + 0.7)^5 - 1)/0.7) = S$
     = $1,086,816

Years To Reach	Your Number	Yearly Goal	Montly Goal	Weekly Goal	Daily Goal	Expected Compounding
1	$1,250,000	$1,250,000	$104,166.67	$24,038.46	$3,424.66	7%
2	$1,250,000	$603,865	$50,322.06	$11,612.78	$1,654.42	7%
3	$1,250,000	$388,815	$32,401.22	$7,477.20	$1,065.25	7%
4	$1,250,000	$281,535	$23,461.26	$5,414.14	$771.33	7%
5	$1,250,000	$217,363	$18,113.61	$4,180.06	$595.52	7%
6	$1,250,000	$174,745	$14,562.06	$3,360.48	$478.75	7%
7	$1,250,000	$144,442	$12,036.79	$2,777.72	$395.73	7%
8	$1,250,000	$121,835	$10,152.89	$2,342.98	$333.79	7%
9	$1,250,000	$104,358	$8,696.51	$2,006.89	$285.91	7%
10	$1,250,000	$90,472	$7,539.32	$1,739.84	$247.87	7%
11	$1,250,000	$79,196	$6,599.68	$1,523.00	$216.98	7%
12	$1,250,000	$69,877	$5,823.12	$1,343.80	$191.45	7%
13	$1,250,000	$62,064	$5,171.96	$1,193.53	$170.04	7%
14	$1,250,000	$55,431	$4,619.26	$1,065.98	$151.87	7%
15	$1,250,000	$49,743	$4,145.27	$956.60	$136.28	7%
16	$1,250,000	$44,822	$3,735.17	$861.96	$122.80	7%
17	$1,250,000	$40,531	$3,377.62	$779.45	$111.05	7%
18	$1,250,000	$36,766	$3,063.81	$707.03	$100.73	7%
19	$1,250,000	$33,441	$2,786.77	$643.10	$91.62	7%
20	$1,250,000	$30,491	$2,540.93	$586.37	$83.54	7%
21	$1,250,000	$27,861	$2,321.77	$535.79	$76.33	7%
22	$1,250,000	$25,507	$2,125.60	$490.52	$69.88	7%
23	$1,250,000	$23,392	$1,949.37	$449.85	$64.09	7%
24	$1,250,000	$21,486	$1,790.52	$413.20	$58.87	7%
25	$1,250,000	$19,763	$1,646.93	$380.06	$54.15	7%
26	$1,250,000	$18,201	$1,516.77	$350.02	$49.87	7%
27	$1,250,000	$16,782	$1,398.51	$322.73	$45.98	7%
28	$1,250,000	$15,490	$1,290.83	$297.88	$42.44	7%
29	$1,250,000	$14,311	$1,192.57	$275.21	$39.21	7%
30	$1,250,000	$13,233	$1,102.75	$254.48	$36.25	7%
31	$1,250,000	$12,246	$1,020.51	$235.50	$33.55	7%
32	$1,250,000	$11,341	$945.10	$218.10	$31.07	7%
33	$1,250,000	$10,510	$875.84	$202.12	$28.79	7%
34	$1,250,000	$9,746	$812.16	$187.42	$26.70	7%
35	$1,250,000	$9,042	$753.54	$173.89	$24.77	7%

So I need to save $1,086,816 at 7 percent compounding to have $1,250,000 after five years. Of course, this number will likely be smaller for you, since you're probably not planning to retire for at least five years. Using this calculation in a spreadsheet, you can determine how much you need to save monthly by dividing this yearly savings number by 12, weekly by dividing the yearly goal by 52, and daily by dividing the yearly goal by 365. Below is the breakdown for the $1,250,000 number that shows the power of compounding growth of investing consistently over time.

It was crazy for me to see these numbers and how saving about $2 more day could help me retire one year faster (years 35 to 34) or that saving $10 more per day could help me retire two years faster (from 25 to 23). No matter how big or small your number, the more money you make and invest, the faster you will get there. It's incredible how fast your money starts growing once you start adding to it. Now that you have your number, you know where you are going and you can start to develop a plan for getting there. But first you need to figure out where you are right now.

RECAP

1. **Planning for retirement is not an exact science, and how much money you need will change as you change.** The key is to set a realistic goal to have some time to work toward it, realizing you will need to adjust it over time.

2. **How much money you need ultimately depends on the type of lifestyle you want to live.** What does a perfect day look like to you? It likely takes less money to live a life you love than you think. Money matters only if it helps you live a life you love.

3. **The younger you are, the less money you need to have saved before you can retire, given you have a much longer compounding period for your investments.** Because of compounding, the earlier and more you invest, the faster your money will grow.

4. **To maximize the odds of your money lasting for the rest of your life, you need to adhere to a set of specific guidelines, including:**
   - Save at least 25 times your expected annual expenses.
   - Defer taking your investment gains as long as possible by using side or passive income.
   - Have one year of expenses in cash on hand.

- Live on as little of your investing gains as possible.
- Preserve as much of your investment principal (the money you originally contributed) for as long as possible.

5. **Use your current expenses to estimate your number.** Once you've figured out your expected annual expenses, you can calculate your base number by using a 25x or 30x multiplier, as well as adjusting your number to include future onetime expenses. You can also use your projected future expenses for a more precise target number.

6. **That $60,000 vintage car is actually costing you $486,989 in the future.** Any time you buy something, you are both trading hours of your life for it and sacrificing the future potential of that money.

7. **Rule of 72: Divide 72 by your expected compounding rate (7 percent) to determine how many years it would take for your money to double.** At 7 percent compounding, 72/7 percent = 10.2 years, so at that compounding rate your money will double every ten years. Thus, if you invested the $60,000 instead of buying the new car, your money would be worth $120,000 in ten years, $240,000 in twenty years, and so on.

8. **Consistent recurring income reduces the amount of money you will need and can rapidly accelerate financial freedom.**

9. Break your number down into smaller, more attainable daily, weekly, monthly, and annual savings goals. Adjust those goals based on different stock market return scenarios. Even saving $1 more per day can make a big difference over time.

CHAPTER 4

WHERE ARE YOU NOW?

Getting Clarity on Your Finances

Now that you've calculated your number and broken it down into smaller goals, next you need to see where you're starting from by calculating your net worth. Your net worth is the difference between your assets (i.e., things that have value like cash, your home if you own it, and investments) and your liabilities (i.e., any kind of debt). Your net worth is the most important personal finance number for you to track on a regular basis. I track mine daily and you should, too. Or at least once a week.

If you've never done so or haven't done so in a while, it can be stressful to sit down and take stock of your finances, but you've got to do it. If you ignore your money, you are wasting precious time that you could be using to start building wealth because you can't map out a strategy until you know the facts. Every day you procrastinate you are wasting time. Trust me, while it might be tough to look at your money right now, you'll start to get used to it soon, and someday you'll find you'll even look forward to it. The sooner you start, the faster you'll reach financial freedom.

If you keep saving and investing, your net worth will keep growing, and because of compounding, the growth will accelerate. As you see your investments grow $10 a day, $100 a day, or even $1,000 a day, tracking your net worth actually gets addictive. It will give you motivation to save even more and becomes your score in the money game as you work toward hitting your number. Even if you don't like games, it's incredible to see how fast seemingly small savings add up.

To take the easiest and quickest route to calculating your net worth, simply use the tool I created at http://financialfreedombook.com/tools. If you want to do it old-school, all you need is a pen, some paper, and a calculator. Even if you use the free online tool, I recommend working through the calculation manually as well in order to see how all of the puzzle pieces come together. Feel free to grab a glass of wine, a cup of coffee, or whatever beverage you are into before we start. It will help!

ASSETS

Let's start with your assets. An asset is anything of real value you can sell, but for the purpose of your net worth calculation you don't have to figure out what everything you own is worth—that would take too long and can get very complicated. Here's what to do. Log into all of your bank and investment accounts and write down the balances of each one below. Then make a list of all the stuff you own that is worth more than $100 that you could sell if you needed to for how much you could sell it for. If you paid $500 for your couch but could get only $60 for it now, then it's worth $60. This could include your car, any art you have, valuable jewelry, furniture, or even something like your grandma's nice set of antique dishes. This will also include any real estate you own, though I would calculate that in its own column. Write down the value of each item (if you're not sure, see if you can research it online) and total it up for each category. The sum of all of these things is your total assets.

By way of example, let's take a look at someone else's assets. Julie is thirty and works in an IT department at a large company. She also runs a side business selling vintage clothing online. She makes $70,000 per year after taxes and wants to reach financial independence as quickly as possible. Her number is $1 million. Julie currently has $412,500 in assets.

LIABILITIES

Now you want to calculate your liabilities, which is simply how much money you owe anyone on anything—e.g., any student loan debt, credit card debt, personal loans, car loans, or mortgages. Write these down in the chart below and note the current interest rate you are paying on the debt

	Bank Accounts		Investments		Real Estate		Valuables	
	Description	Value	Description	Value	Description	Value	Description	Value
1								
2								
3								
4								
5								
6								
7								
8								
9								
10								
Totals								
Total Assets								

	Bank Accounts		Investments		Real Estate		Valuables	
	Description	Value	Description	Value	Description	Value	Description	Value
1	Savings 1	$10,000	401(k)	$67,000	Condo	$250,000	Car	$10,000
2	Savings 2	$5,000	Roth IRA	$31,000			Guitar	$2,000
3	Checking 1	$6,000	Brokerage	$9,000			Watch	$500
4	Checking 2	$1,000	SEP IRA	$14,000			Records	$1,000
5	Biz Checking	$4,000					Jewelry	$2,000
6								
7								
8								
9								
10								
Totals		$26,000		$121,000		$250,000		$15,500
Total Assets	$412,500							

FINANCIAL FREEDOM

	Description	Amount Owed	Interest Rate
1			
2			
3			
4			
5			
6			
7			
8			
9			
10			
11			
12			
13			
14			
15			
16			
17			
18			
19			
20			
Totals			

WHERE ARE YOU NOW?

	Description	Amount Owed	Interest Rate
1	Credit Card 1	$7,000	17.50%
2	Credit Card 2	$4,000	22.40%
3	Credit Card 3	$800	15.60%
4	Student Loan 1	$21,000	9.40%
5	Student Loan 2	$13,000	5.50%
6	Student Loan 3	$6,000	7.80%
7	Personal Loan 1	$14,000	5.50%
8	Mortgage	$187,000	4.75%
9	Car Loan	$4,000	4.25%
10			
11			
12			
13			
14			
15			
16			
17			
18			
19			
20			
Totals		$256,800	

in a separate column. This will allow you to quickly see your highest interest rates, which we will use to develop your debt-repayment strategy. Make sure you are honest; don't hide anything. It's important to be transparent with yourself even if it's uncomfortable. No matter how much money you owe, there's a path out and a path to wealth.

While Julie has been good about saving, she also has a lot of debt and owes money to three different credit card companies. She also has three student loans, a personal loan, a mortgage, and a car loan, all reducing her net worth. Here are Julie's liabilities:

To calculate your net worth simply take your total assets and subtract your total liabilities. Julie's net worth is therefore $412,500 (assets) − $256,800 (liabilities) = $155,700. So if Julie sold everything she had at the price she's estimated it's worth and then used that money to pay back all of the debt she has, she would have $155,700 left.

If you don't have a lot of money saved and are still paying off a lot of debt, then your net worth might actually be negative. This can be depressing, but don't worry. When I started my journey, I had more than $20,000 in credit card debt, and many others who've reached financial independence started with a lot more debt.

If your net worth is currently negative, then you will need to *add* your debt to your number. When I first did these calculations, my number was $1,250,000, but I was $20,000 in debt, so I needed to save $1,270,000 plus any interest I would pay on my $20,000 to reach my goal. In reality, with interest I would likely need to save somewhere closer to $1,280,000.

CALCULATING YOUR NUMBER WITHIN YOUR NET WORTH

It's important to note how *your number* and your net worth are different. Your number is the amount of money that you need to have invested so that you can live off the income from your investments for the rest of your life. Your net worth includes (or will include) your investments, but it also includes other assets that might not generate income for you, like your house or your vinyl collection. You can pay for your dinner with investment income, but unless you rent out one of your extra rooms so your house generates rental income, you can't pay for a night out with your home.

To calculate how close you are to your number, take your income-generating investments from your net worth and subtract them from your number. If we go back to Julie's example, let's say Julie's projected expenses are $40,000 per year after taxes, so $1 million ($40,000 × 25) is her target number. While her net worth is $155,700, she has $121,000 in her investment accounts. So she has $121,000 invested toward her $1 million and needs to save ($1 million − $121,000) = $879,000 more. Julie is currently $121,000/$1 million = 12.1 percent toward her number goal.

While she currently lives in her house and doesn't rent out a room, Julie can add real estate income to her calculation if she decides either to rent out a room or to sell her home and invest any profit! Say she rents a room for $1,000 per month, which is $12,000 per year, and she has no plans to sell her house. She can simply subtract $40,000 (her target expenses) − $12,000 (consistent rental income) = $28,000. Now she would need to withdraw only $28,000 from her investments each year, so her number is reduced to $28,000 × 25 = $700,000, or $300,000 less than her original calculation. That's a huge ROI for renting out one of her rooms for $1,000 per month.

You can adjust your own calculation by subtracting any reliable consistent income from your expense target as outlined in the previous chapter. And if Julie takes it a step further and sells her home for, say, a $200,000 profit, she can take that money and invest it tax-free. Even though she now needs a place to live, if she lives in a place where her rent is similar to what her mortgage was, then her expenses won't change and because she invested the $200,000, she now has ($121,000 + $200,000) = $321,000 total invested, which puts her at 32.1 percent of her $1 million goal!

WHAT ABOUT DEBT?

A lot of personal finance books advise you to pay down your debt by paying off the lowest balance first. The idea is that it's easier to pay down a smaller balance than a larger balance and that once you've paid off one debt, you'll feel better and can better handle the rest of your debt over time.

While it might make you feel good to pay down a smaller balance, if you want to retire as quickly as possible, you need to pay down debt in a way that will allow you to save (and invest) as much money as possible—not just pay down the debt as quickly as possible. For that reason, you should start by paying down the debt with the highest interest rate first—no matter how large the balance is.

It's a numbers game, and this is simple math. If you are carrying debt that is accruing at a high rate of 15 to 20 percent (or higher), then your debt is accruing at a faster rate than your investments are likely growing. Typically credit cards (especially store-specific credit cards as opposed to bank-issued credit cards) carry the highest interest rates, while student loans and mortgages tend to carry relatively low interest rates. Just look at the interest rates you wrote down in the chart a few pages ago to figure out where you stand. Pay down the highest interest rate debt first, not the biggest or smallest balance.

Some personal finance gurus also suggest that you pay down all of your debt before you start saving money, but this is often a terrible idea because while you're waiting to pay down your debt, you are missing out on any returns you could get if you had money in the stock market. In many cases, the returns you'd get in the stock market are actually higher than the interest you are paying on your debt. And in theory you could carry some sort of debt (in the form of a mortgage, say) for the *rest of your life*, continuing to pay the balance with higher returns than your investments generate in the stock market. However, most early retirees pay off their mortgage in full before retiring to simply eliminate their monthly mortgage payment from their expenses.

Even though I could easily pay off my home, I have a fifteen-year mortgage on it at 2.625 percent interest, and I am going to keep that mortgage because I'd rather invest my money at 7 percent plus returns than pay it off. Investing in stocks gives me a higher return; I'm also able to take advantage of the tax advantages of home ownership, like the mortgage interest and tax deductions. If the interest rate on your debt is higher than any return you could realistically get on an investment, then you should pay down that debt before you invest, because that debt is compounding more quickly than any money you invest would grow.

Compounding works both ways, so always make the decision that benefits you most based on the numbers. For example, the interest rates on credit cards are usually incredibly high, so it typically makes sense to pay those off before you invest. Say your credit card APR (annual percentage rate) is 22 percent, which means your credit card balance will increase by 22 percent each year. That's *crazy high*, but unfortunately pretty common! As of May 2016, U.S. residents owe $953 billion on their credit cards. Thirty-two percent of credit card holders carry a balance, and the average balance is $7,527. At a 22 percent APR, someone carrying a $7,527 balance will owe an additional $1,655.94, for a total of $9,182.94 at the end of the year. After two years, he'll owe a total of $11,203 and the debt will only continue to grow if he doesn't pay it down.

As I've shown you, the stock market returns over the long term are about 7 percent (in your favor), so that's a reasonable return projection, but still much lower than the 22 percent rate at which the credit card debt is growing. So it makes sense to pay off your credit card first before investing. Even when the stock market is crushing it, it's likely still returning a lot less than 22 percent. This is why credit cards are so profitable for banks—there are hardly any investments where you can get a 22 percent return on your money. If you use a credit card, always do your best to pay off the full balance each month so you don't accrue any interest payments. If you can't do this, then you need to rethink your spending. If you already have debt at 15 percent plus, work to pay it down as quickly as you can before investing in anything.

What about student loans and investing? Once again, it depends on your interest rate. If your student loan interest rate is 10 percent, then it's a tougher choice, since this is close to the average annual return rate you'd earn on your investments, though if you have decent credit, you might be able to refinance that loan and lower your interest rate to 3 to 6 percent. If you can refinance to that level—or lower—then you should probably invest any extra money instead of putting it toward your student loans. Regardless of what you choose to do, you should always make your minimum student loan payment each month. If your interest rate is at or near the 7 percent you can expect to earn on your market investments, then you might choose to pay off your debt a little faster—perhaps make two months' worth of payments instead of just one at a time—and invest any extra cash.

There is one circumstance under which you should always invest no matter how much debt you have or the interest you are paying on it, and that's if your company offers to match a percentage of contributions you make to your 401(k). Typically, a company that offers a retirement plan will offer to match every dollar (or a portion of every dollar) that you contribute to your account up to a certain percentage of your salary (usually between 3 and 6 percent). That is free money, and when you take advantage of it, it's basically like you're getting a 50 to 100 percent return on your investment. You will never get these returns from the market itself, so if you don't take full advantage of a company match, you are wasting an incredible opportunity. If your company offers a match, then you should definitely invest enough to take full advantage of that match. So if your company matches your investment up to 3 percent of your salary, then you should invest at least 3 percent in your 401(k). If your company also matches 50 percent of your contribution between, say, 4 and 6 percent, then you should contribute at least 6 percent. Rule number one about growing your wealth: never leave money on the table.

CHECK YOUR EMOTIONS AT THE DOOR!

Besides politics, religion, or sex, there is probably nothing that people get more emotional about than money. People have literally killed and been killed for money. Families, communities, and entire societies have been destroyed over money. This is too bad, but it's also entirely natural. In fact, when it comes to building wealth, one of the biggest mistakes you can make is letting your emotions get in the way of making a good decision.

Since we embed our history, our emotions, our desires, and our dream into money, it's essential to learn to learn how to be aware and control our reactions to it. This level of mindfulness takes some practice, but the more frequently you interact with your money, the easier it becomes. If you really want to build wealth, you will be more successful if you check your emotions at the door.

When I first started investing, I bought $3,000 worth of stock that I spent a bunch of time researching. It was almost all of my money at the time, so the next day I kept refreshing my phone checking the stock price. I lost about $500 that first day, and it was all I could think about. I could not get it out of my mind. A week later, after losing almost $1,200, I sold it. Over the next few years the price of that stock more than doubled. If I could have kept my emotions in check and played the long game, I would have come out ahead.

Even after that lesson I freaked out many times when the stock market and my investments would be down over the short term. I remember telling one of my friends, "I lost $10,000 in the stock market this week!" In reality, a loss is realized only when you sell your investments. I didn't lose anything, really, because I kept my money invested (and it's still invested!).

This can be super tough, but the more emotional you are, the less you will make, the less you will save, and the tougher it will be to maximize the potential of your money. So try to keep it cool! Trust me, this gets a lot easier over time. There was a day recently when my investments were down $50,000 in one week and it didn't faze me a bit. While most of the media was predicting that the stock market was getting ready to crash, I was cool as a cucumber because I'm in it for the long game. I actually laughed a little bit, remembering how much I used to freak out. The more experience you get with money, the easier it is to keep your emotions in check.

One of the main reasons financial advisors exist is not because managing money is all that complicated (you'll know pretty much everything you need to know after reading this book), but because they know how to stop their clients from making dumb decisions when it comes to money. Financial advisors are full of stories about the panicked phone calls they get from their clients any time the market goes down. Panicking, clients think they should sell all of their stocks to avoid any future losses, but investing is a long-term game, so reacting to every market fluctuation is almost always a terrible idea. So chill and stay focused on the bigger picture. Play the long game.

Not only do you need to learn how not to lose it when the market dips, you also need to learn how to take calculated risks—even get comfortable taking risks. I know people who are so afraid to invest that they just keep their money in a savings account making 1 percent or less, effectively losing money, since inflation rises 2 to 3 percent each year. Sure, you can lose money investing, but losing to inflation is a guaranteed loss! And if you invest intelligently, in most cases the upside is much greater than the downside over the long term. But we as humans naturally fear losing more than we enjoy winning (a concept aptly known as *loss aversion*), which is why some people either don't invest at all or get stuck on an emotional roller coaster—always chasing that next big gain or freaking out and making rash decision on a decline. But investing isn't gambling and there are ways to minimize the risks, as you'll see in the section of this book on investing.

The same happens when it comes to paying off debt. Some people can get so frustrated, scared, or embarrassed by carrying a large debt load that they don't want to invest until they've paid it all down. Even though the numbers show that this is usually not a good decision, they let their emotions about debt get the better of them. Combine this with an aversion to risk, and these people are lucky if they ever grow their wealth at all. So in short, remember that money is just a numbers game—it works the same no matter how you feel or what you believe about it, and the same rules apply to everyone. The sooner you start investing and the more you learn about how money works, the more confidence you will have and the easier it becomes.

DAILY HABITS = RICHES

Most people don't pay attention to their money, so they either end up doing nothing or making a bad decision. Too many people look at their money only once a month or once a year when their taxes are due. They make plans to save what's left over at the end of the month, but life ends up happening and there ends up being very little, if any, money left to save. So they wait until the next month and the same thing happens. Another problem is that many people don't track their spending closely, so either they think they have more money than they do or they just overspend. And once they overspend, it often leads to guilt and fear of money, which are two of the biggest barriers to building wealth.

This is one of the problems with credit cards and one-click online ordering. It's so easy to spend money before you've earned it or if you don't have it. Back in the days before credit cards (pre-1950s), it was nearly impossible to spend money you didn't have. The idea just didn't really exist, unless you borrowed money from some shady dude who'd come after you if you didn't pay. But after banks made it so easy to spend borrowed money, personal debt exploded in the United States. Banks make billions of dollars a year on interest payments from users who don't pay their balance off each month. (Quick tip: If you have any interest charges on your credit cards from the past few months, call up your bank and ask them to be removed. They likely won't remove them if they are more than three months old, but 99 percent of the time they will remove the past few months to keep you a customer. It doesn't hurt to ask and take back your money).

You can avoid this trap by developing a series of habits you do every day to monitor your money and strategize how to grow it. We spend over two thousand hours every year working to make money, but how much time do we spend managing it? All it takes is five minutes a day. It is much easier to control your emotions, evaluate and get comfortable with risk, and make better money decisions when money becomes part of your daily routine. While it might take some time to build a new habit, the lifetime impact of small daily decisions and habits can be massive.

The most effective way to build better habits is to take it one day at a time. This is actually counter to most of the popular wisdom about money, which states that you should automate as much of your financial life as possible in order to minimize your bad decisions. Many experts will tell you to "set it and forget it," because, the thinking goes, the less effort you have to exert, the more likely you will be to do something that can benefit you over the long run.

So many of the personal finance experts out there will tell you the key to wealth is automation, but automation is not enough. Automation is the status quo. It's just the beginning. But it's also how you get complacent. It's thinking that saving 5 to 10 percent of your income is enough. It's not enough. It's just the starting point. If you are saving 10 percent, you need to do everything you can to save 11 percent. And then 12 percent, pushing your savings rate up as much and as often as you can.

It's easy to automate, to coast in life. But coasting won't get you to the next level. Pushing harder is how you get to financial freedom. It's about spending those extra few hours on a Saturday morning before everyone else wakes up working on your side hustle. Financial freedom is not built on complacency. It's built on pushing your boundaries as often as you can. It's about being uncomfortable sometimes. It's about growing and learning and challenging and pushing. And then pushing some more. Happiness is in the journey, the challenge, the growth.

The more active and engaged you are in optimizing your money, the more money you will be able to make and save. This is a lot easier to do if you look at your money every day, but it doesn't have to take a lot of time or feel like a chore. Take my example: Every morning I make some coffee and analyze my net worth using a simple free tracking app you can download at https://financialfreedombook.com/more. I also log into my investment accounts and look at how my portfolio performed the previous day. Then I analyze how much I spent the day before and how much I've spent so far this month to see if I'm sticking to my spending goals; I look at how much money I've made from all of my income streams (including my investments) to see if my savings goals are on track. I also check my bank and credit card accounts to make sure nothing is off, like extra or fraudulent charges or weird fees or if I haven't received a payment I am owed.

Finally, I spend a couple of minutes thinking about additional ways I can make money. Can I find a new client this week? Can I sell a new project to an old client? Does anyone I know need some extra help? Can I sell something on eBay? The whole process takes about five to ten minutes, but the habit is one the most important things I do each day. When I see how my money is growing, I get excited and want to figure out how to make more. When it's not growing or my cash flow is low, it gives me motivation to go out and make more money.

If I fall off track, I know exactly what happened and can fix the problem immediately. Spent too much last month or fell short of my savings goal? I'll try harder this month. Because I know exactly how my money is performing, I can make better decisions about how to earn, save, and spend. Just starting my day this way has helped me save hundreds of thousands of dollars, since I spend a lot less throughout the day. It really works.

You might be thinking, *Every day?* Yup, every day. As you spend more time with your money, your relationship with it will strengthen. Instead of worrying about money all the time, you'll start to feel at peace with it. Money will start to feel familiar to you. It'll be easier to control your emotions and see optimization opportunities you didn't see before. Money will be with you for the rest of your life, so take the time to build a positive relationship with it—a relationship that you control.

While I do miss days every now and then (nobody is perfect), I pick right up the next day. I try to never miss three days in a row, even when I'm on vacation or traveling. Everything that I do and recommend you do daily, weekly, monthly, quarterly, and annually is broken down in great detail in chapter 12. You can use my own habits as a baseline and customize them to fit your own specific goals.

Seriously, just try this for a week and see how you feel. You'll be amazed by not only what you start noticing but how much more in control of your money you feel. How much freer you feel. Soon money will feel like a game, and the more you play, the better you'll get. The more opportunities you'll see. The easier it will be to take calculated risks. And the better you get, the more money you'll make.

RECAP

1. Net worth is the most important number in personal finance and is your financial scorecard. To calculate your net worth, you add up your assets (i.e., things that have value—like cash, your home if you own it, and investments) and subtract your liabilities (i.e., any kind of debt). You should be monitoring it at least weekly.

2. Your net worth is not the same as your number. Your number is the amount of money that you need to have invested so that you can live off the income from your investments for the rest of your life. Your net worth includes (or will include) your investments, but it also includes other assets that might not generate income for you.

3. Calculate how close you are to your number by subtracting your income-generating investments in your net worth from your number.

4. Pay down debt in a way that will allow you to save (and invest) as much money as possible—not just pay down the debt as quickly as possible.

For that reason, you should start by paying down the debt with the highest interest rate first—no matter how large the balance is.

5. If your company offers a 401(k) match, always invest enough to get the match because it's free money.

6. People get too emotional about money. Check your emotions at the door.

7. Daily habits equal riches. It is much easier to control your emotions, evaluate and get comfortable with risk, and make better money decisions when money becomes part of your daily routine. While it might take some time to build a new habit, the lifetime impact can be massive.

8. Automation is the status quo. It's just the beginning. It's easy to automate, to coast in life. But coasting won't get you to the next level. Pushing and growing is how you get to financial freedom.

9. Spend five minutes a day with your money. Soon money will feel like a game, and the more you play, the better you'll get. The more opportunities you'll see. The easier it will be to take calculated risks. And the better you get, the more money you'll make.

CHAPTER 5

NEXT-LEVEL MONEY

How to Build Wealth Quickly

Now that you know where you are and where you're going, you can start building your strategy to get there. While there are many ways to build wealth, they all rely on the same basic three variables (I like to call them levers):

1. Expenses: How much money you are spending
2. Savings: How much money you are saving/investing
3. Income: How much money you are making

This is not rocket science. The more you increase your savings and income and the more you decrease your expenses, the more money you'll have and the sooner you'll be able to reach the next level of financial freedom and financial independence.

The problem with most personal financial advice is that it focuses primarily on two of these three variables: how to reduce expenses to increase your savings. But you can only cut back so much before you feel like you have to live in a cardboard box if you ever want to be financially secure. And no matter how much you cut back or how often you crash on a friend's couch or grab free food from catered company events, the amount of money you can save is limited by how much money you are making.

But there is something deeper here that most books and experts miss. In order to build wealth quickly, you need to maximize the potential of all three levers. By reducing expenses while simultaneously growing your income, you'll have more money to save/invest, which will help you increase your savings rate.

While both are essential, to fast-track financial freedom, increasing your income is more powerful than cutting back on your expenses because it gives you the opportunity to invest more money more often, accelerating the rate of compounding and the growth of your money.

When I was trying to figure out how to make a million dollars by the time I turned thirty, I did the math and realized that even if I saved 50 percent of an annual salary of $50,000 and it compounded annually at 7 percent, it would take me at least twenty-five years to save $1,250,000. And by then, because of inflation, even that might not be enough to retire. Unless you're earning quite a bit of money already, it will be difficult to reach financial independence quickly by savings alone. Not that you can't do it, you definitely can—it just might take you twenty plus years, which is still better than forty years or never!

That being said, saving is extremely important, and the more money you can make, the more money you can save. And if you can become a super saver (the term I use for those who save more than 25 percent of their income each year), you can significantly cut the years you need to "retire."

The higher your "savings rate," the faster you can retire

There are two ways to measure how much you are saving: in dollars and in percentages. When you are looking at the amount of money you're trying to save (your daily, monthly, and annual targets), it makes sense to think of these in terms of dollars, since your number is a set dollar amount. However, when figuring out how much to save, it's more effective to think in terms of percentages, since the percentage of your income you are saving is directly correlated to the amount of time it will take you to retire and it also makes it easier to track and compare how much you are saving over time as your income grows. So it's important to monitor both the dollar amount you are saving and your savings rate, so you can track and optimize the amount of money you are saving and what percentage of your income it is. Tracking both will also motivate you to save more money, since some people respond more to percentages and others to dollars.

Annual Savings	
Bank Accounts	
Savings 1	$5,000
Savings 2	$2,000
Investments	
Pretax	
401(k)	$18,500
Roth IRA	$5,500
After-Tax	
Brokerage	$9,000
Total Saved	$40,000
Income	$100,000
Savings Rate	40%

The percentage of your income that you save and invest is called your savings rate, and the higher your savings rate, the faster you will hit your number no matter what it is. To calculate your savings rate, you want to add up all of the dollars that you save, both in pretax accounts (for example, 401(k)s and IRAs) and after-tax accounts (brokerage) and divide it by your income. Here is an example for how it looks if you have a $100,000 income and are saving 40 percent.

An easy way to monitor your savings rate is to use a spreadsheet that you update monthly or use the savings rate tracking tool I've built. Both can be found at https://financialfreedombook.com/tools

Anita, a lawyer who lived in Chicago, reached financial independence in five years at the age of thirty-three with $756,715 in her portfolio. She did this by saving 85 percent of her income and living on less than $25,000 per year. By saving 70 percent of the incomes Steve and his wife, Courtney, earned from their jobs, they were able to save $890,000 and both retire at thirty-five. Kristy and Bryce retired at thirty-two with over $1 million after saving 70 percent of their combined income. J.P. retired in New York City at twenty-eight with over $2.5 million by saving 80 percent plus of her income. Brandon was able to do it at thirty-four by saving up to 85 percent of his income. I reached financial independence by saving and then investing at least 60 percent of my full-time and side-hustle income to reach $1.25 million.

While the thought of saving over 50 percent of your income might sound crazy right now, it's actually possible for most people if you are willing to make both saving and making more money a priority. As I've previously mentioned, I always viewed savings as an opportunity, not a sacrifice. Or as Brandon sees it: "It's not about deprivation, it's about optimization."

Even if you don't make a lot of money, if you can reduce your expenses as much as possible and increase your savings rate, you can retire much earlier than you would otherwise. Although this is difficult to do, there are incredible stories of teachers, janitors, public service officials, and others who super-saved their way to early financial independence. Literally every 1 percent more you save will decrease the amount of time you'll need to work to reach financial independence. Remember that retiring any time before sixty-two (the traditional retirement age) is early retirement, so cutting one, two, five, or ten years off your retirement is an incredible accomplishment.

Let's see how increasing your savings rate on different income levels impacts how quickly you can reach financial independence. For this example, we'll use my target number of $1,250,000 and an expected annual investment compounding rate of 7 percent. You can do your own calculation using your own numbers at https://financialfreedombook.com/tools.

Take a few minutes to study the savings rates charts below.

As you look at these charts, the relationship between income and savings rate becomes clear. Let's say you want to retire in fifteen years. To reach $1,250,000 in that time, you need to save $50,000 a year. At an after-tax income of $200,000, this amounts to 25 percent of your income and still leaves you $150,000 to live on. You can live a pretty awesome life on that much. If you're earning $100,000, you'd have to increase your savings rate to 50 percent, which is totally doable given that you can live a nice life

NEXT-LEVEL MONEY

Savings Rate	Income	Expenses	Annual Savings	Monthly Savings	Your Number	Years
5%	$30,000	$28,500	$1,500	$125	$1,250,000	60.35
10%	$30,000	$27,000	$3,000	$250	$1,250,000	50.35
15%	$30,000	$25,500	$4,500	$375	$1,250,000	44.6
20%	$30,000	$24,000	$6,000	$500	$1,250,000	40.59
25%	$30,000	$22,500	$7,500	$625	$1,250,000	37.53
30%	$30,000	$21,000	$9,000	$750	$1,250,000	35.06
35%	$30,000	$19,500	$10,500	$875	$1,250,000	33.01
40%	$30,000	$18,000	$12,000	$1,000	$1,250,000	31.26
45%	$30,000	$16,500	$13,500	$1,125	$1,250,000	29.74
50%	$30,000	$15,000	$15,000	$1,250	$1,250,000	28.4
55%	$30,000	$13,500	$16,500	$1,375	$1,250,000	27.21
60%	$30,000	$12,000	$18,000	$1,500	$1,250,000	26.14
65%	$30,000	$10,500	$19,500	$1,625	$1,250,000	25.16
70%	$30,000	$9,000	$21,000	$1,750	$1,250,000	24.27
75%	$30,000	$7,500	$22,500	$1,875	$1,250,000	23.46
80%	$30,000	$6,000	$24,000	$2,000	$1,250,000	22.7
85%	$30,000	$4,500	$25,500	$2,125	$1,250,000	22
90%	$30,000	$3,000	$27,000	$2,250	$1,250,000	21.35
95%	$30,000	$1,500	$28,500	$2,375	$1,250,000	20.75
100%	$30,000	$0	$30,000	$2,500	$1,250,000	20.18

FINANCIAL FREEDOM

Savings Rate	Income	Expenses	Annual Savings	Monthly Savings	Your Number	Years
5%	$50,000	$47,500	$2,500	$208	$1,250,000	52.96
10%	$50,000	$45,000	$5,000	$417	$1,250,000	43.12
15%	$50,000	$42,500	$7,500	$625	$1,250,000	37.53
20%	$50,000	$40,000	$10,000	$833	$1,250,000	33.66
25%	$50,000	$37,500	$12,500	$1,042	$1,250,000	30.73
30%	$50,000	$35,000	$15,000	$1,250	$1,250,000	28.4
35%	$50,000	$32,500	$17,500	$1,458	$1,250,000	26.48
40%	$50,000	$30,000	$20,000	$1,667	$1,250,000	24.86
45%	$50,000	$27,500	$22,500	$1,875	$1,250,000	23.46
50%	$50,000	$25,000	$25,000	$2,083	$1,250,000	22.23
55%	$50,000	$22,500	$27,500	$2,292	$1,250,000	21.15
60%	$50,000	$20,000	$30,000	$2,500	$1,250,000	20.18
65%	$50,000	$17,500	$32,500	$2,708	$1,250,000	19.31
70%	$50,000	$15,000	$35,000	$2,917	$1,250,000	18.52
75%	$50,000	$12,500	$37,500	$3,125	$1,250,000	17.79
80%	$50,000	$10,000	$40,000	$3,333	$1,250,000	17.13
85%	$50,000	$7,500	$42,500	$3,542	$1,250,000	16.52
90%	$50,000	$5,000	$45,000	$3,750	$1,250,000	15.96
95%	$50,000	$2,500	$47,500	$3,958	$1,250,000	15.44
100%	$50,000	$0	$50,000	$4,167	$1,250,000	14.95

NEXT-LEVEL MONEY

Savings Rate	Income	Expenses	Annual Savings	Monthly Savings	Your Number	Years
5%	$75,000	$71,250	$3,750	$313	$1,250,000	47.18
10%	$75,000	$67,500	$7,500	$625	$1,250,000	37.53
15%	$75,000	$63,750	$11,250	$938	$1,250,000	32.11
20%	$75,000	$60,000	$15,000	$1,250	$1,250,000	28.4
25%	$75,000	$56,250	$18,750	$1,563	$1,250,000	25.64
30%	$75,000	$52,500	$22,500	$1,875	$1,250,000	23.46
35%	$75,000	$48,750	$26,250	$2,188	$1,250,000	21.67
40%	$75,000	$45,000	$30,000	$2,500	$1,250,000	20.18
45%	$75,000	$41,250	$33,750	$2,813	$1,250,000	18.9
50%	$75,000	$37,500	$37,500	$3,125	$1,250,000	17.79
55%	$75,000	$33,750	$41,250	$3,438	$1,250,000	16.82
60%	$75,000	$30,000	$45,000	$3,750	$1,250,000	15.96
65%	$75,000	$26,250	$48,750	$4,063	$1,250,000	15.19
70%	$75,000	$22,500	$52,500	$4,375	$1,250,000	14.5
75%	$75,000	$18,750	$56,250	$4,688	$1,250,000	13.87
80%	$75,000	$15,000	$60,000	$5,000	$1,250,000	13.29
85%	$75,000	$11,250	$63,750	$5,313	$1,250,000	12.77
90%	$75,000	$7,500	$67,500	$5,625	$1,250,000	12.29
95%	$75,000	$3,750	$71,250	$5,938	$1,250,000	11.84
100%	$75,000	$0	$75,000	$6,250	$1,250,000	11.43

FINANCIAL FREEDOM

Savings Rate	Income	Expenses	Annual Savings	Monthly Savings	Your Number	Years
5%	$100,000	$95,000	$5,000	$417	$1,250,000	43.12
10%	$100,000	$90,000	$10,000	$833	$1,250,000	33.66
15%	$100,000	$85,000	$15,000	$1,250	$1,250,000	28.4
20%	$100,000	$80,000	$20,000	$1,667	$1,250,000	24.86
25%	$100,000	$75,000	$25,000	$2,083	$1,250,000	22.23
30%	$100,000	$70,000	$30,000	$2,500	$1,250,000	20.18
35%	$100,000	$65,000	$35,000	$2,917	$1,250,000	18.52
40%	$100,000	$60,000	$40,000	$3,333	$1,250,000	17.13
45%	$100,000	$55,000	$45,000	$3,750	$1,250,000	15.96
50%	$100,000	$50,000	$50,000	$4,167	$1,250,000	14.95
55%	$100,000	$45,000	$55,000	$4,583	$1,250,000	14.07
60%	$100,000	$40,000	$60,000	$5,000	$1,250,000	13.29
65%	$100,000	$35,000	$65,000	$5,417	$1,250,000	12.6
70%	$100,000	$30,000	$70,000	$5,833	$1,250,000	11.99
75%	$100,000	$25,000	$75,000	$6,250	$1,250,000	11.43
80%	$100,000	$20,000	$80,000	$6,667	$1,250,000	10.92
85%	$100,000	$15,000	$85,000	$7,083	$1,250,000	10.46
90%	$100,000	$10,000	$90,000	$7,500	$1,250,000	10.04
95%	$100,000	$5,000	$95,000	$7,917	$1,250,000	9.65
100%	$100,000	$0	$100,000	$8,333	$1,250,000	9.29

NEXT-LEVEL MONEY

Savings Rate	Income	Expenses	Annual Savings	Monthly Savings	Your Number	Years
5%	$200,000	$190,000	$10,000	$833	$1,250,000	33.66
10%	$200,000	$180,000	$20,000	$1,667	$1,250,000	24.86
15%	$200,000	$170,000	$30,000	$2,500	$1,250,000	20.18
20%	$200,000	$160,000	$40,000	$3,333	$1,250,000	17.13
25%	$200,000	$150,000	$50,000	$4,167	$1,250,000	14.95
30%	$200,000	$140,000	$60,000	$5,000	$1,250,000	13.29
35%	$200,000	$130,000	$70,000	$5,833	$1,250,000	11.99
40%	$200,000	$120,000	$80,000	$6,667	$1,250,000	10.92
45%	$200,000	$110,000	$90,000	$7,500	$1,250,000	10.04
50%	$200,000	$100,000	$100,000	$8,333	$1,250,000	9.29
55%	$200,000	$90,000	$110,000	$9,167	$1,250,000	8.65
60%	$200,000	$80,000	$120,000	$10,000	$1,250,000	8.09
65%	$200,000	$70,000	$130,000	$10,833	$1,250,000	7.61
70%	$200,000	$60,000	$140,000	$11,667	$1,250,000	7.18
75%	$200,000	$50,000	$150,000	$12,500	$1,250,000	6.79
80%	$200,000	$40,000	$160,000	$13,333	$1,250,000	6.45
85%	$200,000	$30,000	$170,000	$14,167	$1,250,000	6.14
90%	$200,000	$20,000	$180,000	$15,000	$1,250,000	5.86
95%	$200,000	$10,000	$190,000	$15,833	$1,250,000	5.6
100%	$200,000	$0	$200,000	$16,667	$1,250,000	5.36

Years Until Financial Independence

Annual Spending \ After-Tax Annual Income	$25k	$30k	$35k	$40k	$45k	$50k	$55k	$60k	$65k	$70k	$75k	$80k	$85k	$90k	$95k	$100k
$95k																65.8
$90k															64.7	21.4
$85k														63.6	50.3	42.8
$80k													62.4	49.1	41.7	36.7
$75k												61.1	47.9	40.6	35.6	31.9
$70k											59.8	46.7	39.4	34.5	30.8	28
$65k										58.4	45.3	38.1	33.2	29.7	26.9	24.6
$60k									56.8	43.9	36.7	31.9	28.4	25.7	23.5	21.6
$55k								55.2	42.3	35.2	30.5	27.1	24.4	22.3	20.5	19
$50k							53.3	40.6	33.7	29	25.7	23.1	21	19.3	17.8	16.6
$45k						51.4	38.8	31.9	27.4	24.2	21.6	19.6	18	16.6	15.4	14.4
$40k					49.1	36.7	30.1	25.7	22.5	20.1	18.2	16.6	15.3	14.2	13.3	12.4
$35k				46.7	34.5	28	23.8	20.7	18.4	16.6	15.1	13.9	12.9	12	11.2	10.5
$30k			43.9	31.9	25.7	21.6	18.8	16.6	14.9	13.6	12.4	11.5	10.7	10	9.3	8.8
$25k		40.6	29	23.1	19.3	16.6	14.6	13.1	11.8	10.8	10	9.2	8.6	8	7.6	7.1
$20k	36.7	25.7	20.1	16.6	14.2	12.4	11	10	9.1	8.3	7.7	7.1	6.7	6.3	5.9	5.6

After-Tax Annual Income

pretty much anywhere for $50,000 a year. At $75,000, saving $50,000 becomes a lot more difficult, but it's still possible depending on where and how you live. But if you're earning $50,000 or less, retiring in fifteen years is impossible because you simply won't have the money available to save.

Using the chart below you can easily see how many years it will take you to reach financial independence based on your annual after-tax income and your annual spending (expenses). As you can see, the higher your income and the lower your expenses, the fewer years it will take.

This goes to show why focusing on spending and saving alone is not enough to help most people retire early. So with that in mind, let's shift our focus to the really fun stuff—making a lot more money!

THE ENTERPRISE MINDSET

While countless books, articles, and case studies have been written about how to make money, the rich get richer due to one simple reason: they take advantage of as many ways to make and save money as possible. I call this way of thinking the *enterprise mindset* because it closely resembles how businesses make, save, and grow money. They don't waste money or time.

The rich look at money not as a limited resource that they need to maximize (the way most people do), but as a fungible tool that can be used for any purpose. They take advantage of every opportunity to make more money and build wealth in as many ways as possible—by cutting expenses, optimizing their fees/prices, minimizing their taxes, building multiple income streams, and using whatever other ways they can find. They focus on making as much money as possible per minute and hour of their time. Warren Buffett, the world's most successful investor, makes approximately $1.34 million per hour, even when he's sleeping. While it's nowhere near Warren Buffett, last year I made approximately $45 per hour even when I was sleeping!

The good news is that pretty much anyone with an internet connection can adopt an enterprise mindset. Thanks to technology, it's never been easier to monitor, optimize, and earn more money. It's also never been easier to track and optimize exactly how much money you are making per hour. There are many online tools you can use to analyze your investment performance and tools that recommend different ways to optimize that performance. And the tools are only getting better thanks to developments in artificial intelligence and machine learning.

As of this writing, I am testing a number of new tools that analyze your moneymaking, saving, and spending patterns and not only provide optimization recommendations, but can actually automate most of your financial life so artificial intelligence always makes the right money decision for you and then can explain why.

In many cases the right money decision is simply the mathematically correct one. But as I've already shared with you, while automation is not enough, it's incredible to see the potential technology has to help more people make smarter decisions with their money based on actual patterns and actual performance data.

There are also tons of amazing websites where you can learn a new skill you can then exchange for extra money and job sites that list opportunities to pick up some extra cash—whether it's a $50 dog-walking gig or a month-long tutoring project. I just found a gig today that pays $2,000 a month for just a few hour of your time a week to tutor students learning English online. The point is, it's never been easier to adopt an enterprise mindset and make more money, but very few people take full advantage of this fact. Seriously, there are moneymaking opportunities everywhere.

For an up-to-date list of apps, tools, and moneymaking websites I recommend, check out https://financialfreedombook.com/tools.

To make as much money as possible, you need to combine and maximize as many moneymaking strategies as possible. There are four general types of ways to make money:

1. Full-time employment—working for someone else
2. Side hustling—making money on the side
3. Entrepreneurship—scaling your side hustle and/or making it your full-time job
4. Investing—growing your money in the market

Focusing on all four will help you make the most money quickly, and it will also give you the most control over how you make that money.

Instead of relying on one source of income—whether it's a turbulent stock market or an employer who could go out of business or choose to fire you at any time—you will know that no matter what happens, you will still be able to depend on at least one way to make money. If you lose your job but have a side business helping people build websites (this is what I did) or selling handmade greeting cards on Etsy, you don't have to panic. Likewise, if you decide you don't like your nine-to-five, having other income streams can give you the freedom to quit at any time. Multiple income streams give you options, flexibility, and more control.

In later chapters, I'll show you exactly *how* to do all of these things, but first it's important to understand why each of these is critical toward achieving an enterprise mindset.

HACK YOUR FULL-TIME JOB

It's tough to get ahead simply by working for someone else because the amount of money you make is limited by your time and salary, which your employer will try to keep as low as possible because the company (following the enterprise mindset) is trying to keep expenses as low as possible. Because you are trading your time for money, you can make only so much money because you have a limited amount of time.

But there are many benefits to working a full-time job that you can't get anywhere else. Think of your full-time job first as your foundation and then as a launching pad for making more money. Not only does your full-time job pay you a steady salary (which can increase through promotions or raises), but it probably offers a ton of perks like the opportunity to get paid to learn new skills and make connections, as well as benefits that either aren't available outside of the corporate world or extremely expensive to afford on your own. One of the most common is insurance.

Health insurance is obviously extremely expensive in the United States, but companies with a lot of employees can usually get great group rates with lower premiums and better benefits. Plus the company usually covers a portion of the premium, so your share ends up being relatively minimal. Most companies also have human resources departments that can advise you on which plan to pick. They might also offer disability insurance so you don't have to worry about losing your income if you are injured or get sick or have a child (parental leave is usually covered under short-term disability insurance), or life insurance so your loved ones are taken care of if something happens to you.

Plus, as we already mentioned, many companies offer to match contributions to your 401(k), so you get free money you won't get if you work for yourself. You will likely also receive some sort of paid time off in the form of vacation, sick, or personal days. Some companies also offer a bunch of other sweet perks like free or discounted child care or gym memberships, free food, free on-site doctors, free transportation, free educational opportunities—the list goes on. Every time you take advantage of one of these benefits, you free up any money you otherwise would have spent for the same thing. And that's more money you can save. In some cases, the total value of these benefits could easily add up to 20 to 50 percent of your salary, increasing your overall compensation.

Then there's arguably the biggest full-time job benefit of all—the opportunity to work remotely, which in many cases gives you not only more control over your time but also more flexibility to make more money. Thankfully in order to stay competitive and get top talent, more companies are developing more relaxed work policies on working remotely, since so much of our jobs can be done on a computer anywhere. This is a massive opportunity for you and anyone serious about making more money, because it disrupts the linear relationship between money and time.

In many cases, as long as you get the work done when you work remotely, you can do it from anywhere, and you can also fill the slow hours of the day or your extra time by working on your side hustle or other moneymaking projects. Make sure to check your employee contract to see if you have any restrictions on the type of work you can do outside the office. Many companies have a noncompete clause saying you can't work for a competitor company. While this is understandable and reasonable, don't let your company limit your ability to make money outside your full-time job. Everything is negotiable, and as long as you aren't competing with your company, you should have the right to make extra money on the side. Some companies try to limit all of your ability to make extra money or they use scare tactics so you won't, but you shouldn't work for those companies.

One Millennial Money reader Brian has a full-time network administrator job with great benefits and a salary of $100,000 a year, but he works almost 100 percent remotely and it takes him only about fifteen to twenty hours a week to get the job done, so he spends the rest of his time running a small consulting company doing similar work for smaller companies that nets him an additional $150,000 a year.

While he could quit his full-time job and grow his consulting business, he loves the benefits and security that it offers. He's found the right balance, and if one day he does want to jump ship from his employer or he gets laid off, then he's got options. While this might sound like a lucky situation to you, it's not. I see it happening more every day, and you can intentionally design your career like this. This has never been easier to do than today and gives you a massive advantage to make more money on your own terms.

When you max out these employer benefits, you can save an insane amount of money. Brandon, a twenty-three-year-old who worked at Google, lived in a box truck in the company parking lot. Pete and Kara, a couple who also worked at Google, lived in an RV in the parking lot. Since Google pays well, offers great benefits, *and* provides free food, these three enterprising employees were able to live on very little money and save 80 percent of their income.

Of course, even if you like your full-time job, the biggest disadvantage of having to work at one to earn money is that your time is not your own, and the higher your salary gets, the more your employer is going to expect from you in order to justify that salary. That's why even if you make a high salary, it's still worth diversifying your income streams so you can walk away from your nine-to-five if you ever determine it's not worth it.

Later in the book I'll show you how to specifically maximize your full-time job—including how to analyze your market value and value to your company to get a raise, how to make your boss think you're the best employee ever, how to rapidly increase your salary today and in the future, and how to maximize all of your benefits, including opportunities for working remotely.

SIDE HUSTLING TO DIVERSIFY
YOUR INCOME STREAMS

If you really want to make more money, you need to become an entrepreneur. Being an entrepreneur doesn't require that you create a highly successful company and sell it for a billion dollars. You can be an entrepreneur simply by selling something people will buy. If you make any money outside of your full-time job, even if it's an extra $10 a week, then you are an entrepreneur.

A lot of people, before they get on a career track or while they're looking for a full-time job, take odd jobs to make money. They might have a part-time job as a waitress or in retail. Or perhaps they babysit or mow lawns or work in their uncle's body shop. When you don't have a lot of money, you will take any opportunity to make money, even if it's just fifty bucks here or there. Perhaps these gigs aren't dream jobs and maybe they don't have much growth potential, but money is money, right?

It's crazy to me how many people stop side hustling in this way once they get a full-time job. Side hustling—what I define as any way you make money outside of your full-time job—is a relatively simple way to become an entrepreneur and diversify your income streams without taking the risk of leaving your full-time job.

You can also start a side hustle with very little time and money, so the learning opportunities are high, but the financial risk is low. If one of your side hustles doesn't work out, you can try another. The more side hustles you have, the more money you can make, and if you're already earning a full salary from your main job, you can invest 100 percent of your side income, which will automatically increase your savings rate.

No amount of money is too small to invest; even an extra $20 here or there will add up. Even after I started making $300,000 a year, I still watched my neighbor's cat for $60, just so I could invest that money. Even $1 will accelerate the rate of compounding—it's crazy how fast the extra invested income grows. Remember that any extra money invested at 7 percent interest will double every ten years! At least 40 percent of my own net worth has come from investing the money I made side hustling. It would have taken me at least twice as long to reach financial independence without side hustling.

While we will dive deep into side hustling later in the book, to find a great profitable side hustle, make a list of all the skills you have or things you are good at and a list of the things you love to do. Which ones overlap? Evaluate those opportunities first. If you like your side hustles, you will be more likely to stick with them and perhaps even grow them so they become more lucrative. Your side hustle can literally be anything, as long as you make money doing it, and once again thanks to the internet, there are more ways to make money than ever before.

Do you like to crochet? Sell some handmade mittens on Etsy. Do you collect comic books? Auction some off on eBay. Do you like to drive? Become a driver for a ride-sharing company—or better yet, become a driver for all the ride-sharing companies in your city! Like music? Maybe you can work as a DJ or start selling beat packs online. The possibilities are pretty much endless.

However, while there are an infinite number of ways to make money side hustling, not all side hustles are created equal. For example, if you drive for a ride-sharing company you can drive whenever you want, but you are still working for a large company—which, just like a full-time job, limits your income potential.

In order to maximize your side-hustle earning potential, find a side hustle:

1. Where you actually work for yourself
2. That pays you well for your time
3. That you enjoy doing
4. That teaches you new skills (skills are future currency)
5. That has growth potential (you can grow it into a larger business if you want)
6. That has passive income potential (where you can hire others to do the work or set up recurring revenue streams)

My favorite (and most profitable) side hustles are buying and selling website domain names, flipping mopeds and VW campers, building websites, blogging, and running digital ad campaigns.

One of the benefits of side hustles is that they give you the opportunity to explore a bunch of different ideas without needing to commit to any one of them. If you love dogs but find that you hate dog walking, no sweat. Do as much as you want or switch to another hustle entirely. (Cat sitting, I can assure you, is a lot less work.) You can also go to websites like TaskRabbit, Postmates, or Craigslist to see if there are any odd jobs you can do. These require a little more effort, since you constantly have to look for new opportunities, but more money is more money. Remember money is infinite.

The more you side-hustle, the better at it you'll become. For instance, over time, you'll get a better sense of how much you can charge for a service. Plus you'll probably build a stable base of clients who come to you over and over again, and they will also start recommending you to others, so you don't have to spend extra time drumming up leads. This means that you will end up working less (all told) for the same amount of money—or, if you have loyal clients, you may even end up earning more.

One of the biggest benefits of side hustling is that the more you do it, the more you train yourself to adopt an enterprise mindset and the easier it will be for you to identify other opportunities to make money. The most profitable side hustles are those that meet the most market demand but have relatively little competition. The more competition you have, the less you will be able to charge, unless you have some unique competitive advantage that justifies a premium fee. You'll learn which are which as you start experimenting, but over time, you will also start seeing new opportunities to make money you never noticed before. You start seeing moneymaking opportunities everywhere.

You will also discover new ways to grow your existing side hustles to become more profitable. For example, if you're already mowing someone's lawn, why not offer to water their garden and trim their hedges for a little extra money? Side hustling is also a great way to try out being an entrepreneur. In fact, if you really enjoy your side hustle and there's a lot of demand for it, you might decide to turn your side hustle into a full-time job or bigger business.

HIRE PEOPLE TO DO THE WORK AND MAKE A LOT MORE MONEY WITH PASSIVE INCOME STREAMS

The two best ways to make the most money over the long term are to hire other people to do the work for you and focus on building passive income streams. This is why most of the world's richest people are entrepreneurs who started and grew their own companies. Instead of working for money on their own, they have others working for them. Why mow lawns when you can hire someone else to do it and still make a majority of the money?

When you build a business, the value you are creating is not 100 percent dependent on your own time; it can be much greater, because your employees are creating value as well. Building a business multiplies and compounds your power to make money by the number of employees you have.

And keep in mind that your "employees" don't have to be full-time employees; they can be anyone you pay to do the work either once or regularly. Many people have gotten rich by simply paying other people to do the work and connecting demand with supply.

If you are building a business that makes money, you are also building an asset that can appreciate (go up in value), and you might even be able to sell it—recouping all the value you've created or more, and scoring a big payday.

But you don't always need a bunch of employees or a lot of time to make a bunch of money. The best thing about being an entrepreneur is that you have the control, so you can design a business that fits and funds your ideal lifestyle. As you've already learned, the connection between money and time doesn't need to be linear—you can build businesses that make a lot of money but require few (if any) employees and very little of your time. These are known as passive income businesses because you can make money without having to do a lot of active work. If you can find a business or investment that generates consistent reliable passive income (like rental income or stock dividends), then you can even make enough money to offset or cover your monthly expenses. Once you have reliable monthly passive income that you can live on, you've effectively reached financial independence.

Another example of a passive income business is building online courses: You spend time creating and packaging the content, and then you sell it. While you can actively sell your course or knowledge, it can also generate passive income when people find it and buy it online. I know a bunch of people who've created online courses on a niche topic, like taking care of orchids, repairing guitars, or even launching books, who are able to completely live off the income of a course they created over five years ago. Every year they update the content of the course and their audiences just keep growing.

Drop-ship companies are also popular passive income businesses. The idea behind them is that you design a product and completely outsource the manufacturing, ordering, distribution, and customer service, so you don't have to do much. When someone orders your product (for example, through Amazon), then Amazon fulfills the order and you get paid. When inventory gets low, you and your supplier get alerted so you can restock the inventory. Samantha, a woman I know, launched an extremely profitable ultra-lightweight camping company. Almost her entire company is automated. She's able to make $5,000 a month from her business almost all through Amazon, and it takes her only a few hours a month to manage!

While it might sound too good to be true, it's definitely possible to build passive income streams, but since passive income businesses are businesses, they are subject to the same market forces as other businesses; competition, demand, and many other factors can threaten their longevity.

While the statistics are pretty daunting—only 20 percent of businesses last five years and 4 percent last ten years—don't let these dissuade you from starting a side hustle and becoming more entrepreneurial. These statistics are misleading because they don't measure the eventual success rate of an entrepreneur who has launched many businesses. A vast majority of successful entrepreneurs failed the first few times they launched a business. The first two companies that I tried to launch (both were mobile apps) completely failed, but I learned a ton in the process that I was able to use when I launched my successful ventures, which all started as side hustles.

By starting a business through side hustling, you reduce the risk that comes with jumping into full-time entrepreneurship. Keep that full-time paycheck until you've built consistent income streams or you have enough customers to minimize the risk. While I'm not against quitting your full-time job and completely jumping into a great idea, a great idea is not enough. We all have great ideas, but business success comes down to execution—you've got to actually be able to make it happen. I see far too many entrepreneurs quit their full-time jobs to pursue an idea when they don't yet have a strong proof of concept and customers.

Full-time entrepreneurs are often in feast-or-famine mode. When you do well, you can do really well, but a business can be difficult to sustain and especially difficult to build. You are always chasing after that next deal or next paycheck, so in reality, the freedom of self-employment can ironically end up creating a lot of stress.

Business—like life, like investing—is all about taking calculated risks. Risks are smaller when you are twenty-two years old and single and have plenty of time to test, iterate, and rebound if you fail. But risks are obviously much higher if you are thirty-five with two kids and you're the primary income earner. I'm not saying you can't make it happen at thirty-five, but the more risk you are taking, the more proof points you need, and side hustling is the best way to get them without risking your full-time income.

To increase your chances of success as an entrepreneur, start by side hustling and you'll be well on your way to building a large amount of wealth and fast-tracking your financial freedom. If you can build a consistent stream of clients or income sources and have enough savings to fall back on, then becoming a full-time entrepreneur might be the perfect option for you. Your business, just like you, will change over time, and if it's successful, you will have a lot of options. You could decide to keep growing your business, you could turn it into a passive income stream, or you could sell it.

Later in the book I'll show you how to pick and grow a profitable side hustle, how to price and sell your product, how to decide if/when you should go full time, as well as how to turn your side hustle into a passive income stream or lifestyle business that makes enough money to fund and fit into your ideal lifestyle. One that makes you the most money in the least amount of time. Remember, time > money.

INVEST AS MUCH MONEY AS EARLY AS POSSIBLE

Investing income is the ultimate passive income, and this is the main strategy the wealthy use to both get rich and stay rich. The rich also know that $1 invested today will be worth more than $1 tomorrow, thanks to compounding, and that $1 *not* invested today will be worth less than $1 tomorrow, because of inflation. This is the final piece of the enterprise mindset: learning to see the potential growth in every dollar you earn and save. As you know, the earlier and more you invest, the faster your money will grow. This is why I almost always invested money as soon as it hit my bank account; even a few additional days of compounding add up. While you can invest in anything, I've found stock, bond, and real estate investing to be the most manageable and dependable investments.

If you want to increase your savings rate quickly, one of the most effective strategies is to increase it by 1 percent every thirty to ninety days. One percent is small enough that you won't feel it in your everyday life, but significant enough to have a huge impact on how quickly you can reach financial independence.

Let's say you make $50,000 a year (after taxes) and are already saving 5 percent of your income. If you increase that by 1 percent every three months (4 percent a year), you'll be saving 25 percent of your income after just five years. If you continue to increase your savings rate this way until you reach a 65 percent savings rate (which will happen after fifteen years), you'll have $814,349 saved (without factoring in any compounding gains) after twenty years. That's huge! If you follow the same pattern on a $100,000 salary, you'll end up with $1,628,698.

Yes, 65 percent of $50,000 is a lot of money, but if you are always looking for opportunities to increase your income, you will still have plenty left over.

More than 50 percent of my personal net worth has come through investment gains. But relying on just one method—no matter how effective—is risky, which is why the enterprise mindset is so powerful. By diversifying your income streams, consistently looking for new ways to make more money, and investing as much money as possible, you are giving yourself

50,000 (with 1 percent escalations every three months, peaking at 65 percent savings
te) = $814,349

Year	Savings Rate	Annual Percentage Saving Increase	Salary	Total Saved	Expected Rate of Return	Total Investment Balance
0	5%	4%	$50,000	$2,500	7%	$2,675
1	9%	4%	$50,000	$4,500	7%	$7,677.25
2	13%	4%	$50,000	$6,500	7%	$15,169.66
3	17%	4%	$50,000	$8,500	7%	$25,326.53
4	21%	4%	$50,000	$10,500	7%	$38,334.39
5	25%	4%	$50,000	$12,500	7%	$54,392.80
6	29%	4%	$50,000	$14,500	7%	$73,715.29
7	33%	4%	$50,000	$16,500	7%	$96,530.36
8	37%	4%	$50,000	$18,500	7%	$123,082.49
9	41%	4%	$50,000	$20,500	7%	$153,633.26
10	45%	4%	$50,000	$22,500	7%	$188,462.59
11	49%	4%	$50,000	$24,500	7%	$227,869.97
12	53%	4%	$50,000	$26,500	7%	$272,175.87
13	57%	4%	$50,000	$28,500	7%	$321,723.18
14	61%	4%	$50,000	$30,500	7%	$376,878.81
15	65%	0%	$50,000	$32,500	7%	$438,035.32
16	65%	0%	$50,000	$32,500	7%	$503,472.80
17	65%	0%	$50,000	$32,500	7%	$573,490.89
18	65%	0%	$50,000	$32,500	7%	$648,410.25
19	65%	0%	$50,000	$32,500	7%	$728,573.97
20	65%	0%	$50,000	$32,500	7%	$814,349.15

$100,000 (with 1 percent escalations every 3 months, peaking at 65 percent savings rate) = $1,628,698

Year	Savings Rate	Annual Percentage Saving Increase	Salary	Total Saved	Expected Rate of Return	Total Investment Balance
0	5%	4%	$100,000	$5,000	7%	$5,350
1	9%	4%	$100,000	$9,000	7%	$15,354.50
2	13%	4%	$100,000	$13,000	7%	$30,339.32
3	17%	4%	$100,000	$17,000	7%	$50,653.07
4	21%	4%	$100,000	$21,000	7%	$76,668.78
5	25%	4%	$100,000	$25,000	7%	$108,785.60
6	29%	4%	$100,000	$29,000	7%	$147,430.59
7	33%	4%	$100,000	$33,000	7%	$193,060.73
8	37%	4%	$100,000	$37,000	7%	$246,164.98
9	41%	4%	$100,000	$41,000	7%	$307,266.53
10	45%	4%	$100,000	$45,000	7%	$376,925.19
11	49%	4%	$100,000	$49,000	7%	$455,739.95
12	53%	4%	$100,000	$53,000	7%	$544,351.75
13	57%	4%	$100,000	$57,000	7%	$643,446.37
14	61%	4%	$100,000	$61,000	7%	$753,757.61
15	65%	0%	$100,000	$65,000	7%	$876,070.65
16	65%	0%	$100,000	$65,000	7%	$1,006,945.59
17	65%	0%	$100,000	$65,000	7%	$1,146,981.78
18	65%	0%	$100,000	$65,000	7%	$1,296,820.51
19	65%	0%	$100,000	$65,000	7%	$1,457,147.94
20	65%	0%	$100,000	$65,000	7%	$1,628,698.30

$200,000 (with 1 percent escalations every 3 months, peaking at 65 percent savings rate) = $3,257,396

Year	Savings Rate	Annual Percentage Saving Increase	Salary	Total Saved	Expected Rate of Return	Total Investment Balance
0	5%	4%	$200,000	$10,000	7%	$10,700
1	9%	4%	$200,000	$18,000	7%	$30,709.00
2	13%	4%	$200,000	$26,000	7%	$60,678.63
3	17%	4%	$200,000	$34,000	7%	$101,306.13
4	21%	4%	$200,000	$42,000	7%	$153,337.56
5	25%	4%	$200,000	$50,000	7%	$217,571.19
6	29%	4%	$200,000	$58,000	7%	$294,861.18
7	33%	4%	$200,000	$66,000	7%	$386,121.46
8	37%	4%	$200,000	$74,000	7%	$492,329.96
9	41%	4%	$200,000	$82,000	7%	$614,533.06
10	45%	4%	$200,000	$90,000	7%	$753,850.37
11	49%	4%	$200,000	$98,000	7%	$911,479.90
12	53%	4%	$200,000	$106,000	7%	$1,088,703.49
13	57%	4%	$200,000	$114,000	7%	$1,286,892.74
14	61%	4%	$200,000	$122,000	7%	$1,507,515.23
15	65%	0%	$200,000	$130,000	7%	$1,752,141.29
16	65%	0%	$200,000	$130,000	7%	$2,013,891.18
17	65%	0%	$200,000	$130,000	7%	$2,293,963.57
18	65%	0%	$200,000	$130,000	7%	$2,593,641.02
19	65%	0%	$200,000	$130,000	7%	$2,914,295.89
20	65%	0%	$200,000	$130,000	7%	$3,257,396.60

more control over your financial destiny and protecting yourself in the event something disrupts one of your income streams.

If you want to reach financial independence and retire as quickly as possible, you need to go all out. You need to find ways to make as much money, save as much money, and invest as much money as possible. As I'm writing this morning, I just logged into my accounts: I've made about $2,000 in the past forty-eight hours, most of it passively through investment returns. That's how the rich get richer and how you will, too. Make every moment, every day, every year count. Make the most of your time.

One year of hard work this year can buy you five, ten, even twenty years of freedom tomorrow. You need to view saving and investing not as a sacrifice, but as an opportunity. An opportunity to work exceptionally hard for a few years to really build wealth. Life-changing wealth. Freedom wealth.

RECAP

1. Building wealth relies on the same three basic levers.
   - Expenses: How much money you are spending
   - Savings: How much money you are saving/investing
   - Income: How much money you are making

2. Most personal finance books focus too much on cutting back, but while both making money and cutting back are essential to reach financial freedom, making more money is more powerful than cutting back for fast-tracking financial freedom.

3. Savings rate: Measure savings in both dollars and percentages. To calculate your savings rate, you want to add up all of the dollars that you save, both in pretax accounts (for example, 401(k)s and IRAs) and after-tax accounts (for example, brokerage accounts) and divide it by your income.

4. Your savings rate is directly correlated with the amount of time it will take you to hit your number. Even a 1 percent or $1 per day increase can make a difference.

5. Enterprise mindset: Take advantage of every opportunity to make more money and build wealth in as many ways as possible—by cutting expenses, optimizing fees/prices, minimizing taxes, building multiple income streams, and whatever other ways present themselves. Focus

on making as much money as possible per minute and hour of your time.

6. To make as much money as possible, you want to combine and maximize as many moneymaking strategies as possible. There are four general types of ways to make money:

- Full-time employment—working for someone else,
- Side hustling—making money on the side
- Entrepreneurship—building a lifestyle business, growing your side hustle, and/or making it your full-time job
- Investing—growing your money in the stock market and real estate

7. Find a side hustle:

- Where you actually work for yourself
- That pays you well for your time
- That you really enjoy so you'll stick with it
- That teaches you new skills (skills are future currency)
- That has growth potential (you can grow it into a larger business if you want)
- That has passive income potential (where you can hire others to do the work or set up recurring revenue streams)

8. Investing is the ultimate passive income, and this is the main strategy the wealthy use to both get rich and stay rich. While you can invest in anything, I've found stock, bond, and real estate investing to be the most manageable and dependable investments. Invest as much money as quickly as possible. An effective strategy is increasing your savings rate 1 percent every thirty to ninety days, but you should increase it as much as you can.

CHAPTER 6

IS IT WORTH IT?

11 Ways to Think About Money Before You Buy Anything

How much does a cup of coffee cost? If you go to your local coffee shop, you might see that a twelve-ounce cup of coffee is priced at $3 including tax, so your answer would probably be $3. Seems simple enough, so why am I asking this question?

Because that $3 cup of coffee will actually cost you more—potentially a whole lot more—than you think.

It's so easy to spend money nowadays that few people take the time to consider the true cost of each transaction. Swipe your credit card, tap your phone, or press a button and you are on your way. Unfortunately, the easier it is to spend money, the more money people spend, and that leads to consequences most people don't realize.

Saving money is making money. Every purchase you make is a trade-off—spend money on one thing, that's less money you can save or spend on something else. If you want to fast-track your financial freedom, you need to not only understand this concept but learn to consider every financial transaction you make in these terms. What are you actually getting in exchange for your money? Is it worth it? By spending money on X, will that leave less money for Y? If so, is X or Y more important? In other words, how much do things actually cost?

When you spend money, you are not just paying for something with dollars. You're also paying with your time and the future potential of those dollars. You're also adding to the amount of time it will take to hit your number. Everything you buy you are trading for freedom. What's worth more to you—a few extra weeks of freedom or that new coat?

IS IT WORTH IT?

If you want to make smarter decisions about money, you need to be mindful about spending it, and part of being mindful is considering the true cost of everything you buy—or don't buy—and using that to determine whether it's worth it or not.

To do this, you need to start asking yourself questions other than "How much money does this cost?" In fact, there are eleven key questions you can ask yourself before making any spending decision that will help you figure this out. You don't need to ask yourself each question every time you make a purchase, but having them in the back of your mind (or in your wallet or on your phone) will prove a useful check on spending money unnecessarily or mindlessly and will also help you feel more confident about what you do spend your money on.

When you learn to look at money this way, you'll discover that things are actually *much* more expensive than they appear, and you will end up spending less and saving more automatically. While ten questions might sound like a lot to remember, after a little while, they'll become natural a part of your shopping routine. I've also created a simple list you can download and print or save to your phone at https://financialfreedombook.com/tools

CALCULATE AND REGULARLY MONITOR YOUR REAL HOURLY RATE

Before you can start asking these questions, you need to figure out how much money you are actually making. Specifically, how much money do you actually make per hour? This is known as your real hourly rate. One of the goals of this book is to help you make as much money in as little time as possible and eventually have enough passive income so that you no longer have to trade your time for money at all. The higher your real hourly rate, the more money you are making for your time.

Calculating your real hourly rate is essential because it allows you to both see, in real numbers, just how much time you are trading for your money and weigh this information when considering how much something actually costs and whether it's worth buying.

Your pay stub may show that you are getting paid $20 per hour after taxes, but that is only for the time you are sitting at your desk or working at your job. It doesn't account for all of the extra time you spend doing things *because* of your job but outside of it. You spend time commuting, getting ready for the workday, shopping for work clothes, traveling on work trips, de-stressing after work or on the weekends, and probably other things. You're not getting paid for this time even though you would probably spend it differently if you didn't work.

Your nine-to-five job takes a lot more of your time and your life than you realize. When you add all of this time up and include it in your real hourly rate calculation, you will see that you make a lot less money than what your employer says you do.

As you make more money in your full-time job and launch side hustles, your real hourly rate will change, so, as in the case of your net worth, it's important to calculate and monitor regularly. I recommend calculating your real hourly rate for each of your income streams individually and in aggregate ideally once a quarter, or at the very least, once a year. When you know your real hourly rate, you can better evaluate new job and income opportunities as you work on increasing your salary.

While it can be difficult to calculate your exact real hourly rate, since getting ready, commuting, shopping for work clothes, traveling on work trips, detoxing, and so forth will inevitably vary from week to week, a solid estimate is good enough for our purposes. Start by figuring out your base hourly rate—i.e., the amount of money your company says it is paying you for each hour you work. If you are currently being paid by the hour, this is super easy to do, and you probably already know it.

If you're a salaried employee, your pay stub may show an hourly rate, but this is usually calculated based on a 35- to 40-hour workweek, and it's very possible that you work more than this. If this is the case, divide your annual pretax salary by the number of hours you work in a year. Simply figure out the average number of hours you work per week and multiply it by the number of weeks you work (be sure to subtract any vacation or holidays). If you are a salaried employee, the more hours you work, the lower your real hourly rate. So if you work 50 hours per week for 50 weeks per year, then you are working 2,500 hours per year. That's a lot of premium time!

If you make $50,000 a year, that amounts to a base hourly rate of $20 ($50,000/2,500 = $20). If you don't know how many hours you work each week, it might be helpful to keep track of your hours for a few weeks and then figure out an average. Even if you spend an hour each day surfing the internet at your desk because you don't have enough work to keep you busy, count that hour as work because your job is preventing you from using that time for other things.

Now that you have your base hourly rate, you can calculate your real hourly rate. Think about all the time you spend each week commuting to work, traveling for work (if you are a road warrior, this is a killer!) buying clothes for work, attending events, de-stressing from work, or anything else you spend your time on that you wouldn't have to do if it wasn't for your job. Remember that Americans on average spend roughly 53 minutes commuting every day. That means they spend about 220 hours each year commuting if they work 50 weeks per year. That's equal to 27.5 additional 8-hour working days per year! And they're not getting paid for a minute of it.

And if you travel on trips for your work, those hours really add up—just a few overnight trips to conferences of clients can add hundreds of hours a year. When you are at that sales conference in St. Louis you can't be somewhere doing something else, so a regular 8- or 10-hour workday becomes a 16-plus-hour workday with travel. A simple 3-day work trip might end up costing you 48 hours, instead of 24 if you were at home. If you travel all the time for work, you might be really blown away by how low your real hourly rate actually is. I did this calculation for one of my friends who makes $250,000 a year as a business consultant, but he's traveling most of the year. After taxes, because of all the travel and hours he puts in, his real hourly rate is about $25 per hour!! He was so blown away by how much time he was actually trading for money that he changed jobs a few months later.

Use the table below to write down how much time per week you spend working and doing things related to work. Then use this information to calculate your pretax and after-tax real hourly rates by dividing your salary by the total number of hours you spend as a result of your job. Note that you can also easily find your tax rate at https://www.taxfoundation

	Average Number of Hours per Week	Hours per Year = (# of weeks you work per year x hours per week)
Working		
Getting Ready		
Commuting		
Traveling (to clients, etc.)		
Shopping		
Relaxing/Detoxing		
Other		
Total		

Salary	
Effective Hourly Rate: Salary/Total Hours per Year (pretax)	

Annual Tax Rate (Federal + State)	
Effective Hourly Rate: Salary/Total Hours per Year (after-tax)	

.org. I've also built an online calculator you can use to calculate your real hourly rate at https://financialfreedombook.com/tools

Below is a table showing my numbers when I was working fifty hours a week at a digital marketing agency earning $50,000 a year.

Yikes! That's a lot less than the $20 base rate I assumed I was making based on the amount of time I spent at work.

Don't worry if your real hourly rate is less than you realized. In a later chapter, we'll explore how to maximize your real hourly rate, but for now I just want you to know what it is so you can better determine the true cost of what you're spending your money on.

	Average Number of Hours per Week	Hours per Year = (# of weeks you work per year x hours per week)
Working	50	2,500
Getting Ready	1	250
Commuting	7.5	375
Traveling (to clients, etc.)	3	150
Shopping	1	50
Relaxing/Detoxing	8	400
Other		
Total	70.5	3,725

Salary	$50,000
Effective Hourly Rate: Salary/Total Hours per Year (pretax)	$13.42

Annual Tax Rate (Federal + State)	25%
Effective Hourly Rate: Salary/Total Hours per Year (after-tax)	$10.07

Now that you have your real hourly rate, you can start asking yourself the eleven questions that will help you evaluate the true cost of anything. Each one is designed to help you answer the question at the heart of every purchase you consider making: Is it worth it? The answer may surprise you.

QUESTION 1: HOW HAPPY WILL THIS PURCHASE MAKE ME?

When most people want to buy something, they look at the dollar price first and then ask themselves if they want to buy it. The cheaper it is, the easier the decision often is. "This cup of coffee costs three dollars. Do I want to spend three bucks on this cup of coffee?" People in the United States consume 400 million cups of coffee every day—it's a relatively cheap and easy thing to buy without being mindful of it.

But the next time you want to buy something, before you consider the price or whether you can afford it or all of the other questions we will get into below, start by ask yourself a more personal question: "How much value will this bring to my life? How happy will it make me today? How happy will it make me tomorrow and next month?"

Answering this question gets easier over time as you realize that many things you think will make you happy won't. Or the things that once made you happy or you wanted no longer do. This is a money mastery concept because it forces you to make choices based on something deeper. Only you know what truly makes you happy and if it's worth spending money on.

You need to think about your short- and long-term happiness, since next month you might regret buying something that brings you joy today. Answering this question for a cup of coffee is pretty easy. If you love good coffee and having a high-quality cup first thing in the morning sets the right tone for your day, then you'll probably determine that it's worth it to spend $25 on a bag of beans or $3 on a small cup at your local café.

So many personal finance books and money experts recommend cutting back on your daily coffee or daily wine or whatever relatively small indulgences you tend to buy during the week. The idea is that these small purchases add up (a $3 cup of coffee every day is $1,095 a year) and that this money would be put to better use if saved or invested for later. But those small things often make you happy and bring joy to your life and are therefore much more valuable than they appear. Your best friend may not want to spend $25 on a weekly manicure, but if doing so makes you feel good and confident, and you use the time at the nail salon to chill out after a long day at the office, then by all means go for it. Don't give up what you enjoy just to save a few bucks. Trust me, when it comes to the bigger picture, that moment of happiness is likely more valuable than the extra money you are saving.

On the other hand, if you're bored at the airport and start to get a little thirsty, you can use this question to determine how much you really want that organic cold-pressed green juice; you may decide that a free cup of water will do the trick just fine. By the time you find out the green juice costs $14 a bottle, you've already made up your mind not to buy it.

But "Will this make me happy?" might be more challenging for larger purchases like a nice new suit, a car, or even a house. People often spend the most money on big houses, expensive cars, or fancy trips because they feel like it's what they're supposed to do, not because they really want them or the items will truly make them happy.

If you love to drive and have a passion for cool cars, then perhaps spending extra money on a high-performance convertible might be worth it. Then again, perhaps you'll determine that you'd be happier spending less on a car and using the money you saved on an annual trip to Europe. In the end, you may end up spending the same amount of money, but one decision will likely bring you much more joy than the other. If you're unsure, sleep on it or make a personal rule that you won't buy something whenever you are unsure of its value. Buy what you want, what gives you joy, and say no to anything that is "meh" or "maybe" or "I don't know."

So the next time you are walking by the coffee shop or the salon or the wine bar or searching for properties online, ask yourself, "How happy will this make me and is it worth the money?" Or just wait a few days, weeks, or even months and ask yourself the same question to see if you still want to buy it. A popular strategy is to always wait thirty days before any purchase over a set dollar amount—say, $100. Over time this level of mindfulness will help you more easily identify the things worth spending money on and maximize your enjoyment per dollar.

QUESTION 2: HOW MUCH MONEY DO I HAVE TO MAKE TO AFFORD THIS?

Now let's get down to some numbers. When you buy something, you pay for it in after-tax dollars, which means you actually have to make *more* than the price listed in order to afford it. For example if you are in the 30 percent effective tax bracket, that means that 1.5 of the 5 days you work in a week is going just to pay your taxes! It also means that every $1 you make is actually worth only $0.70 in purchasing power.

Depending on the federal tax bracket you are in, as well as how much you pay in Social Security and state and local income tax, the true cost of that $3 cup of coffee is without a doubt more expensive. You likely have to earn at least 20 to 40 percent more than the list price of whatever you buy, so next time you want to calculate the pretax cost of something, use the formula below.

(the advertised price of what you want to buy) / (1 − the percent you pay in taxes) = the pretax cost of the item

Using coffee as an example again, let's say you pay 25 percent of your income in taxes. So:

$3/(1 − 0.25) = $4

In other words, you have to earn $4 in order to afford a $3 cup of coffee. While $1 isn't a lot of money, when you analyze bigger purchases, the difference can be massive. For example, if you pay 25 percent of your income in taxes and want to buy a $40,000 car, you would need to make approximately $53,333 in pretax income to afford it. That's an extra $13,333. A simple way to look at it is, however much you pay in taxes, you'll have to earn that much more to afford something. So if you pay 15 percent in taxes, anything you buy is actually 15 percent more expensive than the list price. If you want to get technical, it's actually more than that because your income taxes don't include the money you need to pay for Social Security and Medicare taxes, which as of this writing adds at least another 7.5 to 15 percent (depending on whether you work for yourself or for an employer) to your tax bracket.

This is just one of the many reasons tax optimization is important, because it makes every $1 you make worth as much as possible. Just reducing your taxes by 5 percent through proper deductions and investing strategies is like saving 2 hours of your time each week, or over 100 hours a year! It's helpful to also think about money in units of time, which brings us to the next question.

QUESTION 3: HOW MANY HOURS OF MY LIFE AM I TRADING TO AFFORD THIS?

As we've already discussed, money is infinite, but time is not. Anytime you are getting paid to work, you are trading time from your life in exchange for money.

The average life expectancy in the United States is roughly seventy-nine, which means the average American lives for 692,040 hours. Since you spend at least a third of your life sleeping, that leaves about 461,360 waking hours in the average American's life. If you are twenty years old and live to seventy-nine, you have about 344,560 waking hours left. If you are thirty and live to seventy-nine, you have about 286,160 waking hours left. If you are fifty, you have about 169,360 waking hours left. And so on.

The next time you go to buy something, ask yourself, "How much of my lifetime am I trading for it? How many hours do I have to work to afford that three-dollar cup of coffee?

The cup of coffee is a pretty small example, and this calculation tends to be more psychologically meaningful for larger purchases, but it works for the coffee, too. Using the after-tax real hourly rate you calculated earlier in the chapter, let's calculate how much of your life you would have to trade for a $3 cup of coffee.

(advertised price) / (after-tax real hourly rate) = number of hours traded

For the purpose of this example, let's use my after-tax hourly rate of $10.79 that I calculated earlier in the chapter.

$3 / $10.79 per hour = .278

Now, .278 of an hour is 16.68 minutes, so I'd have to work about 16 minutes and 40 seconds for this coffee. That's not so bad. I think most caffeine junkies would be willing to work 16 minutes for a good cup of coffee. But what about more expensive purchases? What if I wanted to buy a new car that cost $40,000?

$40,000/ $10.79 per hour = 3,707 hours

That's an insane amount of time! That's 74 fifty-hour workweeks—about a year and a half of working just to buy a new car! Understand that unless what you are buying can appreciate (go up in value), like real estate, then you will have to save more or work longer to reach financial independence if you choose to buy it. Another way to think about it is, if you don't buy that $40,000 car, depending on your number, you might be able to retire up to five years sooner! Is that new car worth five years of your life? At the end of the day, it might be worth it to you to buy the car if it makes you happy and you can answer yes to the next question.

QUESTION 4: CAN I AFFORD IT?

This seems like an obvious question, but so many people live beyond their means and buy things they can't actually afford that it's important to always ask it, especially when you are trying to decide on a big purchase.

Can you afford a $3 cup of coffee? Probably. But what about that $300,000 house? That all depends on your finances and net worth from the previous chapters. It also depends on how much money you have already saved.

When you look at the median net worth of Americans and how much the average family spends each year, it's easy to see that in most situations the answer to the question "Can I afford it?" should be no. In 2016 the average American family's before-tax income was $74,664 and their annual expenditures were $57,311. If we calculate a roughly 20 percent reduction in net income after taxes, that family is left with about $59,731, which means they are barely making more than they spend. Cutting it so close is why the average American household has $15,654 in credit card debt, $27,669 in auto loan debt, and $46,597 in student loan debt.

As a general rule, you should never spend more than 2 to 3 percent of your total net worth on any single purchase like a vacation or a car. If you are just starting out and have a negative net worth, you are going to need to make some steep trade-offs to get ahead financially, like trying to avoid car ownership if you can or buying the cheapest, most reliable used car that you can find. Of course, if having a car is necessary for your job, then you can spend more, but I encourage you to spend as little as possible until your net worth is positive. Try to pay cash for your car—in most cities you can find a reliable used car for under $2,000—so you don't have to pay interest on an auto loan. This might mean putting off a vacation for a while, but remember the impact of your choice today means more time and more freedom tomorrow.

Buying a home is an exception, since unlike most cars, which depreciate (decrease in value over time), real estate typically appreciates, making it a sound investment. It can make sense to take out a mortgage from a bank to buy a home, but you should take out only as much mortgage as you need, not what the banks are willing to give you. Banks are often willing to lend you a lot more money than you should be lending from them because they make money on your interest payments. Unless you are "house-hacking" and strategically using the bank and renter's money to cover your mortgage, then you should only ever borrow the minimum that you need.

I will explain in detail how to assess buying real estate in chapter 11. For now, a quick rule of thumb is that you should spend only 30 percent or less of your after-tax annual income on your mortgage or rent each year. Some financial advisors will say you can spend up to 40 percent of your income on housing expenses, but I think that's too much. Housing is most people's biggest expense, so you should minimize it as much as possible so you have more money to invest.

QUESTION 5: HOW DO PRICES COMPARE IN TERMS OF PERCENTAGES?

That $1 price difference between a $3 and a $4 cup of coffee might not seem like much, but it's actually a 25 percent difference. By looking at the percentage difference, it is easier to assess the actual difference between two dollar amounts.

The next time you're shopping and want to compare multiple products or multiple versions of the same product, consider the difference in price as a percentage rather than in terms of dollars. For example, the store brand of coffee might be $9 a bag and the name brand $12 a bag. Three dollars is not that great a difference, but in this case, it amounts to a 33 percent difference, which is huge. In fact, buying the store brand, in that case, is like getting a 33 percent return on your money. That's insane! You can't get that kind of return anywhere else!

When you focus on the percentage difference between two prices, it's easier to make a value judgment on whether it's worth paying more for one product over another. For me personally, a product needs to be *a lot* better for me to pay 33 percent more for it, but if I determine it's worth it, then at least I know I made my decision using all the information I had at my disposal. It might not be worth it to pay 33 percent more for what is essentially the same coffee (since the difference in quality between store brands and name brands is usually minimal), but it may be worth it for me to pay 33 percent, or even 50 percent or 75 percent, more for coffee that is obviously better tasting.

The easiest way to make money is not to spend it, and you can use this same strategy when trying to save money. For example, how much more does it cost to eat out than it would if you were to prepare the same meal at home? There is a steakhouse in Chicago that I really love. The vibe is good and the apps and drinks are great, but I calculated that the $60 bone-in rib-eye steak costs almost 400 percent more than if I was to buy the same cut of meat for $15 at the grocery store and prepare it at home. That's an insane premium, and since I did that calculation, I've definitely been making more steaks at home. It might be worth it to eat out for a special occasion, since I can't re-create the entire restaurant experience at home, but if I just want a decent steak, a 400 percent markup is hard to, pardon the pun, swallow.

QUESTION 6: CAN I GET IT FOR LESS OR TRADE FOR IT?

This is a simple question that must be considered with any purchase. Of course, getting something for free is always best, and you can find a lot of things for free if you are patient and willing to seek them out. I'm a big fan of Freecycle, a website that lists free stuff and has millions of users. You can find so many things on there if you make it part of your regular browsing. A while ago I found a $300 juicer that a couple never used, a $500 exercise bike, and an amazing desk chair. Also, don't be afraid to barter for stuff. If you have something you don't need anymore, hunt down someone who is willing to trade you for it.

Second, if you can't find something for free, you can probably purchase it used for significantly less than you can new. Literally almost everything depreciates in value after it's been purchased, so you can get significant savings on anything from cars to clothes to computers to books to furniture when you buy used instead of new. I'm not saying you can't buy new things—your money/time trade-off is up to you. I'm just urging you to consider whether you can get the same value for less by buying used. Personally, I rarely find new goods to be worth the premium.

Of course, this doesn't work for food, but you can still seek out cheaper options. Don't spend hours trying to save a few bucks, but investing the time to find the cheapest grocery store or farmers' market in your neighborhood will pay big dividends over time.

Another option to consider is if you can trade or barter for it instead. You might be able to let your friends use your car in exchange for their taking you out to eat once a week. While this is common when we are in college, once we get it out into the real world, we tend to forget that trading and bartering is possible and can be a lot cheaper if we seek it out. I'm always looking to exchange my web design skills for free stuff and have gotten everything from free furniture to dog walks to haircuts to real estate advice and many free meals all by bartering. While I've never done it, I've also met many people who barter for free rent and bank their income, which we'll dive into later in the book.

QUESTION 7: HOW MUCH AM I SPENDING ON CONVENIENCE?

How much would it cost you to make your daily cup of coffee at home?

We all end up paying a really high premium for convenience when we purchase things that include some type of service. The markup on coffee, for example, is nuts, as is the markup on delivery food.

Let's say a one-pound bag of your favorite coffee costs $12. That's about 75 cents an ounce. It takes approximately 0.75 ounce of beans to make an average 12-ounce cup of coffee, so it costs about 56 cents ($0.75 per ounce cost × 0.75 ounce) to brew a cup of coffee at home versus the $3 you'd spend out. That's a convenience charge of 435.71 percent!

You can do these calculations for food preparation pretty easily using a formula similar to the one above. But don't forget to factor in the extra time you spend making a meal for yourself, including the cost of shopping for ingredients, preparing the meal, and cleaning up. You also need to consider if you *can* actually make the meal yourself, which won't be quantifiable but will at least help you figure out the value of convenience. It might not be worth it to pay someone $15 to make you a grilled cheese sandwich or a Caesar salad, but it might be worth it to pay someone $50 to make you a five-star meal that would take you hours to prepare at home. But like everything else, if you love cooking, then it might be worth doing it yourself even if it ends up being a bigger time trade-off. And it also might be healthier!

Or for services like housecleaning or yard work, if your real hourly rate is $40, then it makes sense to pay your neighbor to mow your lawn for $20 an hour or a cleaning company to clean your house for four hours for $120. But if it costs $200 to clean your house for four hours, then it would be cheaper for you to do it yourself. Of course, you might determine it's worth the premium to buy back that four hours so you can use it for other, more enjoyable things. It's all in being mindful of the trade-offs and realizing how much you are paying for the price of convenience.

I encourage you to start calculating your own convenience cost for items you consume regularly. I used to spend $3 on a cup of quality coffee every day until I realized I could get the same benefit for a lot less money if I made the same coffee at home. However, I will still buy a $6 cup of Stumptown (the best coffee ever) from time to time when I travel because I know it will make me happy. I'm also always down to order sushi from a restaurant, since I can't make it at home.

QUESTION 8: HOW MUCH WOULD THIS COST ME EACH YEAR OR FOR THE REST OF MY LIFE?

No matter how small, recurring expenses add up over time, so it's useful to calculate the impact recurring expenses could have each year, over a longer period of years, and for some expenses, for the rest of your life. Also, remember that every recurring expense you have over your lifetime is going to increase your number.

How much does the coffee cost you if you buy it every day this year? Or how much does that monthly gym membership cost annually? A $3 daily cup of coffee adds up to $1,095 a year, or $10,950 over ten years. Not bad for having a cup of coffee every day for ten years. I'd pay it, but maybe after seeing that total, you wouldn't. A $75 monthly gym membership is $900 a year, or at least $9,000 over the next ten years (because the membership fee is likely to increase). If you just go to ride the bike or use the elliptical at that price, it might make more sense to build a gym in and put some equipment in your basement. Your $14.99 a month HBO Now subscription is $179.88 a year. And so on.

After analyzing my expenses, I learned that my weekly Chipotle habit was costing me over $820 a year. That's a lot of money, but when I did my own convenience calculation, I determined it was actually more expensive for me to shop for and make my own lunch. At the same time, it cost me $891 more to buy coffee out than it did to make it at home ($1,095 a year versus $204 a year). When I first did this calculation, my real hourly rate was close to $10, so I made the decision to not trade 89 hours of my life for a to-go coffee habit, but as my income and real hourly rate increased, it's now closer to 20 hours of my life per year I trade for my coffee habit, which is worth it to me.

QUESTION 9: WHAT IS THE PER-USE COST OF THIS ITEM?

This example doesn't work with a cup of coffee, so I'm going to go a little rogue here to illustrate this useful question. If you buy something that you are going to use frequently, then it's worth estimating the cost of the item on either a per-use basis and/or based on how frequently you use it. For example, you might really love grilling and you're deciding between two different grills, one that is $500 and one that is $1,000.

In addition to comparing the dollar price, you can also consider (1) how often you will use the grill each year and (2) how many years will you use the grill. If you use the grill two times a week, that's 104 times each year. If you estimate the grill will last you 10 years, like your old one did, then using it 104 times a year for 10 years = 1,040 approximate uses. Then you can take this number and divide it into the price of the two grills you are evaluating to get the expected per-use or per-year amount, so $500/1,040 uses = $0.48 per use or $500/10 years = $50 per year. If you do the same calculation with the $1,000 grill, then $1,000/1,040 uses = $0.96 per use or $1,000/10 years = $100 per year.

While the $1,000 grill might feel a lot more expensive than the $500 grill, looking at the difference over 1,040 uses, you will end up paying about $0.48 more each time to use a nicer grill, or about $50 more per year. It's up to you decide then whether the $50 extra per year (or $1 a week) is worth it for the nicer grill. If the nicer grill is easier to use, cooks faster, or allows you to cook for more people, it might be an easy decision.

This works especially well when evaluating large purchases like cars, boats, and specialty clothing items that you might wear only a few times (for instance, a tuxedo or a super fancy dress).

QUESTION 10: HOW MUCH WILL THIS MONEY BE WORTH IN THE FUTURE?

If you've made it this far and have started thinking about money differently, you are now my forever homie. These questions changed my life. But there's still one more question you should consider. Ready to geek out? This is my favorite calculation.

Every dollar you spend could have been invested if you hadn't made that purchase, so you should always try to analyze (especially when considering big purchases) what the future value of your money could be if you invested it instead.

Let's look at the future value of the money from the coffee example to determine what the money I spend on something today will be worth in five, ten, and thirty plus years. For an easy way to measure this for any purchase, check out the future value calculator available at https://finan cialfreedombook.com/tools

Using a 7 percent annual growth rate, the $3 we spend on a cup of coffee today would be worth $4.21 in five years, $5.90 in ten years, and $22.84 in thirty years. Those numbers aren't all that impressive, but let's look at the annual cost of that coffee over the same time periods. That $1,095 you spend every year would be worth $8,123.26 after five years, $18,086.70 after ten years, and *$120,859.30 after thirty years!* WHAT?! All those coffee haters out there could be banking mad money!

When you buy anything today, you are sacrificing the opportunity to save and grow that money. Thus with every purchase, you increase the amount of time you need to hit your number. And since money decreases in value over time thanks to inflation, you could end up needing to save more money the longer you wait. This is the negative net effect of spending money versus investing it. Just as every dollar you invest helps you get closer to your number and reduces the amount of time required to hit it, any dollar you spend means you will have to work more and it will take you more time to reach financial freedom. You are losing out when you buy something not just because you spent the money, but because you missed the opportunity for it to grow.

If you save $40,000 by not buying that new car, that allows you to invest the $40,000 instead. Instead of −$40,000 on your net worth, the impact is +$40,000 × 7 percent per year for the next ten, twenty, or thirty plus years. With your +$40,000 investment from not buying the new car doubling every ten years, you'd have $80,000 in ten years, $160,000 in twenty years, and $320,000 in thirty years. So every time you don't spend money and invest it instead, you will be maximizing the net impact of the money.

By asking yourself, "Is this money worth more to me today or in the future?" you will find yourself much more willing to invest money instead of spending it. Which brings us to the most important questions of all.

QUESTION 11: HOW MUCH TIME (FREEDOM) IS THIS BUYING ME IN THE FUTURE?

When I was deep in my own financial independence journey, I calculated that for every $25 I saved, I was buying one day of freedom in the future. So when I saved $100 in a day, I knew I was buying four days of freedom. This made it easier for me to say yes or no when considering a purchase, because I was able to quantify it in units of future time, which represent freedom.

Thanks to compounding, the younger you are, the less money you need to buy a day, a week, or a year of freedom. Since the math is a little too difficult to do by hand, I've created a simple online tool that you can use to calculate, based on your current investment balance, expected investment growth rate, and the average expected inflation rate, how much money you need to buy one day or year of freedom. You can also use it to determine how many days any amount of money you are investing will buy you in the future.

Check out the freedom calculator at https://financialfreedombook .com/tools.

CONCLUSION

While this may seem like a lot to take in, these questions become easier to answer as you practice them, and over time, I guarantee you will start making better financial decisions. Trust me on this. This psychological stuff is powerful! Remember it all comes back to trade-offs—if that cup of $3 coffee makes you happy and you realize that you are trading 16 minutes of your life for it but determine that's a trade-off worth making, then by all means, drink up. But as you apply these questions to annual recurring expenses or bigger purchases, you'll start to question the value of every dollar you spend. Again, this is why the best way to save money is simply not to spend. It's up to you to decide whether it's worth it. Those trade-offs can add up to a lifetime of freedom.

Download a card of these steps you can print out and keep in your wallet or on your phone at https://financialfreedombook.com/tools

RECAP

1. Calculate your real hourly rate, which is how much money you are actually making for an hour of your life after taking out time for getting ready, commuting, traveling for work, de-stressing from work, or anything else you spend your time on that you wouldn't have to do if it wasn't for your job.

2. Ask yourself these eleven questions before buying anything:

   1. How happy will this purchase make me?
   2. How much money do I have to make to afford this?
   3. How many hours of my life am I trading to afford this?
   4. Can I afford it?
   5. How do prices compare in terms of percentages?
   6. Can I get it for less or trade for it?
   7. How much am I spending on convenience?
   8. How much would this cost me each year or for the rest of my life?
   9. What is the per-use cost of this item?
   10. How much will this money be worth in the future?
   11. How much time (freedom) is this buying me in the future?

CHAPTER 7

THE ONLY BUDGET YOU'LL EVER NEED

How to Live for Free and Increase Your Savings Rate at Least 25%

hate budgets. Like, seriously. I think budgets are the biggest reason most people do a crappy job managing their money—they hate budgeting, too. Most personal finance books and financial literacy courses are built around budgeting, but maintaining a budget is too much of a burden and puts too granular a focus on small purchases that, in the grand scheme of things, don't have that great an impact on how much money you have.

Another reason I don't like budgets is because they reinforce the idea of scarcity. They are designed to make you track every penny you spend to the point that you end up feeling guilty if you overspend or spend money on something you don't absolutely *need*.

Budgeting is a lot like dieting: the more guilt you feel, the less likely you are to stick with it. You think, *Well, I've blown it* or *This isn't working*, and give up. Or eventually you start to feel deprived, like you have to cut back on every little indulgence in order to stick to your blasted budget, and you become frustrated or bitter. Instead of becoming a tool for empowerment by encouraging you to be smart about your money, the budget becomes a source of anxiety and stress. Ugh. Budgets are the worst.

While budgets definitely work for some people and small purchases definitely add up, you're not going to save the most money by cutting back on your small expenses. You save the most money by controlling your biggest expenses—namely housing, transportation, and food—and you can do that without the aid of a formal budget. In fact, just by optimizing your housing, transportation, and food expenses, you can realistically increase you savings rate by 25 percent or more, significantly reducing the number of years it takes to hit your number.

Remember Travis, my parents' old friend who bragged about saving 5 percent a year for retirement? Travis will drive forty minutes each way in traffic to save $20 on a case of wine and prides himself on being able to track down deals like this. And yet both he and his wife recently bought new cars for at least $40,000 each. According to various car-buying websites, if they had chosen a two-year-old version of the same cars with less than 30,000 miles on them, they could have saved at least $10,000 on each car. If they bought five-year-old models with less than 60,000 miles on them, they could have saved more than $20,000 on each car, or $40,000 total. That's like getting one car for free! You have to buy *a lot* of slightly less expensive cases of wine to save $20,000 to $40,000.

If Travis and his wife had invested that $40,000, it would be worth $161,549 in twenty years. If he'd forgone that $150,000 addition on his house and invested that money instead, he'd have $605,810 after twenty years. That's a lot of money.

Again, I don't want to pick on Travis. The new addition to his home looks great, and I have no way of knowing how much joy he and his wife get from it. I just want to make the point that we often spend so much time and energy worrying about how to save a few bucks here and there when we could save so much more with relatively little effort by considering a few key purchases. If you figure out how to save the most money possible on your biggest expenses, you won't have to worry so much about the smaller expenses because you'll have saved so much already. And if you invest this money and let it grow over time, you'll end up with even more than what you had to begin with. This is the only budget you ever need, and it will help you dramatically cut expenses while increasing your savings rate so you can reach financial independence earlier.

The average American family spent $57,311 in 2016. This includes $7,203 on food, $9,049 on transportation, and $18,886 on housing. Those three categories alone add up to $35,138, or about 61.3 percent of the total expenditure. That's a huge ratio, but when you subtract Social Security contributions ($6,509 on average in 2016), which Americans are legally required to

Average annual expenditures	2016		
	Avg. American Household	% of Expenses	Savings Opportuniy
Housing	$18,886	32.95%	HIGH
Transportation	$9,049	15.79%	HIGH
Food	$7,203	12.57%	HIGH
Personal insurance and pensions	$6,831	11.92%	LOW
Healthcare	$4,612	8.05%	LOW
All other expenditures	$3,933	6.86%	MEDIUM
Entertainment	$2,913	5.08%	MEDIUM
Cash contributions (gifts, etc.)	$2,081	3.63%	MEDIUM
Apparel and services	$1,803	3.15%	MEDIUM
Total	$57,311	100%	

SOURCE: United States Bureau of Labor Statistics

make, from total average expenditure, the figure comes closer to 70 percent of their total spendable income. Here are the average American household annual expenses across categories:

Looking at these numbers, you can see how reducing your top three expenses of housing, transportation, and food will allow you to save a lot more money. It's unrealistic to think you can save much on personal insurance and pensions (which include Social Security) and healthcare, since those are relatively fixed costs. The rest are the smaller expenses like entertainment, apparel, and other expenditures that you can manage easily if you are mindful about your spending, but because they constitute only a small portion of your total expenditures, they're unlikely to make a huge difference on your overall savings. Your small entertainment expenses are also probably the things that make you happiest.

And when you consider the future value of any money you save on your biggest expenses, the growth opportunity for savings becomes even greater. Reducing your monthly rent by $400 might not seem like much, but $400 over a year is $4,800. If you live in that apartment for three years, you will have saved $14,400. If you invest that $400 monthly savings over the course of those three years, it would be worth $16,558 at the end of that period. After twenty years of compounding at 7 percent, it will be worth $66,873 even if you don't add a penny to it.

If the average American household could cut the $35,138 they spend per year on housing, transportation, and food in half, they could save an additional $17,500 per year. If they invested that $17,500 every year for the next twenty years (approximately $1,458 per month), they would have $835,143 after twenty years. That's a massive savings toward your number.

Where can you save in each of these categories? If you move to a smaller apartment, walk to work, and cook at home, you could potentially increase your savings rate to 50 percent or even higher, cutting decades off the amount of time it will take you to reach financial independence. Below are some suggestions for saving money in these categories. If you want to get really creative, you can even figure out how to live for free. Yes, you read that right: *free*.

HOUSING

The cost of housing accounts for about 33 percent of the average American's budget. Common wisdom is that you can spend between 30 and 40 percent of your pretax income on housing. I have no idea where this advice came from, but everyone says it and it's what I was told when I started looking for my first place. But just because most people spend within this range doesn't mean you have to. In fact, with a little ingenuity, you can spend a lot less, or even nothing, on housing.

Between early 2011 and late 2012, I saved $25,000 by moving from a $1,500-per-month apartment to a smaller $700 apartment. Sure, I had to move a little closer to a busy street, into an apartment half the size, and in a completely different neighborhood, but it still had two bedrooms, and it was more than sufficient for me. The money I saved from that one move is now worth more than $100,000 in investment growth. That was almost 10 percent of my entire number. And the money will continue to grow into the future. In thirty years if it keeps growing at 7 percent per year, the rental savings on that one apartment will be worth $761,225!

But my savings pale in comparison to those of Anita, who in an effort to retire within five years lived with roommates so she had to spend only $700 per month on rent even though she was making more than $200,000 a year at the time as a lawyer. Following the traditional advice of spending up to 40 percent of your annual income on rent, Anita could have technically afforded to spend $6,600 a month on rent, but instead she invested the $5,900 difference and was able to retire at thirty-three.

There are tons of ways you can save money on rent, some more obvious than others. You can move to a smaller apartment, a less desirable neighborhood, or an older building, or get a roommate, which has the added benefit of helping you save money on some of your other expenses. If you do decide to get roommates, you could actually rent out an entire house and charge your roommates a larger portion of the rent for being the one on the lease or for managing the house. Or you can move in with a family member or your parents, who might cut you a sweet deal on rent. Sure, no one wants to live with their parents forever (I sure didn't), but if you are able to save money and invest the difference, it might be worth it to you. The more creative you get, the less money you can spend on your housing expenses.

HOW TO LIVE RENT-FREE

Anita and I saved a ton of money by choosing to pay much less in rent than we could technically afford, but each of us still had to pay $700 a month. We all assume that rent is a necessary evil, but there are tons of ways to live rent-free. In fact, it's never been easier and you don't even have to live in a tent in your friend's backyard.

The three easiest ways to live rent-free are by house-sitting, house-hacking, and bartering. Here's how each one works.

House-sitting is really simple and requires no money. At any given time in the United States, tons of people are looking for someone to look after their house and their pets while they travel. And in exchange for being an awesome house sitter, you get to live for free. In the past, you could really do this only if you knew someone—a neighbor, coworker, or family friend—who was looking for a house sitter. But today there are dozens of websites where you can set up a profile and search for hundreds of house-sitting gigs near you. This means if you're proactive, you can find a house to sit any time or any place, even when you travel, or even house-sit full-time in the city where you live. Sure, you might have to jump from place to place, but hey, it's free! In many cases, you might even get paid to house-sit, which is even better.

Some of the best house-sitting websites are TrustedHousesitters USA, House Sitters America, HouseCarers, Nomador, and MindMyHouse. All of them are super easy to use. Some charge a small membership fee that's worth it to find free housing opportunities. Just set up a profile, get your background checked (most websites provide this service for free), and start searching for opportunities. Once you've done it a few times and have received good reviews, it will become even easier for you to find opportunities. In many cases, you'll be able to stay in places you could never afford on your own, like huge houses in Colorado or million-dollar brownstones in Brooklyn. While it's usually easier to house-sit as you travel, you can also find a long-term stay for a year or two if you are looking to stay in the same place. Yes, if you're single, house-sitting in this way will be less complicated because you don't have to worry about accommodating anyone else, but if you have a family, sometimes you can bring them with you.

If you want to get even more adventurous, you can live for free internationally by setting up free housing using websites like Workaway and Help Exchange, both of which allow you to connect with people globally who are looking for help in exchange for free housing and even food in some cases. You can find opportunities on organic farms or houseboats, for example, and there are other amazing opportunities to live somewhere else for free. It might take you a little time to find the best situation, but if you are mobile you can live for free almost anywhere in the world.

House-hacking requires a little more effort than house-sitting, as well as some money to get started, but if you do it right, you can save and even make a lot of money. All it comes down to is buying a piece (or multiple pieces) of real estate and renting any rooms or units you don't live in to other people. By doing this, you get someone else to cover your mortgage so you end up living rent-free or even making money. Plus because real estate typically appreciates in value over time, the investment itself will increase your net worth and make it easier to reach financial independence.

And if you can manage to pay off (or have someone else pay off) your mortgage by the time you hit your number, you won't have to worry about rent at all because you'll own the property outright. How cool is that?!

The easiest way to start house-hacking is to buy a two- or three-bedroom apartment or house and rent the additional rooms out to your friends or other tenants; you should charge them enough to cover your monthly mortgage payment. If you prefer not to live with roommates full time, you can rent out additional rooms on sites like Airbnb. If your monthly mortgage is $1,000, you could rent out one room for $100 a night for ten nights to cover the cost and live by yourself for free for the rest of the month. Another benefit of starting this way is that two- and three-bedroom apartments tend to appreciate faster than studios and one-bedrooms, so if you want to buy real estate anyway, this ends up being a better long-term investment.

You can also buy multiple apartments or even entire buildings; it's actually a lot easier than it sounds. Adam, a Millennial Money reader, bought an entire eight-unit apartment building in Chicago at the age of twenty-four and was not only able to cover the mortgage by renting to other people but also made an additional $2,500 a month in income. In chapter 11, I will go into more detail about the ins and outs of house-hacking and investing in real estate.

Bartering is as simple as it sounds. Become a nanny or summer grounds keeper or pet sitter in exchange for free rent. I know one guy who lived in the basement apartment of an elderly woman's home and lived for free in exchange for maintaining the property and running errands for the owner.

House-sitting, house-hacking, and bartering are all viable options if you want to live for free. Also, you don't have to do it forever. A great strategy would be to house-sit for a year so you can save up enough money for a down payment on a house that you can then turn around and house-hack. By going from house-sitting to house-hacking, you can save money, acquire an appreciating asset, and eventually start getting cash flow from your rental income. Or if you're flexible, you can house-sit your way around the world forever.

TRANSPORTATION

Transportation accounts for about 19 percent of the average American's budget. There are three types of transportation included in this expense category: commuting to work, commuting for day-to-day errands and responsibilities, and traveling for vacation. As I've already mentioned, the average American commutes 53 minutes a day, often in a car. If this is the only way you can get to work, then, well, that's what you have to do. But a lot of what we spend on commuting is wrapped up in owning a car. Americans spend more money on car loans than student loans, taking out over $96 billion in car loans in the first quarter of 2017 alone.

The easiest way to save on transportation costs if you have to buy a car is to always buy used and to always buy the cheapest car you can. And if you can manage it, pay for it in cash so you don't have to pay interest on a loan. The average monthly new car loan payment is $517, and the average length of the loan is over six years. Just imagine the impact of buying a used car for less than $2,000 cash and investing that $517 a month you save on a loan payment. You'd have $46,365 saved after six years and then $187,256 after twenty more years without adding another cent to the principal. That's an exceptional ROI for buying a used car instead of a new one.

Of course, having a car costs money even after you buy it. As of this writing, the average cost of owning a car if you drive about 15,000 miles per year is $8,469 per year. That includes the cost of insurance, gas, taxes, maintenance, parking fees, and other expenses you might incur as a car owner.

If you factor all this in, the best way to save money on transportation is to not own a car at all. I myself am a huge moped and scooter fan. Not only do they cost a fraction of what a car does, but mopeds get almost 100 miles to the gallon. Plus they look cool and are fun to ride. The least expensive forms of transportation are walking, followed by biking. In late 2012, I moved closer to my office so I could walk to work and estimate that over the past five years I've saved more than $40,000 by not driving.

Public transportation is also a great option if you live in a city that has it. Trains, buses, and even ferries cost no more than a few hundred dollars a month and don't require insurance or maintenance costs. Plus you don't have to do the work of driving! You can use that 53 minutes each day to read a book or take a nap, listen to a podcast, or even earn some extra cash by selling something online or working on one of your side gigs.

If you have a couple of friends or neighbors that drive the same direction as you, then carpooling is a simple way to cut costs, one that might be even more affordable than public transportation. Another option is ride-sharing using a service like Uber, Lyft, or Waze. In some locations, ride-sharing might even be cheaper than owning a car. I know people in Los Angeles, one of the most car-dependent cities on the planet, who use ride-sharing services to get everywhere because they're so inexpensive.

THE ART OF TRAVEL-HACKING

Get out and explore the world. It's never been easier to travel for less. While travel-hacking takes some work, with a little effort you can travel for a lot less. The more you travel-hack, the better you'll get. I have paid for only a handful of flights in the past seven years and have traveled to over twenty countries, often in business class, for free. Here's how you can travel both domestically and internationally for less money, and in some cases, even free. Travel-hacking is all about finding the loopholes and using timing, strategic searching, airline reward points, credit card bonuses, and other promotions to reduce or eliminate the cost of travel.

Let me make a disclaimer here—travel-hacking is both an art and a science. It's also always evolving, so the specific offers and loopholes will change frequently, but this will give you a good primer. The best way to get updated information is to check out travel-hacking forums online. Here are some of my favorite travel-hacking tips.

1. **First, before you search for any flight, you need to make yourself untraceable by the airlines and travel websites so they don't show you a higher price when you search again.** Airlines use variable pricing and adjust it based on your browsing history. Simply turn off cookies in your browser and open an incognito browsing window.

2. **Travel when no one else wants to travel.** You can often save at least 50 percent plus on flights, hotels, and everything else if you travel during the off-season. It's easy to google when the peak travel season is for any location. I always try to travel to the destination one to two weeks before or after peak season so I can still get the good weather, but with fewer tourists and for less money. Try to fly in on a Wednesday or out on a Tuesday for the cheapest flights.

3. **Buy one-way tickets, which can often be cheaper than round-trip tickets.** Look for a one-way deal and book it immediately when you find it (any deal will likely disappear immediately when you close the window). It's often worth spending the extra time to look for the cheapest one-way ticket and not restricting your tickets to one airline. I frequently fly out on one airline and back on another, or into one airport and out another.

4. **Buy tickets one at a time if you are family, because airlines often have only one or two tickets at a certain price, so if you try to buy four tickets, you will immediately get bumped to a higher pricing tier.** While it takes more time to buy one ticket at a time, it can save you a lot of money and is often

worth the time. Be sure to make note of the seat you have chosen so you can pick seats for the members of your party together. You can also go back afterward and link your tickets together so one of your party doesn't get bumped while the others are boarded.

5. **Try to fly out of the biggest airport that you can, since the bigger the airport, the cheaper the prices are.** It's often worth taking a bus or train or driving to a bigger city to get a better flight deal. New York City, for example, is one of the cheapest airports to fly out of in the world. Get creative by looking at one-way flights in and out of different cities, airports, and airlines.

6. **Set-up a fare monitor using services like AirfareWatchdog, Skyscanner, and Hopper to get alerted when the fare for your ideal trip drops.** Also track all of your miles and credit card reward points using a free service like AwardWallet.

7. **Sign up for travel email newsletters from publications and travel search engines like Expedia and Travelocity.** There are some crazy deals you can find if you are flexible and ready to act quickly when you get the email. There are also premium emails that you can sign up for that do the hunting and deal-finding for you. If you travel a lot or want to travel a lot, these premium flight deal- and travel-hacking newsletters are worth checking out.

If you want to travel-hack at the highest level, you'll want to use credit card rewards and perks to maximize your free travel opportunities. You should do this only if you are responsible with credit cards and if you can pay off your balance each month. This is how I've gotten many of my free flights. Here's how travel hacking with credit cards works:

1. **First you need to find your base credit card(s) (one for personal and one for your business if you have one).** Sign up for

a really good travel miles/points credit card and use it to buy everything so you accumulate miles/points whenever you make a purchase. Since you will use your base card most often and will likely keep it for multiple years, you should find one that gives the best rewards and will give you multiple points for specific categories like three times points for travel expenses or five times for grocery expenses. If you travel a lot, get one that maximizes the benefit of travel spending. Most credit cards waive their fees for the first year and then charge between $99 and $500 for each subsequent year, but they often come with additional benefits that mitigate the fee. For example, my base credit card has a $350 annual fee, but I get a $300 travel credit against it and I can use it to get into airport lounges for free, so I end up getting a lot more value than the $350 I spend. Using my base personal and business cards, I accumulate at least 400,000 points/miles per year, which is good for over $5,000 in free domestic or international travel.

2. **Next, start looking for promo mile cards, which you will sign up for to get the promotional onetime sign-up bonus (typically 40,000 to 100,000 miles/points) and then cancel afterward.** You get the bonus when you spend a minimum amount, usually about $2,000 to $4,000 over the first three months of having the card. I hit this threshold by moving all of my expenses over to the new card and using it exclusively until I get the bonus. Most of these cards waive the fee for the first year, so you can cancel after you get the bonus and never pay a fee. Be careful with your credit score, since opening and closing multiple credit card accounts can lower it temporarily. Don't do this right before applying for a mortgage or a loan. There are also certain restrictions on how many credit cards from one bank you can typically apply for. I apply for only three to five new cards per year, with a mixture of personal credit cards and business credit cards. Most years I get about

300,000 to 400,000 bonus miles doing this, which is another $4,000 to $5,000 in free travel per year.

3. **Once you get the bonus, most credit card companies let you transfer the points/miles to your favorite airline.** Some airlines give you better exchange value for your miles than others—1:1 is typically the best you can get, meaning you can transfer 1 credit card point for 1 mile. Once the miles have been transferred, you can start looking for super-saver deals, which allow you to get a ticket for the least number of miles. Sometimes there are promos in which miles are worth more or certain trips are discounted—like a flight from New York to London that's normally 50,000 miles round-trip might be 30,000 miles, or a first-class ticket that's usually 300,000 miles might be discounted to 120,000. The deals are always changing, and while it's a pain to keep looking and reading forums for an alert, the savings can be massive. While I'm not nearly as hard-core as some travel hackers, I've routinely gotten first-class round-trip tickets to Europe, which normally cost $5,000 each, for around 100,000 miles. When I'm interested in going somewhere I start looking for travel awards five months before the trip. Sometimes they won't be there one day but will the next.

While this might sound crazy at first, it's actually pretty easy to do. It takes a bit of time to learn and then do, but the time/money value can be insanely high and you get to explore the world. No matter what you do, make sure you spend only as much on your credit card as you can pay off every month. The value isn't there if you have to pay interest on any carryover balance.

FOOD

You can probably cut your food budget by a lot, but you need to consider whether the savings are worth your time. If you're making a ton of money at your full-time job or with your side hustle, it might not be worth it to go too far out of your way to save on food. You might not want to spend an extra hour shopping to save $10 if your real hourly rate is $50, unless of course you really like shopping or you have specific dietary restrictions. The same goes for using coupons, cooking, or eating out. This is also where the convenience and other calculations from the last chapter can be really helpful. And of course, not everything needs to be a cost decision—if you just really love cooking or shopping or cutting coupons, then do it!

Some simple ways to save money on food include buying collectively with your roommates or neighbors or growing your own food (yum!). While it takes more time to do the latter, you'll get the added benefit of spending time outside and eating healthy, and if you grow more than you need, you can sell it or trade it for other food. When I was a vegan, I actually grew lettuce in my kitchen for an entire year and saved at least $30 a week. It also tasted amazing.

Another way to save money on food is to buy in bulk. But make sure you do your own calculations. I recently found items that, on a per-unit basis, were cheaper at Whole Foods than at Costco! Always look at that little number on the price tag that states how much an item costs per unit (typically per ounce) to do a one-to-one comparison. Buying in bulk will also insulate you from inflation, since prices on many staples go up over time. Another option for products you use often is to check out Amazon's subscribe-and-save service, which allows you to save 10 percent by ordering regular deliveries of your favorite foods and staples.

Obviously food prepared at home tends to be cheaper and healthier than food you get eating out, but not always. If you do decide to eat out, there are lots of ways to save money with just a little effort. Join the restaurant's meal club, search for sign-up promos for food delivery apps, hunt for "buy one, get one free" promos, split an entrée and an appetizer, always order water (restaurants make a ton of money on sodas and drinks), and so forth. Another easy way to save money at your favorite restaurant is to buy gift cards for those restaurants online through a discount reseller. This can add up to an immediate 5 to 25 percent savings.

Where can you save or completely eliminate your biggest expenses? Save as much as you can and invest the savings. Then save as much as you can on the smaller expenses without taking away the things you love. Boom. This is the only budget you'll ever need.

RECAP

1. You don't need to budget. You can likely save at least 20 percent or more per month by cutting back on your three biggest expenses— housing, transportation, and food.

2. The cost of housing accounts for about 33 percent of the average American's budget. Save on your housing by moving to a cheaper home or renting out your extra rooms or entire home. Other options are living for free by house-sitting or buying a home and house-hacking. House-hacking is when you buy a two- or three-bedroom home and rent out the additional rooms to offset, completely cover, or even make money on your mortgage. You can also house-hack by buying multiple units in the same building and renting them out to cover the cost of your own.

3. Save on transportation by walking and biking whenever possible. If you don't really need a car, then don't buy one. If you do have to have one, always buy used.

4. Get out and explore the world. It's never been easier to travel for less. While travel-hacking takes some work, with a little effort you can travel for a lot less. The more you travel-hack, the better you'll get.

5. Save money on food by growing your own, cooking at home, buying in bulk, bartering with your neighbors, and hunting promos.

CHAPTER 8

HACK YOUR 9-TO-5

Use Your Full-Time Job as a Launching Pad to Freedom

n this chapter, I'll tell you what your boss never told you and teach you how to use your full-time job as a launching pad to make a lot more money in a short amount of time. Most people view their full-time job as a silo: they show up, do their job, connect with coworkers through lunch or office small talk, put in as little time as possible, and then head home. But this is a mistake.

Optimizing your full-time job is essential if you want to make more money and hit your number in as few years as possible. While working for someone else is not the quickest path to wealth, there are many benefits that come with it that you won't get working for yourself. Even if your dream is to strike out on your own, you would be wise to keep your day job and take as full advantage of it as possible until you can make that dream a reality without having to worry as much about making money.

This isn't about liking or not liking your job; it's about having the freedom and enough money to "retire" when you want. No matter where you are in your career or what job you have, if you approach it with the enterprise mindset, you can significantly reduce the amount of time it takes you to hit your number.

Depending on where you are today and how aggressive you plan on being, it might take five, ten, twenty, or more years to hit your number, so you need to balance your short- and long-term strategies. The goal is to get as much money out of your job as you can today and then look for opportunities to keep increasing it over time.

Your short-term career strategy should be focused on increasing your market value (what someone is willing to pay you) and maximizing your salary and benefits, including any opportunities to work remotely or create your own schedule (which can give you more control over your time). Your longer-term career strategy should be built on taking advantage of the access you have to information and other people by networking, building skills, and learning as much as you can, so you can increase your value and learn everything you can about how your company (and others) make money so you can apply it to your future full-time jobs, side hustles, and business ventures.

SHORT-TERM STRATEGIES

Your three short-term strategic goals are to maximize your benefits, make as much money as quickly as possible (so you can invest it!), and give yourself more flexibility with your time. Here's how to do it.

Maximize Your Benefits

Let's look at your benefits first, since they are the easiest to maximize. If your company offers them, your benefits can be incredibly valuable in giving you or more flexibility or helping you save or make more money. But you need to take full advantage of them. Only about 34 percent of Americans actually pay attention to the materials they receive about their benefits, which is like leaving free money on the table. Taking full advantage of your benefits can easily add 20 percent or more to your entire compensation.

While the health insurance, dental insurance, vision coverage, life insurance, disability insurance, HSA (health savings account), FSA (flexible spending account), transit benefits, and 401(k) matching contributions offered by your company are probably fixed, other benefits—such as how often you can work remotely—are probably negotiable. You can also negotiate additional vacation time, transportation support, and reimbursements for other expenses. A recent Millennial Money reader was able to get his company to cover his cell phone and internet bill, since he uses them for work, saving him over $150 a month. If you consistently add benefits to your salary negotiations, over time you could have a really sweet package.

You should always take advantage of all insurance and tax-advantaged benefits that your company offers. Almost all the insurance benefits your company offers are worth participating in, since your employer is likely picking up part of the cost (free money!). You should also take advantage of as many pretax benefits as you can by contributing to an HSA, FSA, or 401(k) or opting into pretax transit offers if you drive or use public transit to get to work. Because the money you contribute to these accounts is taken from your pretax dollars, by participating in them, you reduce your taxable income, which means you'll pay less in taxes at the end of the year. This is especially useful if you have to spend the money—on things like transit or healthcare costs—anyway. Don't worry: we will go into detail on how to maximize your tax-advantaged investment accounts (like a 401(k)) in the investing chapters.

Some companies provide health savings accounts (HSAs) to help employees pay for high-deductible health insurance plans. When you enroll in one, you can contribute a certain amount of pretax dollars to pay for your medical expenses, and if you don't spend it in a given year, you can roll it over and it will keep accumulating.

This is one of the main differences between an HSA and an FSA (flexible spending account). While an FSA (if offered by your company) can be used in conjunction with any insurance plan, you lose any money that you don't spend at the end of the year. Plus the contribution limits for FSAs are typically lower than they are for HSAs. As of 2018, individuals can contribute up to $3,450 ($4,450 if you are over fifty-five) per year to an HSA. If you have a family, you can contribute up to $6,900 ($7,900 if you are over fifty-five). Since you'll never lose the money, max out your HSA contributions to reduce your tax burden and to provide peace of mind, since you'll know you'll always have the money to pay for medical expenses when you need it. You can also use your HSA as another tax-advantaged investment account because you can keep your money invested and growing until you retire or need it.

We've already covered how you should maximize your 401(k), but for the sake of driving the point home, always contribute enough to get your employer match (more free money!). After that, you should try to max out your contribution—to both save on taxes and invest as much as you can for the future. Later, in the investing chapters, I'll discuss exactly how to invest in your 401(k).

Sure, there are confusing terms and sometimes a lot of fine print, but most companies have a human resources department that you can use to help you answer any questions. HR reps are trained to help you understand and make the most of your benefits. Ask for a full list of your employer benefits, since there might be some that you don't know about (like company profit sharing) or that you missed in the benefits packet. A simple thirty-minute meeting can generate a huge return on your time.

After you've maximized your benefits, the next step is to negotiate even better benefits. Benefit negotiation is typically easier to do at a smaller company, but even if you work for a big company, it's worth a shot trying to negotiate benefits that ultimately support your ideal lifestyle. Remember your bosses want to keep you, so they are likely to make reasonable adjustments to your benefits to keep you at the company.

The benefit that can have the biggest positive impact on your life is whether or not you can work remotely, and if so, how often you can do it. While you might really enjoy being a part of an office culture, you might not want to be in your office for eight hours a day five days a week. Or perhaps you hate commuting every day or you find the office distracting, so you want to work remotely as much as possible. While there might be some downsides to working remotely 100 percent of the time, since you might not be able to network as effectively as you would if you were in the office, it's all about finding and trying to negotiate the right balance for you.

In 2016, 43 percent of the American workforce worked remotely at some period during the year, which is the highest number in history. Even the U.S. government is jumping on board: now 3.1 percent of federal employees work remotely full time. Plus, according to the annual 2016 Gallup State of the American Workplace report, workers who spent three to four days of their week working remotely had the highest rate of employee engagement, so you can actually make the case to your boss that you'll be a better employee if you can work at home at least part-time.

While it might be hard to negotiate three to four remote workdays a week, you can start small and work up to a more robust remote benefit over time. Your ability to work remotely will ultimately depend on your current role in the company, the strength of your performance, and your value to the company. For example, if you're an assistant, you likely won't be able to work from home that often, if at all, unless, say, your boss also works remotely or is out of the office. But if you are in sales or marketing and perform well, you might be able to negotiate a really sweet deal. The stronger your performance and the greater your value to your company, the more likely your supervisor will be open to your working remotely. If you want more flexible remote-work privileges, don't be afraid to ask. This benefit costs your employer nothing, and given the research into how work flexibility improves engagement, it may even increase your productivity and value to the company.

Brandon, who walked away at thirty-four, was able to negotiate the ability to work remotely full time as a web developer, allowing him to travel and have almost unlimited flexibility while still having a full-time salary with bonuses and benefits. Because he didn't have to commute or buy work clothes, he saved a bunch of extra money that helped him reach financial independence faster.

Drew, who lived in Chicago, worked in software sales and had sold over $2 million in business for his company. During his performance review, he said the only way he would stay was if he received a $100,000 raise and could move to Los Angeles to live with his girlfriend and work remotely. His company wanted to keep making money, so they eagerly agreed. Now, while his coworkers have to brave the cold Chicago winters and sit in an office all day, he wakes up and takes his dog for a walk on the beach in the morning and hops on a few calls during the day. He also just spent a month in Japan and was able to call in easily (with a few calls in the middle of the night!).

While Drew's example is a little extreme, the lesson here is clear: If you are valuable to your company (and you likely are!), you can make a strong case for the benefits that you want. The more in demand your skills are, the more flexibility you are likely to get, but even if you are new or young, you can still negotiate for flexibility benefits. As long as you are doing a good job and your company wants to keep you, they will likely be willing to work out an arrangement that keeps you happy and working for the company. Work remotely and bank the extra money and extra time!

Not all remote-work opportunities are equal. Most jobs that will allow you to work remotely are salaried positions, although there are some hourly jobs, like customer service or virtual assistant jobs, that you can do remotely. But if you're working a salaried job, your boss won't be measuring how many hours you work, just whether you get the job done and do it right. If you can get your work done in four hours and don't have to stick around an office all day, you can use the rest of the time to do all manner of things—work on side hustles, take a nap, have lunch with a friend or colleague, whatever. And even if you do get paid by the hour, you'll still save time and energy by not having to commute or get ready to go to an office job every day.

Or you can be like the Bay Area programmer who confessed on Reddit that he automated his $95,000-a-year salary job so that it required him to work only two hours a week. His entire job was done using scripts that responded to certain tasks and emails, so he wrote a program that did this work for him. While the ethics of this approach are certainly questionable, there is no argument that he did the job he was hired to do.

How to Actually Get a Raise

There are few things more important to securing your financial future than getting paid as much as you can. Your lifetime earnings are significantly impacted by every raise that you get, and a single raise could mean reaching financial freedom years faster. This is because your future earning potential is impacted by your base salary today. Most people are underpaid in their roles, but many don't do anything about it. Eighty-nine percent of Americans believe they deserve a raise, but only 54 percent plan to ask for one in the next year.

Less than 10 percent of all the employees I've managed in my career ever asked for a raise or bonus. Whether it was fear or laziness or something else, I still can't believe more of them didn't ask for a raise. While it's definitely true that some people aren't motivated by money, you never want to leave money on the table. If you don't ask, then you'll likely never get paid what you are actually worth or maximize the value of your time. Actively pursuing salary increases will make a huge difference in your overall lifetime pay and hasten your ability to reach financial independence.

There is a constant tension at work between employers and employees. As an employee, you want to get paid as much as possible, but your boss (and your boss's boss and everyone else up the food chain) wants to pay you as little as they can while still keeping you on board. Optimizing your salary means figuring out the upper limit that your boss would be willing to pay you and going for it. It's a consistent and far-from-perfect process, but with the right information, you can dramatically increase your chances of getting paid more. And the sky's the limit.

If you want to make more money in your full-time job, it doesn't matter how hard you work or how busy you are or how much time you spend desk or the hours you put in. What matters most is the perception of your value by your company (aka what your boss and boss's boss think!) The more valuable they perceive you to be, the more money you can make. Without a doubt, there are many things your boss and your boss's boss didn't see that you were doing or accomplished. It's up to you to tell your story and show your value.

You need be your own advocate; your boss is trying to save money, not pay you more. Sure, your boss wants to keep you around, but as a human resources director once told me, "You want to keep your employees happy enough." Another former colleague told me, "You want to pay them just enough so that they stay, but still feel like working for that next raise or bonus." It may sound cold, but this is how businesses make money.

Here's the plan. Grab a folder and be prepared to record or print out information on your market value, your value to your company, when you go beyond the responsibilities outlined in your job description, and any competing offers of employment you've received. Your goal is to have a file of information you can use to make the case that you deserve more money. While you don't have to give this to your boss, it helps to have it in front of you when negotiating in case you need to use some of your supporting evidence. For example, you might want to pull out a printout of salaries paid for your position at other companies that shows you are being underpaid. Or you might want to pull out an email from a recruiter telling you how much you could make at another company. You can also use the same information if or when you want to look for a new job.

Not only will having this information help you accurately determine how much you should be getting paid, but it will also show your boss that you are prepared, that your request is based on data, and because you made such an effort, that you are serious about staying with the company. The more prepared, organized, and compelling your case is, the more money you will be able to get in your current and future roles.

Getting paid what you're worth is about how the market, your company, and you value your time. You might find that after running the numbers and analyzing the market, you are no longer willing to trade your time for what your company is paying you. This might be the catalyst for finding a new job or building an entirely new career. How much is an hour of your life worth? How much money are you willing to trade for it? Keep this in mind throughout the evaluation and negotiation process. This is more than a job or a salary, it's your time and your life energy.

Here's a simple four-step process to figure out if you should ask for a raise (the answer is almost always yes!) and significantly improve your chances of getting one:

1. Figure out your current market value (aka what other companies are willing to pay for someone with your skills and experience)
2. Figure out how valuable you are to your company (aka how much money your company makes on you, how much it would cost to replace you, and how much you go above and beyond your role).
3. Determine how much to ask for and the right time to ask.
4. Ask.

Let's walk through the process in detail. This exact process has helped many Millennial Money readers make more money in their full-time jobs, including one who got an $80,000 raise!

1. FIGURE OUT YOUR CURRENT MARKET VALUE

Companies are always trying to stay competitive, and they want to be able to hire the best talent, so your boss and your company are always trying to keep track of an employee's market value. You should be doing the same at least a few times a year because the demand for your position and your skill set are constantly evolving.

Your market value is what another company would be willing to pay you to do your job, and in some areas like marketing or programming, your market value changes depending on the supply and demand for your position in your city. Your market value also increases as you build new skills and gain more experience. The higher the demand for your skill set, the more money you can and should make. And market demand can vary dramatically according to which city or country you are working in, so no matter where you live, you could potentially get paid more money doing your same job working remotely for a company in another city.

To find out what your current market value is, you need to do three things.

First, look how much others in your role in your city are getting paid. There are many tools online that can help you do this, but my favorites are the Glassdoor, LinkedIn, and Indeed salary checkers. Make sure you do searches for your job title and any other roles that are similar. Print out all of the comparison salaries and put them in your case-making folder. If you have a weird job title, then search by skills, not titles, and talk to a recruiter who can help you align your skills and role with a job title and comparative salaries.

Second, contact recruiters who work in your industry. In most industries, there are recruiting firms and recruiters who are hired to fill open positions at companies. Simply search for "recruiting company [industry you work in]." The best thing about recruiters is that they are paid by the companies looking for employees, not by the potential employee or candidate. So you don't have to pay recruiters for information; they want to help you so they can place you in a job with a company and get paid by the company.

Because these recruiters specialize in your industry and are close to the market, they can tell you based on your experience and skills how much you can and should be getting paid. Ask the recruiter specifically what the salary range is for someone with your skills, then print out their messages and put them in your case-making folder. I recommend talking to at least two or three recruiters at different firms because they will have different viewpoints; thus you'll have multiple salary reference points to include in your analysis.

Third, look for research put out by recruiting firms, industry groups, and associations in your industry. Most industries have firms and associations that publish salary guides, many of which include handy tables to help you calculate salaries specifically in your city based on a multiplier. Just search for "[your industry] salary guides" in Google and boom—there will probably be a report as a starting point. Print them out and put them in your folder.

As a bonus, when/if you want to leave your company and over time, having relationships with recruiters can open some amazing (and high-paying) opportunities. And even if you don't want to leave your company, a recruiter might find and send you an opportunity that you can't refuse. Brian, a twenty-seven-year-old Millennial Money reader in Syracuse, New York, hit me up and asked me how he could find a higher-paying IT job. He was burnt out and underpaid, making $42,000 in a job that should have paid $50,000 plus. I recommended that he contact IT recruiters to see how much his skill set was worth and if there were any better opportunities. He ended up talking to a recruiting firm who had connections in New York City and found him a job making $90,000 working remotely from home. That's a huge life upgrade for Brian, just because he reached out to connect with recruiters in his industry.

Finally, while this can be a slippery slope, if you are interested in maybe jumping ship to a higher-paying job at another company, then it's useful to connect with other competitor companies to learn more about their open roles and compensation opportunities. Many hiring managers will be willing to talk with you if they think you might leave your current company and you could be a good fit for them. You can even go through the entire process of trying to get another job and use a competing offer from another company in your negotiation with your boss. This is particularly helpful if you've asked for a raise previously and been denied, or if you are willing to leave your company. I've seen this work really well, helping people get a much higher salary at their current company, and I've also seen it backfire, where the boss actually fired the employee because he didn't like feeling bossed around. (The good news is that the employee was able to get a nice severance and take a new higher-paying job.) So you shouldn't do this unless you are actually willing to leave your current company.

2. FIGURE OUT HOW VALUABLE YOU ARE TO YOUR COMPANY.

The second type of value you need to calculate is your value to your company. This is a little more difficult than calculating your market value, but here's how to do it. You should try to make a qualitative and quantitative assessment.

First, calculate how much it would cost your company to replace you. The cost of hiring a new employee—especially salaried employees—is really high in most industries. To determine the cost to replace you, you can use the same metrics companies use. Companies typically use either the percentage of salary method (e.g., 16 percent for hourly employees) or six to nine months of a full-time salaried employee. If you make $60,000 per year as a salaried employee, it could cost $30,000 to $45,000 to replace you.

Also, the more experience and unique company knowledge you have, the more valuable you are. Your boss likely knows what it would cost to replace you and your value to the company, so use this to your advantage when asking for a raise. Some bosses might give you an immediate $5,000 or higher raise if they thought you would leave because they know it would cost $20,000 or more to find your replacement and they don't want to lose all of the experience and knowledge you've gained working for the company. Most people should be making a lot more money, but they underestimate their value to their company and don't ask for more money because they fear they'll lose their job. In reality, your company would likely actually pay you a lot more to keep you and the value you bring to the culture and business.

Next, if you work for a company that makes money off clients or customers, you should to try and calculate how much money your company is making off your work or how much money you have made your company. If you work in a law firm, ad agency, or other field where you have a personal or blended hourly rate your company charges for your time, then this should be easy. It should also be easy if you are in sales and know how much business you have generated for the company.

This is not possible for all jobs or industries. For example, if you are a teacher or work as part of a larger team, you might not be able to put a dollar value on your contribution. But if you work in an industry that services clients, figure out how much your company is charging them for the service you are offering and deduct you average hourly wage from the fee to determine your company's margin on your work. For example, if you're an electrician and your company charges $300 per hour and you get paid $30 per hour, your company is making a $270-per-hour profit on your time. That's a great return on your company's investment in you!

Of course, this calculation doesn't factor in your company's overhead, which includes other expenses your company has to fork out to run the business, like paying rent and utilities, hiring support staff, and offering benefits. While it varies by company, a standard way to estimate the impact of a business's overhead on your compensation is to add 30 percent to your average hourly rate. Using the same electrician example, 30 percent of $30 per hour is $9, so with overhead, your company's total cost is $39, but they are charging $300. So they are making $261 per hour, or an 87 percent margin on your time. If you are making your boss three to four times what they spend on you a year, you can probably easily justify a salary increase.

If you are in a sales role and receive less than a 15 to 25 percent commission on your sales, then you should ask for a raise. While average sales commissions vary widely by industry, I have personally met way too many salespeople who get only a 5 percent commission. That means your company is getting a 95 percent return on your sales. If you are a good salesperson, most bosses are willing to give you a higher commission (at the risk of losing all of your sales if you leave). I strongly recommend that you negotiate for at least at 15 to 25 percent commission. If you're already at 15 percent, try to negotiate an increase to 20 percent; if you're at 25 percent, try to negotiate an increase to 30 percent.

Your company is probably making a lot of money off you; if not, they wouldn't be in business. Most sales commissions should be negotiable because it's mostly upside for the company, since they make money if you stay but don't if you leave. Use this information to make the case for getting more money or as motivation to launch your own competing business so you can make the $300 per hour, not just the $30.

Victor, a twenty-six-year-old Millennial Money reader from Milwaukee, works in sales for a manufacturing company. After reading one of my posts, he reached out and told me that he had brought in over $1.5 million in new business over the past year, but makes only $45,000 and no commission. I recommended the strategy in this chapter to him, and while he wasn't able to get a commission, he was able to get a raise to $125,000. While his market value was about $50,000 in Milwaukee, he was able to ask for a lot more.

And while an $80,000 raise is big, the impact it can have on Victor's reaching his number is huge, since $80,000 over the next twenty years is an additional $1,600,000 in earnings, and even more if he invests all the extra money (which I hope he does!). And if Victor decides to move to another company, he's likely to make even more than $125,000, compounding the impact of that single salary raise. It's incredible how a single raise or pay bump can help you reach financial independence years faster.

Finally, you want to look at what you've actually helped the company do since you received your last raise or started with the company. While you are getting paid to do a job, doing a "good job" might not be enough to get a raise or bonus beyond the standard 1 to 3 percent cost-of-living increases some company's give. You need to show how you've gone above and beyond your job description or helped the company succeed in a way that wasn't expected.

Look specifically at any big milestones *you directly* helped the company reach or any big projects or responsibilities you've had outside of your job description. How can you show (and ideally measure) how you've gone above and beyond the call of the job? Have you taken on extra clients, or are you managing more employees and responsibilities? Are there new skills you learned that helped you take on more responsibilities? Did you refer new clients even though you're not a salesperson? Did someone else leave and you picked up some or all of their work?

Make a list of all of the things you did, new skills you learned that you used in your role, and any successes you had outside your job description so you can show how you did more than just a good job. Even better, every time you go above and beyond your job description, keep track of the date and task in an online doc, on a piece of paper, or on your phone. Then when the time comes to negotiate, you'll have a record you can pull from. Now you definitely don't want to bring up everything in your negotiation; just pick a few specific examples that represent a variety of ways and times you went beyond your job description and added value. Sell your story.

3. DETERMINE HOW MUCH TO ASK FOR AND THE RIGHT TIME TO ASK

As you've already learned, thinking about money in terms of percentages and dollar amounts impacts your perception of savings. It also impacts how your boss will think about your asking for a raise. Typically, you are more likely to get a bigger raise if you ask in terms of percentages instead of dollars. This is because the percentage will feel less tangible to people. Think about it: If you are making $50,000, what feels more substantial to you—getting a 10 percent raise or $5,000 more per year? Probably the $5,000, since you (and your boss) can immediately imagine what the extra $5,000 could buy. It has tangible value, whereas 10 percent is an abstraction or representation. What can you buy with 10 percent?

Just to keep you at your company, your boss might give you at 5 percent raise, but if you want 10 percent or more you will need to make a compelling case using the data you've gathered. You can also take more risks if you have another position lined up. I personally believe that 10 to 15 percent is the perfect amount to ask for unless you are being wildly underpaid based on your market and company value. If you do find that you are really underpaid (to the tune of 20 percent plus or more), then you can go in with your research and ask for a raise that pays you at least the market rate for your position. Ask for the upper bound of the salary range.

If you are getting paid significantly under your market value, then you realistically could get a raise of 20 percent plus to the market level by making the case using the data you found online and from recruiters. That's an incredibly high ROI for just doing a bit of research. If your company wants to keep you (and they have the money), they will give you a raise to get you at market rate. Not all companies will be in a position to give you a raise, and some will be but will say no. Even if you ask, there are many excuses bosses use to say they can't give you a raise—like we didn't hit our numbers, sales are down, or we don't have the budget. It's up to you to decide if you believe them and if you're willing to stay under those circumstances.

A lot of employees don't know when to ask for a raise or ask at the wrong time. When you ask can have a huge impact on whether or not your boss says yes. First, look at where you are in your career and your responsibilities. It's important to monitor your market value and value to your company regularly—at least twice a year and more if your job responsibilities change.

If you've done all the research and are determined to ask for a raise, the next step is to think about the actual timing. The best times to ask for a raise are during your annual performance review, at the end of your company's fiscal year (if you don't know when this is, you can ask HR), after your workload has increased because of recent employee turnover, or after you've spearheaded a company initiative that turned out to be a huge success. Here's why:

During your annual performance review, your boss is already thinking about your value to your company. If you come with your market-value research, you are significantly more likely to get a higher raise. At the end of the company's fiscal year, your boss is thinking about next year already, and as long your company is performing well, then you are more likely to get a yes. If your company isn't performing well, then it's unlikely you will get a raise, unless your company determines they really need to keep you to get the numbers up.

Another good time is if your responsibilities have significantly changed or your workload has increased because of employee turnover or consolidation. Under these circumstances, the last thing your company wants is another employee to leave, so they might pay you more to keep you.

Likewise, if you launched an initiative or project that is now a big success, now is another good time to ask. Ride on your accomplishments.

The next step is to pick the day and time. On a random Tuesday at four P.M. when your boss is stressed out is not a good time. On a Friday afternoon before a holiday or right before your boss is due to go on vacation is not a good time. Monday mornings are also not good, because who actually like Monday mornings?

Research shows that the best time to ask for a raise is Friday morning. The reason is because your boss is, like you, relatively relaxed and excited about the weekend. Psychology research also shows that people tend to be more generous in the morning before noon.

No matter what day or time it is, you definitely want to feel out your boss's mood. Your boss could be stressed, upset, or focused deeply on something else. If bosses are distracted or stressed, they aren't going to listen to you the same way they would if they were more focused. Find a time when both you and your boss are in a good mood. While these guidelines can be helpful, your best opportunity could come at any time. Be ready.

4. ASK.

So you've decided on the perfect time and are ready to ask? Here's how to maximize your chance of getting a yes. First you need to decide whether to schedule a meeting or just stop by. The decision should depend on your relationship to your boss, the boss's style, and your style. Some bosses are really buttoned up and don't like surprises; in this case you should schedule a meeting. Send your supervisor an email saying you want to chat for fifteen to twenty minutes and ask when he or she is available. If your boss is more free flowing and spontaneous, then just stop by and ask to chat.

Next you need to have a specific percentage in mind. You should ask for a raise that puts you in at least the 90th percentile of salary ranges for your position in your city. If you are making your company a lot of money and you have the data to back it up, your company might pay you at lot more to keep you, so don't be afraid to ask for more than you want so you have some room to negotiate. The worst that can happen is he or she will say is no or give you less than you ask for.

Once you're in the meeting, start the conversation by telling your boss how much you enjoy working for him or her and the company. Share something that really excites you about a project or the direction of the company. By doing this, you put the company (and your boss) first in the conversation. Next, explain why you are asking for a raise: "Recently because of *x, y,* and *z,* my responsibilities have really increased" or "I was recently analyzing my market value based on my experience" or "I was recently contacted by a recruiter who said that based on my experience, she could get me a position making \$X." Then go for the ask. Say something like "I would really like to stay at here, and I see a bright future here, so I'd like to ask for a raise of *x* percent." Don't talk too much or oversell it. Respond to what your boss says. He or she might ask you a few questions and/or tell you he or she needs to think about it. It's fine to not get an immediate answer, but if your boss does ask for time to think about it, set a limit on it. "That's fine. Is it possible for you to get back to me by Friday or next Monday?" Some employers will try to drag it out; you might not hear back from them for weeks or at all. If this is the case, you might be better off looking for another gig. If they do make an offer on the spot that's not what you want, keep the conversation going and then add more to your case—but only if they offer a counteroffer or say no.

Most employees don't know they probably have the upper hand and are more valuable to their boss and their company than they realize. If you ask well and for a reasonable amount, your boss will likely appreciate the thought you've put into the process and your desire to stay at the company. In most cases the worst that can happen is the answer is no. Don't be afraid, and definitely don't leave money on the table or undervalue your time or the impact you're having on your company.

Keep Researching Your Value

Even after you've negotiated a raise or gotten a new job, you should continue to monitor your market value, company value, compensation, and benefits at least a few times a year. You should also sit down and analyze your future market value—i.e., the amount of money you will get paid if you stay on your current career trajectory. Look up the salaries of the roles you will move into over the next three to five years. For example, if you are a junior graphic designer but want to be a creative director in the next five years, look at the path to get there and the amount of compensation you can expect. Look for similar jobs you could get that have higher earning potential and pick up any new skills to increase your chances of getting there. It's remarkable how much more some jobs pay than others even when they require similar skillset and the availability of data makes it easier to aim for higher paying jobs. If you don't like your current career trajectory, deviate from it as soon as you can. Plan your path and you'll be much more likely to get there.

Doing this analysis every so often will also help you to keep an eye out for lots of opportunities, not only to get a raise, but to get a new job or strike out on your own. And you'll be better at determining your real market value over time.

LONG-TERM STRATEGY: SKILLS + NETWORKING = MONEY

While your short-term strategy is built to maximize today, realistically you still have five, ten, or twenty or more years working until you hit your number. Your longer-term strategy should therefore be focused on building your own value by learning as much as you can, leveraging mentors, building a network and an audience, and acquiring in-demand skills you can use throughout your career and life.

Skills are the currency of the future, meaning that the more valuable skills you can learn now, the more valuable you will be and the more money you will make later on. The higher the demand and the more diverse your skill sets, the more money you can make and the more options you will have. There's also a ton of value in building and blending two different and seemingly opposing skill sets. For example, you can make more money if you know how to code and can also sell, or if you have graphic design and analytics skills, or Excel and marketing skills. The more diverse and well-rounded your skill sets, the more money you'll make and the easier it will be to side hustle. One of the best graphic designers I know is actually a full-time veterinarian, but she enjoys designing on the side. She learned most of it through free YouTube videos.

Without a doubt one of the most important and valuable skills you can and should learn more any job is how to sell. Selling and winning business is a highly valued and highly compensated skill set in any company and also essential if you want to build a profitable side hustle.

Many of the jobs in the future don't exist yet (digital marketing didn't even exist twenty years ago), but by building diverse skill sets and continuing to learn and grow, you'll thrive in the future. Look at your skills today and both start filling in the gaps for the job you want tomorrow and learn new skills that interest you. There will likely always be demand for selling, communicating, marketing, branding, designing, coding, and synthesizing data in some form.

When I was twenty-four, the first job I got to move out of my parents' house was at a small digital marketing agency in Chicago. Once I decided to get into digital marketing, I made the choice to apply only to jobs at small companies so I would be closer to the action. This was the huge turning point in my career. It was during this year that I went from making $50,000 a year as my full-time salary to over $300,000 through my side hustles. In the eleven months I worked at the agency I showed up early and stayed late to meet with almost every person at the company to learn how they did their jobs. It was through these conversations and relationships that I was able to learn about branding, copywriting, creative design, website design, front- and back-end programming, writing proposals, search engine optimization, and the single skill that would ultimately help me make the most money: selling.

Even though my job was running Google advertising campaigns, I sought out the head salespeople, Dave and Jade, who responded to inbound inquiries about our services and reached out to companies that were looking for a new website or digital marketing help. I spent as much time as I could with them. You'll be amazed, once you start asking questions, how willing most people are to help, especially since you are both working for the same company. Within a few months, they started including me in new business pitches and I closed one of the biggest and most profitable clients in the agency's history in my second pitch! I was hooked, and I learned more in that one year than I had learned in my entire life, all because I was curious.

A quick tip that will pay huge dividends in your career and life: Reach out to one new person a week and ask them out to lunch, even if their job has nothing to do with yours. Tell them you want to learn about what they do and offer to tell them more about your role. Take the time to actually get to know the person—schedule your coffee or lunch or chat for at least an hour. One hour is enough time and will force you to go beyond simple pleasantries. Learn as much as you can about the person and their role. How can they help? How can you help them?

I started doing this in 2011 and it was really hard for me at first, since I'm a natural introvert. But it got easier over time. If you take one new person out for lunch or coffee per week, after a year you'll have had hour-long conversations with fifty new people. That's fifty connections you can learn from and use as a resource throughout your life. If you don't want to do it every week, that's cool—even once every couple of weeks or once a month is useful. Just like compound interest, the value of relationships, connections, and knowledge also grows and compounds over time.

Meeting with so many people will also help you see patterns in seemingly unrelated things. This will help you identify ways to make your company better, connect two people you think will get along well, learn the value of a new skill set, uncover new resources, and even identify money-making opportunities you've never seen before. It will also naturally open up business opportunities as you discover how you can help others and your network starts making connections for you. I've been able to make at least $500,000 through side-hustle client referrals as a result of those early lunches with my coworkers.

Keep building new skills, asking questions, connecting, and keeping an eye open for new opportunities. Most of the best full-time moneymaking and side-hustle opportunities will come through your existing network, since it's both easier to sell into and get help from. Many of the best jobs are given to people who have an in or know someone at the company, not through a blindly submitted job application online.

Now that you've optimized your full-time job and are ready to use it as a launching pad, you need to start making money in your extra time through side hustling. This is when you can really ramp up your savings, learn new skills, and start making a lot more money on your own terms.

RECAP

1. Your full-time job is an incredible income opportunity and you should use it as a launching pad by maximizing your benefits and salary opportunities while building other income streams.

2. Maximize your benefits. Meet with your HR team to determine what benefits you have and how to maximize them. Almost all benefits are worth participating in. Look into HSA, FSA, 401(k), continued learning, various forms of insurance, and remote-work opportunities. If you are unhappy with a benefit, try negotiating for a better one. Not maximizing your benefits is like leaving money on the table.

3. Maximize your salary. Your company is trying to make as much money for your time as they can, so use this to your advantage when negotiating for a raise. Research and print out information on your current market value, value to your company, and any competing offers of employment you've received. The net impact of even a single raise will be huge over your career.

4. Figure out if you should ask for a raise by analyzing the current market demand for your skills and experience. You can do this simply by looking at salary comparison websites like Glassdoor, contacting recruiters, and reading industry salary reports. If possible, then try to calculate your value to your company and what it would cost to replace you (it's probably a lot!). Also try make a list of everything you did above and beyond your job description.

5. Determine how much to ask for and the right time to ask. You are more likely to get a bigger raise if you ask in terms of percentages instead of dollars. If you are getting paid significantly under your market value, then you realistically could get a raise of 20 percent plus to the market level by making the case using the data you found online and from recruiters.

6. Pick the right time and ask. Two good times are during your annual performance review and if your responsibilities have changed significantly. Research shows that the best time to ask for a raise is Friday morning. The reason is because your boss is, like you, relatively relaxed

and excited about the weekend. Research also shows that people tend to be more generous in the morning before noon.

7. Keep researching your value and your future market value—i.e., the amount of money you will get paid if you stay on your current career trajectory. Look up the salaries of the roles you will move into over the next three to five years. If you don't like what you find, pivot as soon as you can.

8. Skills + Network = Money. Skills are the currency of the future. The more valuable and diverse your skill sets are and will be, the more money you will make. Keep building your skills and your network and they will pay huge dividends over time

CHAPTER 9

MORE MONEY IN LESS TIME

How to Start a Profitable Side Hustle

M att is a twenty-five-year-old graphic designer living in Chicago who makes $55,000 per year at his full-time job. He loves his coworkers and the vibe at his company and has no plans to leave. But one thing most of his coworkers don't know is that Matt makes an additional $200,000 a year from his side hustle—a dog-walking company that he launched three years ago while still a student.

Matt started walking dogs for $5 a walk as a way to make some extra money in between classes after seeing a posting on a school message board. He was walking up to ten different dogs each week, but as more people moved into his neighborhood, he started to attract more business than he could handle. To satisfy demand, Matt set up an limited liability company (LLC) and hired a few other students to walk dogs as well. Now he's making four times what he earns at his office job just from this simple business idea.

Matt is also saving a ton of money because he pretty much lives like a student. He still lives in the apartment he had in college and invests almost 100 percent of the profit he makes side hustling. Making $55,000 and saving 20 percent of his salary per year ($11,000) at a 7 percent annual growth rate, Matt would have needed about thirty-three years to hit his $1.5 million number. And as you know, after thirty-three years, he'd actually need a lot more than that to retire. But because of his side hustle, Matt's currently on pace to have $1.5 million saved by the age of thirty (in just five more years).

In the last chapter, we talked about how to optimize your day job, but if you want to make a lot of money quickly, you need to diversify your income streams by developing one or more side hustles—moneymaking ventures outside of your full-time job. In this chapter, you'll learn how to identify, start, and grow profitable side hustles that can help expedite your journey to financial independence.

It's one thing to make a few extra bucks on the side so you can go out to a nice dinner or buy a nice pair of shoes, but if you want to reach financial independence as quickly as possible, you're going to need to up your side-hustle game. You need to move beyond simply trading your hours for a limited amount of money and transition to thinking about side hustling using the enterprise mindset.

The enterprise mindset requires looking for as many opportunities to make money as possible, which means investing all the money you make. You need to put your side-hustle money in investments so it can work for you. Every side-hustle dollar you invest reduces the amount of time it will take to hit your number. It would have taken me at least two to three times longer to reach financial independence if I hadn't invested almost 100 percent of my side-hustle income.

Side hustling is great because you can make money—sometimes a lot of money—doing pretty much anything. You can mow lawns, walk dogs, shovel snow, babysit, make deliveries, or chauffeur people. You also no longer need to be present to start a side hustle, since making money online has never been easier. You can code online, tutor, launch a blog, flip products on eBay or Amazon, participate in focus groups, or do an infinite number of things. But few people use side hustling to its greatest potential, which is all about making a lot of money and then investing it to make it grow. If you are making money on the side, but not investing it, then you are wasting time by not making nearly as much money as you could.

While I had always had side jobs growing up, it wasn't until 2010 that I really started side hustling seriously solely so I could have more money to invest. Before that point I would have just spent the extra money (which is why I was broke at twenty-four!), but once I learned about the future value of money, I was hooked. At the time, I was working at the small digital marketing agency making $50,000 per year. On the side I was spending most of my free time (about forty additional hours a week) making as much money as I could doing (mostly) things that I really enjoyed, like:

- **Building websites for law firms.** My first project was a $500 gig I found through Craigslist, and three months later I sold a $50,000 project using the same template! One lawyer introduced me to another, and I never had to do much selling, since my business came mostly through referrals.

- **Flipping domain names.** This was definitely my most profitable side hustle. Domains are the real estate of the internet and are still significantly undervalued in my opinion. I was able to buy a lot of social media, legal, money, and education-themed domains early in domain auctions. I routinely was able to buy a domain for less than $50 and resell it within a year for $2,500 plus. That's at least a 4,900 percent return in my investment. Of course, not all domains sell for that much or at all, but overall, it's been the perfect side hustle, and I'm still doing it! I own over 800 domains as of this writing, and they are just getting more valuable. The average price for a mid-tier domain has jumped from $400 to $2,500 in the past three years alone.

- **Running digital marketing campaigns for law firms and real estate agents.** In addition to building websites for law firms and real estate agents, I was also able to command up to $500 for any qualified lead I was able to capture for them through my ad campaigns. At one point I thought hard about scaling this business, but I didn't enjoy it enough to do so.

- **Doing search engine optimization projects.** I really love SEO because optimizing websites to rank on Google is both an art and a science. SEO is the compounding interest of digital marketing because the small adjustments and optimizations you make grow exponentially over time. It's challenging, competitive, fun, and profitable. While SEO is more of a commodity now than when I started doing it, it's more in demand than ever, and if you are good at it, you can make a lot of money. I've designed SEO strategies for hundreds of websites through the

years and learned a ton that has also helped me grow Millen
nialMoney.com.

- **Flipping vintage mopeds and Volkswagen campers.** I have
  been buying and selling both VW campers and mopeds since I
  was in college. I've sold more 1970s vintage mopeds than VW
  campers, but when I find a good deal on a camper, I don't hesi-
  tate. I love VW Westfalia Campers from the 1970s and 1980s and
  have owned two over the past ten years. They have gone up quite
  a bit in value over that time and keep going up!

I also did a bunch of miscellaneous things like selling concert tickets,
watching my neighbor's cat, reselling high-end office chairs, writing white
papers (detailed or authoritative reports), doing research, and even babysitting occasionally. No job was too small.

I was always looking for ways to make more money, and most of my
investment gains have been made on money I made side hustling. It's also
worth noting that all of my side hustles were things I didn't learn in school,
need a college degree for, or have to work through another company to do.

There are two ways you can make money side hustling: you can work
for someone else or work for yourself. If you are side hustling for someone
else, the money you can make will always be limited by the number of
hours you have in the day. It's really tough to get off your nine-to-five job
and hop in a Lyft to drive all night. Sure, it gives you flexibility and freedom, but no matter how much you drive for Lyft or deliver for Postmates,
you'll always be limited to your own hours and will make only as much
money as those companies are willing to pay you. In other words, these
gigs are not scalable.

Working for yourself allows you to make a lot of money doing something that you love and gives you more control. Matt could have easily
worked for someone else's dog-walking company and made $10 per hour,
but by launching his own company, he gets to make money, not only on
the time he spends walking dogs, but also on the time his employees spend
walking dogs. Then he invests it so the money grows even more. I'm not
saying it's not worth walking dogs for another company so you can invest

a few hundred extra bucks a month; any additional money you invest will help you reach financial independence sooner. It's simply not as lucrative as working for yourself.

When you work for someone else, you don't set your rates, but if you start your own business, you can (at least to a point that the market will bear). For example, even if you're a babysitter, you'll earn more money working for yourself and establishing your own stable of clients than you will signing up with a day care or babysitting service. And over time you may be able to charge more because your clients will come to trust you and perhaps you can offer an additional service—like tutoring or prepping dinner for the family. Plus you will get 100 percent of the profit (minus any overhead) instead of sharing a portion with your employer. If you really want to make a lot more money, you can start hiring other babysitters to do the work for you and take a share of whatever they make. The point is, working for yourself gives you more control over your money and your time and the opportunity to grow your business if you want to.

PASSIVE INCOME AND THE MONEY/TIME TRADE-OFF

If you want to make money side hustling, you need to evaluate how much time you are realistically willing to commit to it, because how much time you have will determine the types of side hustles you can launch. Some side hustles take a lot more time to get off the ground than others. For example, if you have an amazing idea for a new mobile app but you don't know how to code, it's going to take a lot of time to get that idea off the ground. But walking dogs in the evenings or on the weekends doesn't require anything more than the ability to walk.

This doesn't mean that if you're busy, you can't find time to side-hustle. It just means that you should calibrate the difficulty of your side hustle based on the amount of time you have and also try to find more time.

If you want it badly enough, you're going to find the time. If you tell me you don't have enough time to carry out a side hustle, I'm going to ask you how much time you spend streaming TV shows per week, watching sports, going out with your friends, playing video games, or just lounging around. I'm not saying don't do the things that you love, just if you look at everything you do in a regular week, no matter how busy you are, I'm sure you can find the extra time if you really want to make more money. Look at your calendar and look for areas where you could free up time. Remember you're investing more time today to open up more freedom in the future.

Chris, one of the members in my community, reached out for advice on when he could find the time to start his side-hustle idea (which was actually a really good idea). He told me that he was the grand marshal of his local marathon, led a local runner meet-up, was on multiple nonprofit boards, volunteered as a tutor, played in a pickup basketball league, and was training for a triathlon, all while working a fifty-hour-a-week full-time job and having two kids. The answer was simple: Chris needed to let a few responsibilities go (not his kids, obviously!). It all comes back to priorities and trade-offs. One of great things about side hustling is you can go at your own pace, but realize that you should calibrate your expectations based on how much time you spend. Also note that your side hustle might require a lot of time to start, but then less time to maintain. Just because you are working every Saturday getting your side hustle off the ground doesn't mean you will need to work every Saturday or Saturdays forever! Looking at Chris's schedule, we were able to find eight hours a week for him to get started.

Cut back to the essentials. If something doesn't give you joy and you don't "need" to do it, then cut it out. I'm not saying you should spend all of your time working on your side hustle, I'm just showing you how you can find more time if you want it. It's up to you if you do. There are going to be five primary areas in your life where you can free up more time, and here's how you do it.

Mornings

I'm not a morning person at all, but I never used it as an excuse, and the morning became and is still is my most productive time period in the day. I've found two to three extra hours in the morning to be prime working time because it doesn't allow me to make any excuses as other priorities come up during the day. You don't have to get up at four A.M. or anything crazy like that. I'll get up around five-thirty or six and get cranking. It's quiet and I can watch the sun rise and focus on myself and my side hustles first. You might be thinking two to three hours isn't much time, but two to three hours of really focused time in the morning before your partner or kids wake up really adds up. That's an extra ten to fifteen hours a week, which is plenty of time to launch and grow a successful side hustle. The key is to really focus—turn off the TV, social media, everything—and get down to work. Schedule your morning time. Take it seriously and the investment each morning will compound over time.

Evenings

The next best time to work on your side hustle in the evenings, although it can be more challenging than working in the mornings because you've had a busy day and might be tired. But this is when you can really rally and spend some extra time on your side hustle. While it's really tough to find extra time every night, even working for a few hours in the evening a few days a week will really add up. Instead of catching the game or going out for drinks with friends, spend time working on your side hustle. If you can, schedule this time in your calendar for the weeks and months ahead so you can commit to it. The more you prioritize yourself and your side hustle, the more you're going to accomplish. There are also going to be those nights when you really get into the flow; those are the nights when you should ride it as long and stay up as late as you can. If you are feeling super productive, then stay up, but if you aren't, then don't force it. Energy preservation and management is key.

Weekends

Weekends are prime side hustle time. Don't waste them. Seriously, when I was twenty-four I realized that I was wasting a ton of time going out to boozy brunches every Saturday, which were not only expensive but took a lot of time, and I'd always need to take a nap when I got home! So in reality almost every Saturday I was using up seven to eight hours of time just for brunch. I cut back from brunch every weekend to once every two to three months, and instead on Saturdays I started waking up at seven A.M., walked my dog, and then dove into work until two or three in the afternoon. Then I took the rest of the day, and often the rest of the weekend, off.

Saturdays became my most productive day of the week. Sure, I could have rested or gone out with friends, but it meant more to me to work on my side hustles. Putting in at least eight hours per weekend on your side hustle adds up to over four hundred hours of additional time each year. If you really enjoy your side hustle, this won't feel like work and you won't feel like you're sacrificing your Saturday. Also you don't have to work every Saturday; even two Saturdays a month can make a big impact.

Take a Vacation, Sick, or Remote-Work Day

Once a quarter or whenever you want to do it without compromising your full-time job, take a vacation or sick day to work on your side hustle. These days are extremely valuable and you should take them when you need an entire day to focus on your business. For example, I know some people who take sick days when they are making a big push like the launch of a new website, course, or podcast, or implementing a big marketing plan. When you do take a sick day, get up early and use your day off as productively as possible—put in an eight-, ten-, or even fifteen-hour day that day to get the highest ROI for your time. I also know many people who use their remote-work privileges to work on their side hustle, since all their bosses care about is that they get the work done. Dedicating days like these to your side hustle can really fast-track your progress.

The In-Between Moments

Then there's all those in-between moments when you can find an extra ten, twenty, thirty, or even sixty minutes here and there. It's how you make the most of your commute or your lunch hour; it's for when you're traveling, when you're sitting in an Uber, or you're waiting for an appointment. If you can stay focused, these small blocks of time can also really add up. Whether it's writing a blog post on your phone in the back of a cab or taking calls when you have a few extra moments, make the most of them to work on your side hustle. Or take twenty minutes to just breathe deeply and decompress, which might be the most valuable way to spend a few extra minutes. No matter how you spend your in-between moments, just be intentional. Make the most of it.

Even an extra hour or two here and there will add up. I've gone through this exercise many times with my coaching clients and members; they always end up finding at least an extra five to ten hours a week, and in some cases, an additional twenty or more hours extra a week they can use to build a side hustle.

I know you're busy, but you can still make a lot of money with the extra moments you do have. No matter how much time you have, the key to making the most of your time is to focus on taking the steps and making the decisions that are going to have the highest ROI on your side hustle. Don't waste time—optimize it. Focus on making and saying yes to the decisions that push you forward and no to everything else. Be honest with yourself. It doesn't matter how hard you work, what matters more is how you use your time. No one is going to watch over your shoulder to make sure you're working. You've got to want it.

Given that you have only a limited amount of time, the most lucrative side hustles are ones that generate passive income—that is to say, money you can earn without actively having to do anything. This is why scaling your business is so lucrative; it allows you to make money in your sleep (while your employees walk dogs, babysit, or whatever else). Passive income is amazing because it completely disrupts the traditional idea that you need to trade your time for money. You can build a passive income business with or without employees.

But passive income side hustles can be tough to build (there's no such thing as free money, after all). Many will require significant setup time and then a solid marketing/sales strategy. A good way to build a passive income stream is by selling something that you spend a little time creating but that people can buy for a long time without you having to put in much (if any) additional work. A few examples of potential passive income ideas are building an online course, launching a drop-ship product on Amazon, creating an app, writing a book, or launching an apparel item. Then there are semi-passive income streams like blogging, since you make money on

Monthly Side Income	Annual Side Income	25x multiplier (reduces your number)	30x multiplier (reduces your number)
$250	$3,000	$75,000	$90,000
$500	$6,000	$150,000	$180,000
$1,000	$12,000	$300,000	$360,000
$1,500	$18,000	$450,000	$540,000
$2,000	$24,000	$600,000	$720,000
$2,500	$30,000	$750,000	$900,000
$3,000	$36,000	$900,000	$1,080,000
$4,000	$48,000	$1,200,000	$1,440,000
$5,000	$60,000	$1,500,000	$1,800,000
$6,000	$72,000	$1,800,000	$2,160,000
$7,000	$84,000	$2,100,000	$2,520,000
$8,000	$96,000	$2,400,000	$2,880,000

content that you previously published but don't have to update. Most of my own blogging income comes from blog posts I wrote two or three years ago.

These types of businesses are great for early retirement because you can build a passive income business that generates enough or more than enough money to cover your monthly expenses—potentially giving you the ability to "retire" sooner or at least take a mini-retirement of a few months or years to follow your passions. Remember that any amount of consistent stable recurring monthly income will reduce your number and could even cover your entire monthly expenses.

When evaluating passive income opportunities, focus on those things that people will always need, not just a fad. For example, people will always need to eat, sleep, get their dogs walked, find babysitters, get their lawns mowed, and travel from point a to point b. They will always want to be entertained, to learn, and to be inspired.

But any type of business can go out of business, so it's really difficult to build a long-term sustainable passive income stream outside of rental income. The world changes quickly and so does demand; what people are buying today might not be what they buy tomorrow. There are many online businesses that were making a lot of passive income but then all went out of business when Google updated its algorithm and they no longer showed up in searches, or Facebook changed its newsfeed and they could no longer get traffic. Sure, these passive income sources might help you travel the world for a year (which you should definitely do if you want), but you might not be able to live off them forever.

But passive income can definitely help you hit your number faster, because not only is it additional money you can invest, but it also takes less of your time so you can spend the rest of your time making money in other ways (or just chilling out).

TAX ADVANTAGES OF SIDE HUSTLING AND ENTREPRENEURSHIP

Another benefit of having a side hustle is that you can deduct many of the expenses of running and growing your side hustle, making it more cost-effective to get it off the ground. The $100 you spent to build a website and print business cards is all tax deductible on your personal tax return. When you travel to a conference that aligns with your side hustle or have lunch with a potential client or collaborator, it's tax deductible. As your side hustle grows and becomes more integrated into your daily life, there are many tax advantages to having an LLC (limited liability company). While you don't need to have a formal company established to deduct expenses, there are limitations on the amount and types of tax deductions for something you do as a "hobby" as opposed to a business.

This is one of the many reasons you should consider creating an LLC to use for your side hustle. If you are at the stage where you are starting to make money side hustling and you are ready to take it more seriously, it is probably worth investing the money (typically about $300 to $400) to create your own LLC company.

There are many benefits to setting up an LLC for your side hustle, including the ability to set up a business bank account, open a credit card to use for expenses, and build credit for your business. Having an LLC also gives you additional legal protections, helps you to separate and protect your personal and business assets, allows you to pay yourself a salary and manage employee and contractor expenses, and gives you more opportunities for tax deductions. It's also a great branding and business building opportunity, since you will be perceived as more legitimate to potential clients and customers. It also makes it easier to scale your side hustle if you decide to grow it into a larger business. So if you are planning to take your side hustle seriously, definitely set up an LLC and run all of your business expenses and income through it. It also makes taxes a lot easier!

Keep all of this in mind as you walk through the process of creating your own side hustle ideas, which you are going to do next.

THE SIDE-HUSTLE EVALUATION FRAMEWORK

While I recommend you start with one side hustle so you don't spread yourself too thin at first, because you are your own boss, you can test out a lot of different ideas to find one you really love and/or that makes you the most money.

While you can sell pretty much anything, you will probably sell either a product or a service—your own or someone else's. But one thing to keep in mind as you explore new ways to make money is that ideas are a dime a dozen. I had the idea for Uber a full four years before the company launched, but why didn't I become a billionaire? Because ideas don't mean anything if you can't or don't execute them. As you brainstorm side-hustle ideas while walking through this chapter, be realistic about which side hustles you have the time, skills, and motivation to take on.

After coming up with a few ideas using the framework in this chapter, just get started. Don't overthink it. You will figure it out as you go. Remember, you aren't stuck with any of your ideas—you can always move on to another one if it doesn't work. I've outlined four steps to help you choose your next side hustle.

1. Analyze your passions and skills.

To identify a new potential side hustle, you should consider what you are passionate about and what skills you have. While you can make money doing pretty much anything, it's a lot easier to make money doing something you love or at least like. Not only are you more likely to stick with something you enjoy, but it also won't feel like work. Sure, you can just have hobbies and do things for fun, but why not make money doing them if you can?

Think about what you really love to do and whether you can monetize it. Do you love crafting or making things? Samantha works as an account manager at a digital marketing agency during the day, and on nights and weekends she makes beautiful handmade dream catchers, which she sells for $50 online. One of Samantha's dream catchers was recently featured in a prominent magazine, and now her waiting list has ballooned to six months. She's in an amazing position and debating whether or not she wants to take her business to the next level and hire a few other people to build dream catchers with her. This is a great problem for Samantha to have—she's making money doing something she loves and has the opportunity to grow the business if she wants.

Do you really love music? Maybe you should gig more, sell your beats, produce your friends, get a promotion gig for a local venue, launch your own promotion or management company or record label or music blog. Adam was so into music he launched a blog called Run The Trap that made $4,000 a month, allowing him to quit his full-time job in digital marketing and follow his passion to launch a music management company. He's launched artists who have played Coachella and others who are touring the world. Now Adam is traveling around the world living his dream lifestyle and making a lot of money; he is well on his way to being financially independent by the time he's thirty-five. This all started from a simple blog side hustle.

Do you like to write? In 2005 while working in the defense industry as a software engineer, Jim Wang started the personal finance blog Bargain eering.com. Because he loved writing, he kept at it on his own pace and slowly started making money, figuring out the blogging business as he went. Eventually he was able to make enough money to start blogging full time. Five years later, the blog was acquired by a public company for $3 million, and Jim immediately reached financial independence at the age of thirty-four.

Do you like to code? Brandon launched a Chinese-to-English travel translator iPhone app in 2010 as side hustle while working as a computer programmer. Once he built it, he was able to make about $500 per month in passive income for years. And while $500 might not seem like much, because it was passive income, it required almost none of his time, and Brandon invested all of his side-hustle money, which helped him reach financial independence at the age of thirty-two.

Do you really love traveling? Maybe you should launch a private custom travel company that helps people book custom vacations or consult with people who are trying to plan their dream travel experiences, or coach people on how to travel hack, or write a travel blog, or get a side gig marketing one of your favorite destinations in your city. Brian Kelly, aka The Points Guy, loved traveling so much he started blogging about it, posting reviews of destinations, travel deals he found, and advice on how anyone can use credit card bonuses and airline points to travel for free. Now the guy makes millions of dollars a year to travel and write reviews and recently sold his blog for a reported $25 million. At the age of thirty-five he could retire at any time.

Do you really love connecting people? Tyler worked in technology sales and liked connecting with people so much that he launched a recruiting firm as his side hustle. In his spare time, he started finding his friends new jobs at companies his other friends worked for. The pay is incredible: companies will pay Tyler 20 percent of the first-year salary of any employee he places with them. So if he places someone who has a $100,000 salary, he makes $20,000. This means Tyler could make an extra $5,000 to $15,000 per month pretty easily. The venture has been so successful that he now does it full-time and the money easily covers his monthly expenses.

Now more and more of Tyler's friends and connections are looking for new jobs and more companies trust Tyler to find good talent. He's absolutely crushing it. And he can work from anywhere in the world, a perk that he takes full advantage of. A few months ago he worked from the base camp of Mount Everest in Nepal and then jetted over to party in Hong Kong.

Next you need to think about your skills. The best side hustles are the ones for which you already have the skills required. Think about each and every skill you have as well as things you enjoy doing that could potentially be monetized. You probably already have skills that you don't realize can be used to make money. You might be thinking about "skills" as something that you use for your job or something that you've been formally trained in or learned at school. But there are many kinds of skills that you can sell. For example, while you might not work in child care or education, you might be amazing at and love working with kids. What's stopping you from babysitting or launching a day care center? You might be taking many of your skills—like driving or doing laundry or cleaning or cooking or landscaping—for granted.

Another effective way to start side hustling is to simply take the skills and expertise you've acquired from your full-time job and sell them on the side. I know many full-time lawyers, accountants, web programmers, digital marketing managers, editors, copywriters, and designers who sell the same services they perform in their day jobs on the side. This is a great way to make extra money and help people who might not be able to afford the premium prices your big law firm or digital agency charges.

Before you do this, of course, you need to make sure your company doesn't have a conflict of interest policy that restricts your ability to take on outside work. Many companies allow you to take on outside work as long as it's viewed as noncompetitive—meaning it's not a service for an industry that your company serves or works with, nor is it directly for a competitor. If your employer does have a strict policy that restricts your ability to do side work, sit down and explain specifically how and why you want to make money on the side and why it's not a conflict. Your company might grant you a provision, or if they don't, you should seriously consider moving to a company that doesn't restrict your ability to make money in other ways.

I made most of my own side-hustle money selling digital marketing and website design services to companies that either couldn't afford to work with the digital agency I worked for or that my company wasn't interested in working with. So while my agency was working with hotels and car companies, I was working with local law firms, doctors, and real estate agencies on the side. Same services, but instead of the money going to my company and the partners, it all went to me.

As you think about side-hustle ideas, consider specializing in a particular niche. While doing so will limit those you sell your services to, the benefits of niche specialization tend to outweigh the risks.

While I could have built websites for anyone, I purposefully focused on law firms and Realtors. In my nine-to-five I worked only with universities. Focusing on only a few niches made it easier to get referrals, build connections, and position myself as an expert in those industries. Many people spread themselves too thin and try to get clients anywhere they can, but the more specialized your audience and more money your target market has, the more money you can make. The most profitable consultants I know all have a niche focus and have worked hard to become an expert in their niche. One digital marketer I know, Trevor, serves only Canadian orthodontists; he got hooked in with the primary association they all belong to and has an insanely profitable business as the expert on digital marketing in that niche.

No matter what niche you pick, it's never been easier to sell your expertise online, either in the form of one-to-one consulting services, group consulting or training, or other formats like online courses. Just as in your full-time job, the more valuable and in demand your skill set, the more money you can make selling it as a side hustle.

This is also an easy first step to becoming a full-time entrepreneur, since you could realistically sign up enough side clients and start making enough money to launch your own full-time venture. This happens all the time in many industries. So take stock of the skills you are getting paid for in your full-time job, and if you like doing the work, or at least like doing it enough so you will stay motivated to do it outside of your full-time job, it's a great place to start side hustling as well as make new connections.

What New Skills Do You Want to Learn?

Side hustling can also be a great way learn new skills and pursue a new career in an industry that you have very little experience in. As long as you can add value and meet the needs of the person who is paying you, then you can sell your service to someone. Of course, you can't sell something you know nothing about, but all you need to know is more than the person you are selling to and you can learn the rest as you go. There is nothing quite like a paying client to motivate you to learn how to do something.

This is how I learned how to build websites. While I knew basic HTML, I was able to learn how to build WordPress, Drupal, and Joomla websites for free on YouTube. It took me only a few weeks to learn, and I was getting paid to do it. You can learn almost anything on YouTube now. You no longer need a degree or formal training for many industries. There are many free or inexpensive online courses on literally anything, making it easier to acquire and master new knowledge. It's never been easier in history to rapidly learn new skills and use them to make more money. Your success isn't guaranteed just because the information is available, but two things will make it happen: curiosity and focus. We've entered the era of lifetime learning. The more you learn, the more money you'll make. Always keep learning.

No matter what you want to learn, find someone who needs that skill, sell it to them, and keep filling in your own knowledge gaps. This is an awesome way to build up skills and experience and test out a new career track without having to go back to school or dive into a full-time job.

Think about what you love doing—everything you love doing. Your hobbies, your passions, and your skills. Look at your skills in and outside your full-time job.

Can you get paid for any of them?

Could you launch a course teaching other people how to do it?

Could you sell it locally?

Grab a piece of paper or open a spreadsheet and create two columns. In one column, list all of your hobbies/passions, and in the other, list your skills. Then narrow down the skills list by crossing off skills you don't enjoy. If you notice overlap between the two lists, start with those ideas that allow you to combine your existing skills with your interests. If there isn't any overlap in the lists, start with your skills first and then work to build the skills required to make money on your passion. Here's an example to show how it works.

Kyle is a twenty-six-year-old marketing manager at an engineering company. While he makes decent money at his full-time job, it's really not his passion and he doesn't want to work there forever. He wants to start a side hustle in which he can make some additional money and do something he loves. His dream would be to be his own boss so he could travel more, so his goal is to find a side hustle that has full-time potential. Here's a list of Kyle's hobbies/passions and skills.

Hobbies/Passions	Skills
Design	Excel
Electronic music	Writing
Traveling	Copywriting
Running	Editing
Volunteer Tutoring	Facebook Advertising
Cooking	Photoshop
Reading	Outdoor survival skills
BASE Jumping	
Mountain Climbing	
Microbrewing	

Looking at the two lists, you can easily see there is some alignment between his hobbies and his skills, which makes selecting a potential side hustle much easier. For example, Kyle loved design and has Photoshop and copywriting skills, so he could start doing freelance design work for local businesses or through an online freelance marketplace like Upwork and then use positive client referrals to grow his business. He could also combine a few of his other passions by doing some design work for a microbrewery. You can also see overlap in Kyle's love for mountain climbing and BASE jumping with his outdoor survival skills, as well as design and marketing. If he is really skilled at climbing, he could start leading trips or launch (and market) his own company that organizes mountain trips and excursions.

In addition to the skills he already has, when Kyle launches a business he will likely learn other skills like business accounting, contracts, and negotiation, which he can then market on their own. One of the best benefits of side hustling is that you can use the opportunity to learn while you're making money, increasing the number of skills that you can monetize. Remember that skills are future currency and will make you more valuable and give you more ways to make money in the future.

2. Evaluate the moneymaking potential of your side hustles.

Now that you have a list of potential side hustles, the next step is to narrow them down to the ones that can make you the most money. This starts with looking at market demand. The higher the market demand for your service or product, the more money you can make. Market demand is determined by supply and demand, or the number of people who want to buy something (customers) and the number of people selling it (competitors).

In Matt's example, he was able to make a lot of money because the demand was high and growing (a lot of new people with dogs were moving into the neighborhood) and the supply was low (there weren't enough dog walkers servicing the area). He saw the market opportunity.

Matt also recognized that most of the other dog walkers in the neighborhood were like him—just one person working with a few clients. If there were a bunch of dog-walking companies in the neighborhood, then he wouldn't have had the same opportunity. But there weren't any big competitors and he also had something that a company trying to get into the neighborhood didn't have: connections with many of the local tenants, who ended up connecting him with other people they knew who needed a dog walker.

Before you start any business, you should analyze and understand market demand, because if people don't want what you have to sell or too many other people are selling it, then you won't make any money.

When it comes to something like dog walking, you are competing mostly on price (as opposed to the type or quality of service being offered), and when you are competing on price, people often choose the cheapest option. Thus every dog walker ends up making less money as more dog walkers enter the market. Anyone can walk a dog, so the amount you can charge is limited. Sure, you'll be able to get a few jobs mowing lawns or shoveling snow or babysitting, but it will be a lot tougher to compete and build a business in these markets.

If a market is too competitive, you aren't going to make much money unless you offer something your competitors can't. This doesn't mean you can't make money in this market; it just means that you will need to find a way to add extra value so people will choose you over your competitors and/or pay more for your service. For example, with a dog-walking company, you could walk earlier in the morning or later at night than your competitors, or you could offer longer walks, grooming, boarding, or training sessions (if you have that skill).

There is one exception to the rule of supply and demand: People are willing to pay more money for your service when they already have a relationship with you. Business is about relationships. If people trust you, they will buy from you. This is why you should start your side hustle in your community or work to build relationships in online communities. No matter what side hustle you want to launch, you are going to have an easier time selling into a network you are already a part of and with people you know. It's all about the referrals and positive references.

This is why an early mover advantage for Matt was so essential. He already had relationships in the community. When you are first in a market you can build relationships that will be difficult for another company to replicate after you have already gained traction. This is where Matt really excelled—he saw the market opportunity and moved quickly to build more relationships using his existing referral network.

Sure, there are now other dog-walking companies in Matt's neighborhood, but he has more business than he can handle through word of mouth and a few simple promotions. Matt offered a free dog walk to anyone who referred him to a new client. All it took was a couple of existing clients referring him to other potential clients on their local community or building message boards. Because the demand is so high and his reputation is strong, he doesn't have to do any marketing.

It's also worth noting that busy people are typically willing to pay a lot of money just to take tasks off their plate. So if you or one of your current or former clients can convince them you can solve their problems, then they are less likely to check with competitors before they hire you. Many people have made a lot of money offering a simple service to people who have money and are too busy to do it themselves.

As you build your side-hustle list, think about who will buy your product. If you think you can make money on it, then just get out and start trying to sell it. The market will tell you if there is demand because either people will buy from you or they won't. Since most side hustles won't involve a whole lot of capital to start, you can just launch it and see where it goes. I don't recommend new side hustles where you have to spend a lot of money or need buy expensive tools to start. Keep your up-front investment as small as possible. There is little downside to testing out new moneymaking opportunities when all you are trading is a little bit of your time.

If you are launching an online product or service, then an online survey is essential. If you don't already have an online audience/community, focus on building the community first. It's extremely hard to sell an online product without an existing audience. As you build your community and connect with others, send them a simple survey to gauge their interest and test your product or service idea. You will learn a ton from asking people what they think about your idea and if they would buy it from you.

Another benefit of asking people for feedback both online and off-line is that because they have already engaged with you, they might be interested in buying from you. Once you start asking people for feedback, the people who want to buy will step forward. If they trust you, people will also start recommending you to others they think could benefit from your service or product.

It's also worth trying to find someone who has already built a successful business like the side hustle you want to start. Seek out people who've already done it and learn everything you can from them. It could save you years of time. There are many older successful entrepreneurs who would love to get coffee or grab lunch with you and tell you about their experiences. Depending on the type of side hustle you want to launch, you could even reach out to a potential competitor and offer to intern for a few months to learn about the business.

Another great way to analyze market demand for almost any type of product or service is by using Google Search data. Because so many people use Google Search, by analyzing Google Search patterns you can get a statistically valid analysis of market demand across almost any geographic area in the world. If you want to launch a dog-walking company in Syracuse, New York, take a look at how many people are searching for "dog walking" or "dog walker" on Google in the area. Look at how the search volumes are changing year over year. Is demand going up or going down? While you won't be able to access all of the data unless you are a Google advertising client, there is a free version that will give you enough info to get started. Simply search for the Google Keyword Planner tool.

In addition to analyzing Google Search data, you should also take the time to look at who your competitors would be for each of your side-hustle ideas. Doing competitive analysis is essential—it will tell you not only who your competitors are but also how much they charge, what their specific services or products are, how they are marketing their products/services, and what they don't do. I also recommend secret shopping with any of your potential competitors. Fill out an inquiry form on their website or call them. Ask them more about their services and what they charge. Get as much info as you can. It will all be useful intelligence as you build your own side hustle. It will help you figure out what to charge and what you can do differently from your competitors to stand out.

If there are tons of competitors and the market looks oversaturated, then you might want to pick another side hustle with less competition. Or be honest with yourself about what your unique value or differentiator could be. Why should someone buy from you instead of someone else? Of course, not every side hustle needs to turn into a big profitable business, but simply realize that if there are a lot of competitors, it can be tougher for you to sell your product, and as a consequence, you might make less money. It can also be tough and expensive to reach potential customers in a market that is already super competitive.

If there is no one else offering what you want to offer, then the reason is either because no one is willing to buy it or you've stumbled on a re-markably good side-hustle idea and might have an early mover advantage. No matter what your side-hustle idea is, the more you know about your competitors, the easier it will be for you to market and sell your own ser-vices. What is different about each of your competitors? How are their services different? Why can some charge more than others? What can you offer that is unique? All of this detective work will help you better price your own services and fees.

3. Figure out what to charge, get your first sale, and get paid as much as possible.

There are essentially six things that dictate how much you can charge:

1. The skill required to perform the task or your relative skill level as compared to your competitors
2. Demand
3. How much your competitors are charging
4. Added value (that is to say, any additional services or bonuses you offer)
5. Perceived value (based on your reputation or how valuable your offering is to the customer)
6. How much someone is able to pay (generally people/compa-nies with more money can pay you more). You'll often make more money selling to people who have more money.

Let's dive a little deeper into each of these.

First, the more in demand your skill set, the more you can charge for your service, since there are a limited number of people who can do it. You can charge more for website building than for dog walking, and if you are an especially talented coder, you can charge more than another coder for the same service.

Second, the greater the demand for what you are offering, the more you can charge. While being a dog walker is pretty easy, lots of people need dog walkers, so demand in many places is high. But demand is market dependent, meaning it's dependent on a specific location, so the demand for dog walkers may vary greatly by city and neighborhood.

Third, how much you can charge depends on how much your competitors are charging. You can only charge so much more than your competitors, and you'll need to add a lot of extra value to do so. Often when you are launching a new product or service, you'll want to price lower than your competitors at first, in order to capture customers looking for a lower price. However, there's risk in pricing your services too low, since it's much easier to lower prices than raise them in the future. This is yet another reason why it's so important to determine and communicate what makes you different from your competitors.

Fourth, you want to add as much value as possible. But this matters only if the client or customer can see it. Making more money is not about how hard you work or how many things you get done or how busy you are. It's about maximizing the perceived value of your work and doing it as efficiently (i.e., in as little time) as possible. The more valuable your clients consider your work, the more money you can make. Since people are the buyers, *what they think matters most.*

Finally, companies and people that have more money are more likely to pay you more for your services. The more affluent a neighborhood, the more you can make walking dogs. The bigger the company, the greater the resources they have to pay for your service. For example, a few months after I built a $500 website for a small law firm, I built a $50,000 website using the same general template for a large law firm. It actually took me less time to build the $50,000 website, but the larger firm had more resources at their disposal and they saw a bigger upside in having a nice website. The value I provided to both was the same, but the client who paid $50,000 perceived that value as greater. While intelligent pricing is an art and science, you can get a good sense for what the market is willing to pay based on what your competitors are charging and by going out and selling. If all you get is pushback and can't sell, lower your prices or realize that maybe you can't compete.

Some side hustles are going to make you a lot more money than others, so it's important to determine what your target rate per hour is. Just as when you calculated your real hourly rate in chapter 6, you'll want to have a target hourly rate to shoot for with your side hustle. As you write down your ideas and analyze your potential competition, write down how much money you could realistically make for each venture. If you've valued your time at $20 per hour for your full-time gig, you probably want to get at least $20 per hour if not more for your side hustle.

I'm just going to come out and say it—most people when they are side hustling, especially when they are first starting out, charge way too little for their services or products. Don't undersell yourself. Sure, you want to have an attractive offer so you can sell your first few clients or customers, but after you've sold your first few, you should increase your prices.

One of the goals of this book is to help you make the most money for your time, so you should be charging as much as you feel slightly uncomfortable charging and what your customer feels a little uncomfortable paying (but not so uncomfortable that they walk away). As one of my mentors once told me, "If the client isn't pushing back on the price, then you aren't charging enough."

You should charge as much as the market is willing to pay, no matter what service or product you are offering. If it's too high, people won't buy, but if it's too low, people might not buy either (because they perceive the value or quality of what you are offering as low). Or if it's too low, you'll have too many customers. In most cases, it's better to have five customers paying you $20,000 than five thousand paying you $200. In both scenarios you make $100,000, but it's a lot easier to manage five customers than five thousand.

You want to price so you can control supply and demand. If you normally build three websites a month, but you feel like building only one website this month and there is demand for your service, see if you can double or triple your prices. If demand is really high, then you are in an awesome position and can charge whatever you think people are willing to pay.

Another way to price your services is based on a percentage of the growth in profit that you help drive. If you are selling a product or service for someone else, then you offer to charge based on the amount of profit you help drive or for a cut of the revenue. If you are confident in your services, you can offer to work for only a cut of the revenue or profit, so your clients pay only if you make them money, and the more you sell, the more money you make.

I once did some work for a Bluetooth headset company and charged them 20 percent of the profit that my ad campaigns generated, which ended up being really profitable for a few months until they decided to do it themselves! It's definitely a pricing model worth considering if you are in advertising, marketing, or selling and have confidence in your ability to increase your client's revenue. It's higher risk but higher reward, and the sky's the limit.

Getting Your First Sale

Now that you've got a great side-hustle idea, how do you actually get clients? While this depends on the type of product or service you are selling, generally the easiest way is to sell into the same community (online or offline) you surveyed to analyze market demand. If people already know you, they are much more likely to buy from you.

However, whether someone knows you or not, one thing can significantly increase your chances of making a sale—telling your story. At the heart of selling any product or service is your story. We are all human, and selling is all about connecting with people. The better and more your story connects with someone, the more they will trust the value and service you can provide them. Your about page is the most important page on your website.

Oh, yeah, no matter what you are selling you will definitely need a nice website. Don't worry, you can create one easily with WordPress in about an hour. The better your website looks, the more legitimate you'll be perceived to be and the easier it will be to sell your product. Your goal is to share your story to potential customers so they can both learn who you are and connect with you. Share a personal story why you decided to start your business. What was your aha moment or what inspired you to launch it? Why are you passionate about it? What is your goal or mission with the company? Also share some stories about connecting with your customers and what you've learned in running the business. The more personal you are, the more likely you will form a connection. Look at your competitors and write a better about page. There are far too many boring about pages, so showing your personality and passion will give you an advantage.

Don't worry about selling to a lot of people at first. Just focus on selling your first client or first product. While you might launch the best product or service ever and might immediately end up with more sales than you can handle, it's more likely that you will have a tough time selling your first few clients or products. This is normal and actually to your advantage, since you will want to grow your side hustle at a pace you can handle. One of the worst things for a young business is to oversell and not be able to handle demand.

While it can be tough to sell your first client or first product, if you do it correctly, your first customers will be the most valuable customers you ever have. Selling slowly at first will help you do two essential things that can significantly increase the potential of your business having success.

You should always overdeliver for your first clients. Give them as much value as possible. Go above and beyond to make them happy, even if it takes a ton of extra time, because you will want/need your first clients to be your references. Having a great reference will make selling your second client or product much easier. Your future customers will be more likely to buy from you if they can talk to a satisfied customer. The first website I ever built was for a lawyer in Chicago whom I found on Craigslist and used as a reference for the next two years. Just that one reference helped me sell over $500,000 in business. He was my first and most valuable client.

Your first clients can also provide invaluable feedback on your product or service that can help you refine and improve it. Make sure to always ask for feedback on what your customer liked and what you can do better. Don't forget to ask and always offer some small incentive—something for free to encourage them to share their experience! The better your product or service gets and the happier customers are, the more money you're going to make. Happy customers tell other people why they're so happy, and before long you'll have built a referral network that does the selling for you. There is nothing more valuable than a happy customer.

Another way to attract new customers is to partner with a business with which you align but don't compete. For example, say you have a snow removal business. You can contact the local lawn-mowing or landscaping companies in your community who don't offer this service. Build a relationship with them and create some exchange, whether monetary or otherwise, so that they will recommend your service to their customers. Leveraging other people's networks can rapidly launch or grow your side hustle. Just tapping into one network is all you could need to significantly expand your side hustle.

4. Know when to scale.

You should consider scaling (growing) your side hustle if you have been able to consistently sell your service or product and have been making a profit for the past six months, or if the demand for your services or products has exploded quickly. If demand is higher than you can meet on your own, or if the demand is consistent and you don't want to do the work, then you should consider hiring others to do the work for you. If demand is low or growth is slow, you should hold off on hiring anyone new, since the last thing you want to do is hire employees and then have nothing for them to do.

By hiring employees, you can shift from just selling your own time to brokering others' time. The better your team is at doing the work and the more efficient they get, the more you can eventually charge your clients, and you will end up making a lot more money for doing absolutely no extra (and possibly even less) work. The more you can distribute the work, the less you have to work, and the faster you can grow your business.

If you do decide to scale, you can do it at your pace; you don't have to build a huge company unless that's what you want. You don't have to go out and hire a bunch of employees. In fact, I recommend that you start slow by hiring one or two contract employees, instead of committing a lot of resources to full-time salaries and benefits. Try to keep your overhead (employee costs) as low as possible until you've got a good handle on the economics and growth opportunity of the business. And when you do decide to bring on your first few employees, try to hire what I call "believers," people excited about the opportunity and the business. Finding someone who actually enjoys the work and believes in your vision will be more valuable and helpful than just hiring an employee who just watches the clock. Not only are they likely to go the extra mile, they will stick with you as you grow and help drive more growth.

I also recommend you think hard again about what kind of life you really want and what trade-offs you are willing to make for money. The transition from being a solopreneur to being an entrepreneur is tough. As we've already discussed, there are many challenges to being an entrepreneur, and while you will still be the boss, having to hire and manage a team, as well as increase your sales to pay for your growing team, can add a lot more stress to your life than just managing yourself.

Having employees takes your responsibility to an entirely new level: you start feeling responsible not only for your own livelihood but also for the livelihoods of your employees and their families. That's a lot of responsibility.

This was a massive transition for me. Going from employee to employer was a lot more work than I had anticipated, and it also pushed me away from the work I loved (building websites, marketing products, and competing at the forefront of digital marketing) to spending most of my time doing administrative and management work, like dealing with the complexity of human emotions in an office where people spend more time with their coworkers than their families.

But research shows that even when they work more hours, self-employed workers are actually happier, largely because when you work for yourself you have the freedom to innovate and you're more engaged in solving challenges and grow your own business. The best thing about having your own business is you can do whatever you want. You might want to grow your business to be as big and profitable as possible, or you might want to build what's known as a *lifestyle business,* which is essentially a business that fits into your ideal lifestyle. Lifestyle businesses are about having an ideal balance of money and time, and they can give you the opportunity to hit your number faster and generate consistent cash flow to cover your monthly expenses (and maybe more).

Matt estimates that he could double the size of his dog-walking business, but he isn't willing to trade more of his time to manage it. He's got a good balance and is able to manage his full-time job and his side hustle and still have time to travel with his girlfriend. And he's still on track to hit his target number of $1.5 million by age thirty.

Remember, side hustling is also about the time/money trade-off, so it's up to you to decide how much time you are willing to trade today to make more money to invest in the future. Yes, you will need to make some sacrifices, but the size of the sacrifice is ultimately up to you. If you're committed to walking away early, remember that any time you spend making money today will buy you back that same amount of time (or more) in the future.

If you want to make a bunch of money, you're going to have to say no sometimes. You can't expect to make millions of dollars watching Netflix or going out every night. When I was side hustling really hard, I turned down offers to hang out with my friends sometimes, but I still found time to chill with my homies. I just built it around my side hustling. Sometimes I even hired my friends to help or brought them along. The choice is ultimately up to you, but I have no doubt that once you start earning money side hustling and seeing it grow, it won't feel like a sacrifice at all.

RECAP

1. **You need to diversify your income streams by developing one or more side hustles—moneymaking ventures outside of your full-time job.** Side hustling is great because you can make money—sometimes a lot of money—doing pretty much anything. It also typically required very little investment to get started, and it's easy to test multiple ideas.

2. **Side hustling to invest will fast track your investment growth.** Every side-hustle dollar you invest reduces the amount of time it will take to hit your number. No job should be too small. Every extra $1 invested helps and speeds up the process.

3. **There are two ways you can make money side hustling: you can work for someone else or you can work for yourself.** If you are side hustling for someone else, the money you can make will always be limited by the number of hours you have in the day. Working for yourself allows you to make a lot of money doing something that you love

and gives you more control over your money and your time and the opportunity to grow your business if you want to.

4. **You need to evaluate how much time you are realistically willing to commit to it, because how much time you have will determine the types of side hustles you can launch and how much money you can make.**

5. **The most lucrative side hustles are ones that generate passive income—that is, money you can earn without actively having to do anything.** Passive income completely disrupts the traditional idea that you need to trade your time for money. You can build a passive income business with or without employees.

6. **You can build a passive income business that generates enough or more than enough money to cover your monthly expenses.** This gives you more flexibility and potentially the opportunity reach financial independence very quickly.

7. **The Side-Hustle Evaluation Framework**
   - Analyze your passions and skills.
   - Think about what you love doing and look at your skills. Can you get paid for any of them? Could you launch a course teaching other people how to do it? Could you sell it locally?
   - Evaluate the moneymaking potential of your side hustles.
   - Figure out what to charge, get your first sale, and get paid as much as possible. There are five things that dictate how much you can charge:
     1. the skill required to perform the task or your relative skill level as compared to your competitors
     2. demand
     3. how much your competitors are charging
     4. added value (e.g. any additional services or bonuses you offer)
     5. perceived value (based on your reputation or how valuable your offering is to the customer)
     6. how much someone is able to pay (generally people/companies with more money can pay more)
   - Focus on building a lifestyle business—knowing when and how to scale

CHAPTER 10

THE SEVEN-STEP FAST TRACK INVESTMENT STRATEGY

Accelerate Your Moneymaking Money!

nvesting is the ultimate form of passive income and the accelerator of financial freedom. It's how you make money on your money without having to exchange any of your time.

The simple investing strategy presented in this chapter is designed to help you reach your number as quickly as possible. It is designed so you or anyone can implement it, no matter how much money you make or investing experience you have. It's worth nothing this strategy is specific to U.S. citizens, but you can still invest in the same investments, just not the same types of accounts.

Many people find investing daunting or confusing, so they don't invest, invest in dumb things, invest way too little, or pay financial advisors large fees when they could easily manage their investments themselves.

Don't get distracted by more advanced or flashy strategies or complicated language. The important thing is not to become an investing wizard, but to get your money growing as soon and as efficiently as possible. The longer you wait, the more time and money you are wasting, and as I've mentioned many, many times in this book, every day of compounding matters. Start today. Seriously, you don't need to figure out everything before you start investing.

Let me start by clearing up a popular misconnection: investing is not gambling. When you invest, you are putting money in something that gives you a reasonable chance to get that money back or see it grow. When you gamble, you are relying solely on luck to get a return. Also, unlike with gambling, when you invest, you can control many of the variables that impact whether you make money and that can limit performance.

This strategy is built on five key concepts you can directly influence:

1. Minimizing risk
2. Minimizing fees
3. Minimizing taxes on your contributions
4. Maximizing returns
5. Minimizing taxes on your withdrawals

While all investing carries risk, and you can't control the market, the economy, or the performance of a stock, the simple investing strategy in this chapter can help you get the highest return for the level of risk you are comfortable with and maximize your chance for success.

Don't worry, it won't take long for you to find your sweet spot—the point at which you are invested in a way that will make you as much money as possible while still letting you sleep at night. Over time, you'll also get more comfortable taking calculated risks to make even more money.

You can invest in a wide variety of things like art, wine, commodities, currencies, cryptocurrencies, domains, furniture, collectibles, businesses, and tons of other things. While you can make money investing in any of these things, for the purposes of this chapter, we're not going to focus on investing in physical assets (like art, wine, or collectibles) or speculative financial instruments (like cryptocurrencies).

Never invest in anything you don't understand. Don't put your money in investments that your friends or family or a financial advisor or someone you just met told you to invest in without understanding exactly what you are investing in and what the risk/reward trade-off is. Beware of trendy or too-good-to-be-true investments, things that promise a 20 percent return each year or something that is unlikely to happen over the long term. No matter how much you trust the people making an investment recommendation, focus on simple financial instruments that generate consistent returns over time. The core of your investment portfolio should be made up of stocks (shares of actual companies), bonds (money that you are lending someone), and real estate (properties). These are the easiest, most dependable investments, and they can make you a lot of money.

While you can hire a financial advisor or company to manage your investments, as you've learned throughout the book, the more you control your own financial life, the more money you can make. You can and should implement this strategy yourself, and realistically you can manage it in less than an hour a month.

Financial Advisors, Fiduciaries, and Robo-Advisors

If you need help investing, you can hire a fee-only financial advisor for a few hours to help you set up your accounts. You should work only with advisors who charge on an hourly or project basis, not based on AUM (assets under management). When you are charged based on AUM, your advisor is getting a percentage of your investments (typically 1 to 3 percent) to work with you, whether they make money for you or not, and the impact of those percentage withdrawals, like any other investment fee, will negatively compound overtime, thus reducing the total long-term value of your investment.

Also make sure any financial advisor you work with is a fiduciary, which is an advisor who is legally required to advise you in your best interest, not their own. If they aren't a fiduciary, they can sell you anything they want even if it's not in your best interest, which is pretty common, since many brokers receive commissions for selling certain products. Whenever you talk to financial advisors, ask if they are a fiduciary and if they receive commissions on investment products; if they say yes, don't work with them. Check out XY Planning, a network of financial advisors who charge by the hour that include some early retirement experts.

Another option is to work with a low-fee company commonly known as a robo-advisor that uses algorithms to invest your money and keep you accountable. I've personally tested a number of robo-advisors, and you can easily save your money and do everything they do on your own. But if you decide you absolutely need help managing your investments, working with a robo-advisor like Vanguard Personal Advisor Services, Betterment, or Wealthfront are good options. Just be mindful of the fees and the type of support you get. I personally like Vanguard's service because it has a low fee and you are also able to talk to a financial or tax advisor at any time if you have questions.

THE SEVEN-STEP FAST TRACK INVESTMENT STRATEGY

This investment strategy is designed to help you to minimize taxes, minimize risk, account for inflation, and maximize your returns. It's very close to the exact investing strategy I personally used, with some improvements that I've discovered since becoming financially independent and recommendations I've gathered from others who've fast-tracked their financial freedom.

This investment strategy is designed to be done in order, so follow each step as presented. If you follow these instructions and maximize your savings rate so you're investing the absolute greatest amount of money you can, you will turbo-boost your chances of hitting your number quickly. It's also a strategy you can follow for the rest of your life.

Please note: All of the contribution limits mentioned are current as of 2018, so check for the most up-to-date limits on the IRS website so you can maximize your contributions. There are also different contribution limits depending on if you are single or married.

STEP 1: SEPARATE SHORT-TERM AND LONG-TERM INVESTING GOALS

You should be investing differently depending on whether you need the money in the short term (within the next five years) or the long term (after five years). Most of your money should be invested for the long term so you can live off it for the rest of your life.

Short-Term Investing

Because the stock market can fluctuate quite a bit over any five-year period, if you want to buy a house in the next few years, redo your kitchen, or take that amazing trip to Italy that you've always wanted, then you want to put that money in investments that are less volatile. While your investments won't grow as much as they could if you took more risk, they also won't lose as much money; you don't want the value of your money to fall 20 percent because of a stock market dip right before you need it.

Most people hold their short-term investments in cash in a savings account so they can access the money immediately. This is an okay option if it helps you sleep at night, but most savings accounts grow at less than 1 percent per year, so you will actually be losing money to inflation (which grows 2 to 3 percent per year).

It's always safe to keep some of your investments in cash in case of emergencies in what's commonly called an *emergency fund*. Traditional wisdom recommends you save at least six months of your living expenses in cash in a simple savings account or money market fund. This allows you to have access to cash whenever you need it without having to sell any of your investments, which can be useful in case of an emergency or if you lose your job. If you believe you have a secure job and/or you have cash flow from multiple income sources (making you less reliant on one job), or if you have access to cash in other ways, then you might be okay saving less than six months' worth of expenses and investing the extra money in stocks or bonds instead.

Personally, I've always kept less than two months of my living expenses in cash because I want to keep as much money in the market and growing. But I'm comfortable doing this because I have multiple income streams as well as the ability to use credit cards strategically (since my monthly cash flow can cover paying them off) to cover any emergencies. In a worst-case scenario, you can always withdraw money from your Roth IRA account, since you've already paid tax on the principal and won't be penalized for doing so. I've always viewed my Roth IRA as a backup emergency fund. Remember the more money you have invested, the more it can grow.

Another safe short-term option is to put your money in a CD (certificate of deposit). CDs are offered by banks and will give you a guaranteed interest rate, likely around 2 percent, for a fixed period of time. But CDs force you to lock up your money for typically between one and five years, and you'll get penalized if you take the money out early, so you don't get the flexibility of cash if you need the money in a pinch. However, one strategy you can use is to set up what's known as a CD ladder, which is when you open CDs so they are maturing on a consistent basis, typically every year, so you can then use the money if you need it or just reinvest it in another CD.

A better option is to keep your short-term investments in bonds. A bond is a form of debt issued when a company, government, or municipality needs money. It's a loan with a guaranteed interest rate attached. When you buy the bond, you are loaning money to whoever issued it for a certain period of time at a fixed interest rate. Because the interest rate is fixed (meaning it's set by the bond issuer and doesn't change over time), bonds are known as fixed-income investments, so you can count on the returns as long as the issuer doesn't default on the loan. High-quality bonds (where the borrower, such as the U.S. government, is likely to pay it back) are traditionally viewed as less risky investments than stocks because their interest doesn't change the way a stock price does.

If you want to invest in bonds, you don't need to go through the hassle of buying bonds directly. You can easily buy them through a bond fund (which holds a lot of bonds to diversify your risks and maintain an expected rate of return). Check out the Vanguard Total Bond Market Index Fund, which invests in a diversified group of investment grade (aka high-quality) bonds. This particular fund contains about 30 percent corporate bonds and 70 percent government bonds. Bond funds are low risk but carry a higher potential return than most savings accounts. This allows you to at least keep up with inflation (and potentially beat it). Between 2012 and 2017 the Vanguard Total Bond Market Index Fund has returned approximately 2 to 3 percent each year. When you have money invested in a bond fund in an after-tax account, you can withdraw the money at any time. You will just be responsible for paying taxes on the gains.

If you want to take a little more risk, you could invest your cash in a fund comprised of both stocks and bonds like the Vanguard Wellesley Income Fund, which invests in approximately 60 percent bonds and 40 percent stocks, so you can generate a higher return (with slightly higher risk). Over the past year (2017–2018), the Wellesley has returned 10.20 percent; over the past three years, 6.45 percent; and over the past five years, 7.31 percent. That sure beats the 1 percent or less that most savings accounts offer. If you have access to consistent secure cash, then don't keep your money on the sidelines unless you plan to actually retire in the next few years and will need to live off your investing income. As you get closer to early retirement you should increase your cash fund from six months of living expenses to twelve.

Long-Term Investing

No matter when you start investing, a majority of your money should be invested for the long term (30 plus years), because even if you plan to retire earlier than that, you will want to keep the money growing so you can live off it forever. *Buy and hold* is the name of the long-term investment game. Because you have a longer time horizon, short-term fluctuations in your investments don't matter as much because you have a longer time to recover. The best place to invest for the long term is in the U.S. and international stock markets.

The rest of the investing strategy presented in this chapter is designed for long-term investing.

STEP 2: FIGURE OUT HOW MUCH MONEY YOU HAVE TO INVEST

As you already know, the higher your savings rate, the more money you can invest and the faster you'll hit your number. Sit down and think about how much money you can invest each day, month, quarter, and year. Set a foundation—a baseline number that you are going to invest in each account over each period.

Whether it's getting a percentage withdrawn from your paycheck and deposited into your 401(k) or having a certain amount transferred from your bank account into your portfolio each month, automate as many of your deposits as you can into each account. But remember, automation is just the start. Don't just set it and forget it. Try to push your investing foundation as high as you can as frequently as you can by escalating the amount you are withdrawing from your paycheck and the amount of your side-hustle income you are contributing.

Try to escalate your investing rate at least 1 percent every thirty days (trust me, you won't feel 1 percent increases) and reevaluate every six months. Keeping this habit up, you will save at least 12 percent more every year. If 1 percent feels easy, then try for 2 percent, 5 percent, or larger increases. Once you start investing more, saving becomes a lot easier. The hardest part for many super savers, myself included, was going from 0

	Jan	Feb	Mar	Apr	May	Jun	July	Aug	Sep	Oct	Nov	Dec	TOTAL
Income													
Full-Time Income	$5,000	$5,000	$5,000	$5,000	$5,000	$5,000	$5,000	$5,000	$5,000	$5,000	$5,000	$5,000	$60,000
Side-Hustle Income	$1,000	$1,000	$1,000	$1,000	$1,000	$1,000	$1,000	$1,000	$1,000	$1,000	$1,000	$1,000	$12,000
Total Income	$6,000	$6,000	$6,000	$6,000	$6,000	$6,000	$6,000	$6,000	$6,000	$6,000	$6,000	$6,000	$72,000
Investment Accounts													
Tax-Advantaged													
401(k)	$900	$900	$1,200	$1,200	$1,200	$1,200	$1,200	$1,200	$1,200	$1,200	$1,400	$1,500	$14,300
Roth IRA	$200	$500	$500	$400	$500	$500	$500	$500	$500	$700	$700	$700	$6,200
SEP IRA	$50	$50	$50	$50	$50	$50	$50	$50	$50	$50	$50	$50	$600
Non-Tax-Advantaged													
Brokerage Account	$0	$0	$0	$0	$0	$0	$0	$0	$0	$0	$0	$0	$0
Target Savings %	20%	21%	22%	23%	24%	25%	26%	27%	28%	29%	30%	31%	31%
Target Savings $ Monthly	$1,200	$1,260	$1,320	$1,380	$1,440	$1,500	$1,560	$1,620	$1,680	$1,740	$1,800	$1,860	$22,320
Target Savings $ Daily	$40	$42	$44	$46	$48	$50	$52	$54	$56	$58	$60	$62	$744
Actual Savings $	$1,150	$1,450	$1,750	$1,650	$1,750	$1,750	$1,750	$1,750	$1,750	$1,950	$2,150	$2,250	$21,100
Actual Savings %	19%	24%	29%	28%	29%	29%	29%	29%	29%	33%	36%	38%	29%
Savings Rate +/- Goal	-1%	3%	7%	5%	5%	4%	3%	2%	1%	4%	6%	7%	-2%

percent to 20 percent, but at a 20 percent investing rate you really see your money starting to grow, which is motivating and makes going from 20 percent to 50 percent a lot easier.

If it's easier for you to think in dollars instead of percentages, try to invest as much as you can every day. In 2011, I started trying to invest an extra $50 a day into my retirement accounts on top of my contributions that were automated. As I started making more money, I would invest as much as I could each day, sometimes as much as $200 extra some days when I made extra money. Once I had invested the money, I didn't miss it and enjoyed seeing my account balances grow. Remember even one extra dollar invested every day will make a difference. Push yourself to invest as much as you can every day. Remember it's an investment in the future you!

Below is a simple spreadsheet format you can use to plan and track your savings rate. In this example, the person's target savings goal was $18,360 by the end of the year, which equals a 25.5 percent savings rate. But they were actually able to save $21,100, which is 29.3 percent. Using a simple spreadsheet like this and/or the tools I've built to help you track your information on can help you push to save more.

You can find the editable spreadsheet at https://financialfreedombook .com/tools.

STEP 3: DETERMINE YOUR TARGET ASSET ALLOCATION

Next you need to determine your target asset allocation, which is the percentage of each asset (e.g., stocks, bonds, and cash) you have in your investment accounts. Your target asset allocation determines the level of risk/reward of your investment portfolio and is one of the most important investment decisions you will need to make. No matter which target allocation you choose, you will need to monitor and maintain this asset allocation across all of your investment accounts.

Typically, stocks are riskier investments than bonds, so the more stocks you hold in your portfolio, the risker it is, meaning the more it could go up or down in value. Bonds fluctuate less than stocks, meaning they have less risk but also less reward potential. And cash is cash, so it's not going to go up in value much and, as you've learned, will likely lose value over time due to inflation.

So having a portfolio invested 100 percent in stocks is riskier than having a portfolio invested 60 percent in stocks and 40 percent in bonds or 40 percent in stocks and 60 percent in bonds. If the stock market goes down, the more you have invested in bonds, the less your portfolio will likely go down, but the more you have invested in bonds when the stock market goes up, the less it will increase in value.

The typical advice is that you should set your bond allocation to your age (that is, if you are thirty, you should have 30 percent of your investment profile in bonds), but age-driven asset allocation recommendations are misleading because they assume you will retire in your sixties and seventies. While they might work for many people who don't want to retire early, they might not work for you and can expose you to too much risk and minimize your returns.

The best way to pick your target asset allocation is to estimate how long it will be before you need to use the money (that is, when you are going to need to live off your investment growth).

The longer time horizon you have before you need to withdraw your investments, the risker your target asset allocation should be, because you have more time to weather short-term ups and downs and participate in the long-term potential gains. Here are two simple rules to follow:

1. The further away you are from retirement and the longer you plan to keep your money invested before withdrawing it, the more risk you should take, so the greater your stock allocation percentage should be (e.g., 100 percent stocks/0 percent bonds or 90 percent stocks/10 percent bonds).

2. The closer you are to retirement and the sooner you need to live off your investment balance, the less risk you should take, so the greater your bond allocation percentage should be (e.g., 70 percent stocks/30 percent bonds, 60 percent stocks/40 percent bonds, or 40 percent bonds/60 percent stocks).

If you are ten or more years away from retiring, I recommend you invest 100 percent in stocks for now. When you are five years from retiring, then depending on how well the market is performing, you will want to readjust your asset allocation to be more conservative. After you retire (that is to say, when you get to a point where you want to live completely off the returns of your investments accounts) and depending on how long you need the money to last, you will want to shift your asset allocation to focus on generating consistent income with less risk. But if you aren't actually planning to retire completely, you can maintain a higher level of risk in your portfolio and continue to let the money grow at a higher rate.

Brandon, who reached financial independence at thirty-two and is now thirty-six, keeps 100 percent of his portfolio invested in stocks because he is still making money from his side-hustle blogging and he's confident in the long-term prospects of the U.S. stock market. As I write this at thirty-two, I also still have 100 percent of my investments in stocks for a similar reason: I am still making money and also believe in the long-term growth of the stock market. If I didn't have any additional income, then I would likely switch to a more conservative allocation closer to 70 percent stocks and 30 percent bonds. There is no hard-and-fast rule—your target asset allocation will fluctuate as you invest more money and your plans change.

On the other hand, Kristy and Bryce, who reached financial independence at thirty-one and thirty-two, respectively, and are now in their mid-thirties, are more conservative and have shifted their investments to 60 percent stocks and 40 percent bonds so they can get a fixed amount of pretty much guaranteed income. No matter what happens in the stock market, their investments are set up to generate between $30,000 and $40,000 in dividends and fixed income while maintaining their investment principal. They prefer the security over the growth potential, but since they do have 60 percent invested in stocks, they can still participate in the gains as the stock market goes up, just at a lower rate than Brandon or I do. J.P., who reached financial independence at twenty-eight, is also conservative, but not as much as Kristy and Bryce. She has about 70 percent of her portfolio in stocks and 30 percent in bonds/fixed income.

Here are asset allocation recommendations based on your age and years to retirement. While I still recommend you use years to retirement

Age	Years to Number	Stocks	Bonds	Cash	Age	Years to Number	Stocks	Bonds	Cash

Asset Allocation Recommendations Until You Hit Your Number

Age	Years to Number	Stocks	Bonds	Cash	Age	Years to Number	Stocks	Bonds	Cash
20	5	100%	0%	0%	35	5	70%	20%	10%
20	10	100%	0%	0%	35	10	80%	20%	0%
20	15	100%	0%	0%	35	15	80%	20%	0%
20	20	100%	0%	0%	35	20	80%	20%	0%
20	25	100%	0%	0%	35	25	80%	20%	0%
20	30	100%	0%	0%	35	30	90%	10%	0%
20	35	100%	0%	0%	35	35	90%	10%	0%
20	40	100%	0%	0%	40	5	60%	30%	10%
25	5	100%	0%	0%	40	10	80%	10%	10%
25	10	100%	0%	0%	40	15	80%	10%	10%
25	15	100%	0%	0%	40	20	80%	10%	10%
25	20	100%	0%	0%	40	25	90%	10%	0%
25	25	100%	0%	0%	40	30	100%	0%	0%
25	30	100%	0%	0%	45	5	60%	30%	10%
25	35	100%	0%	0%	45	10	70%	20%	10%
25	40	100%	0%	0%	45	15	80%	20%	0%
30	5	100%	0%	0%	45	20	80%	20%	0%
30	10	100%	0%	0%	45	25	100%	0%	0%
30	15	100%	0%	0%	50	5	60%	30%	10%
30	20	100%	0%	0%	50	10	60%	40%	0%
30	25	100%	0%	0%	50	15	60%	40%	0%
30	30	100%	0%	0%	50	20	70%	30%	0%
30	35	100%	0%	0%	55	10	60%	40%	0%
30	40	100%	0%	0%	55	15	60%	40%	0%

as the guide, I've also included baseline age asset allocation recommendations since they are a good reference point if you are just starting out.

Please adjust these as you see fit, and also remember that you should adjust your asset allocation as you get closer to wanting to retire. How you set your allocation is up to your appetite for risk/reward and what helps you sleep at night. To help you determine your own target asset allocation, the chart below shows the past performance of each allocation percentage over the past one, five, ten, and twenty years. For the stock investments, the money is invested in the Vanguard Total Stock Market ETF (VTI) index fund and the bond investments are in the Vanguard Total Bond Market ETF (BND) index fund.

As you can see, over the past ten years, the returns of a 100 percent stock portfolio would have outperformed the returns of a 100 percent bond portfolio by 4.54 percent per year. In the past year, the same 100 percent stock portfolio would have returned 17.54 percent more than a 100 percent bond portfolio. While these types of returns of course aren't guaranteed, these are solid benchmarks you can use to select your own target asset allocation.

After you determine your target allocation, you should maintain it across all of your investment accounts. This doesn't mean that if your target asset allocation is 60 percent stocks/40 percent bonds that you have to have 60 percent stocks/40 percent bonds in every investment account; it just means that your total allocation across all accounts hits those target percentages. You could have 100 percent of your 401(k) in stocks and 80 percent of your IRA in bonds, but it could average out to 60 percent/40 percent depending on the amount of money you've invested in each. The easiest way to monitor your allocation is to use a free net worth investment tracking app that you can find at https://financialfreedombook.com/tools

Once you set your investments up (or adjust them) to align with your target asset allocation, you should try to maintain this allocation as you invest more money and the market fluctuates. Maintaining your allocation will help ensure that you get the highest returns possible based on the level of risk you are willing to take.

Readjusting your allocation rates so they align with your target allocation is known as rebalancing and should be done quarterly (four times a

THE SEVEN-STEP FAST TRACK INVESTMENT STRATEGY

Bond/Stock Performance Over Past 10 Years at Each Target Asset Allocation

Stocks	Bonds	Annual Percentage Return			
		1 Year	3 years	5 years	10 years
0%	100%	3.62%	2.18%	2.04%	4.18%
10%	90%	5.37%	3.07%	3.39%	4.63%
20%	80%	7.13%	3.96%	4.74%	5.09%
30%	70%	8.88%	4.85%	6.09%	5.54%
40%	60%	10.64%	5.74%	7.44%	6.00%
50%	50%	12.39%	6.63%	8.80%	6.45%
60%	40%	14.14%	7.52%	10.15%	6.90%
70%	30%	15.90%	8.41%	11.50%	7.36%
80%	20%	17.65%	9.30%	12.85%	7.81%
90%	10%	19.41%	10.19%	14.20%	8.27%
100%	0%	21.16%	11.08%	15.55%	8.72%

SOURCE: Vanguard.com data as of 12/31/17

year). For example, because of market fluctuations or automated investing, your 60 percent/40 percent target could become 80 percent/20 percent if, say, stocks go way up and increase in value exponentially over bonds.

For instance, let's say you invest $100,000 in 80 percent ($80,000) stocks and 20 percent ($20,000) bonds. Over the next several months, the stock market averages a return of 20 percent, which means you end up with $96,000 in stocks. Meanwhile, bonds averaged a return of 3 percent, so you have $20,600 in bonds for a total portfolio of $116,600. Your allocation is now weighted 82.3 percent in favor of stocks and 17.6 percent in favor of bonds, so your target of 80/20 is off, exposing you to slightly more risk.

This is why it's important to rebalance four times a year. Simply sell some of the assets you have too much of (in this case, stocks) and use that money to purchase more of the assets you should have more of to get back to your target asset allocation. In this case, you could also buy more bonds to rebalance. In many cases, it's always better to buy more of an asset to rebalance, since you are investing more money and don't have a potential tax consequence for selling your investments. However, if you do decide to sell your investments to rebalance, you should do it within your tax-advantaged accounts so you won't have to pay taxes on the selling and repurchasing of stocks or bonds.

STEP 4: EVALUATE YOUR CURRENT FEES (AND TRY TO KEEP THEM AS LOW AS POSSIBLE!)

Investment fees can have an enormous impact on how quickly your money grows, how much money you'll have within a given time frame, and how many years it will take you to reach financial independence.

Any company that holds or manages your investments is going to charge a fee to do so, and there are typically multiple layers of fees when investing. For example, if you invest in your company's 401(k) plan, you pay a fee to the company that manages the plan and also to each company that manages the investment vehicles inside the 401(k). Also be on the lookout for what are known as *load fees,* which are extra fees that some 401(k) or 403(b) management companies sometimes charge if they are smaller. And that's just for your 401(k). You will have fees for all of your investments and investment accounts.

The more you pay in fees, the less money you have compounding, and while 0.5 to 1 percent of your investments might not seem like a lot, it adds up over time. Remember that compounding works both ways, so every 0.1 percent in fees negatively compounds year after year. Fees also have a bigger impact the younger you are, since the impact of the fees has longer to compound.

I was recently talking with a married couple, whom I'll call Jim and Jane. Jim and Jane are both lawyers and work 70 plus hour weeks and travel constantly, leaving their kids at home with a nanny. They are both making a lot of sacrifices to make a lot of money, but when we started discussing their investments, they eventually admitted that they were working with a financial advisor who charges them 1 percent of their investment assets every year to manage their accounts, even if their investments are down.

During the conversation, they confessed that they really didn't know what they were invested in. "But our money is growing," they told me. "And we are happy enough with our advisor, who is one of Jim's longtime friends from college."

While I don't have the couple's entire financial history, I do know that they have at least $1.5 million in investments and they are in their early forties, so here is a very realistic scenario to show the impact of their investment fees on their portfolio. Let's assume they started with $100,000 in investments and contribute $75,000 to their investments every year for twenty-five years (about the time they have before they reach the traditional retirement age of sixty-two to sixty-five). Check this out:

Fund 1: Investing directly in stock market index fund charging 0.04 percent in fees

Fund 2: Investing in actively managed funds (1.2 percent fee) with a financial advisor (1 percent) fee, for a total fee of 2.2 percent.

As you can see, because of the 2.2 percent in investment fees they were charged, they lost 29.2 percent of their investment returns over that twenty-five-year period. If they invested in a simple index fund with low

Fund 1	Fund 2
After- Fee Investment Value	
$5,178,096	$3,687,812
$ Lost in Fees	
$−33,325	$−1,523,609
% Lost in Fees	
−0.6%	−29.2%
Fee Savings (Fund 1−Fund 2)	
$1,490,284	

fees that tracked the U.S. stock market instead of working with a financial advisor and investing in actively managed funds, they could have $1,490,284 more when they retire! That's a massive amount of money they could have if they just paid a little bit more attention and invested in mutual funds with lower fees and managed their investments themselves.

Even if you don't have millions of dollars to invest, a small difference in fees can potentially subtract hundreds of thousands of dollars from your potential earnings. Fees also matter once you do retire, because if you are living off 3 to 4 percent of your investment gains and your investments are growing an average of 7 percent per year, then taking out another 1 percent for fees means you will be able to keep only 2 to 3 percent of the investment gains in the market.

If you have investment accounts, I encourage you to check your fees right now by looking at your investment statements and the prospectus of each fund you invest in. Fill out the annual fee chart below. For investment accounts note the percentage you are being charged to have your investments managed, as well as any additional administrative fees.

In the account column, list the type of account (e.g., 401(k) or IRA); in the investment column list the investment (i.e., the name of the fund, stock, or bond invested in); in the company fee column, list the annual fee the company holding your investments *charges to hold the investment.* This is typically an annual management fee charged by the 401(k) company your employer uses or an annual fee the company who manages your IRA might charge.

Next, list any investment fees a *company charges to manage the actual investments* (for example, what the mutual fund company charges to run the mutual fund). The company that manages the investment (Vanguard, for example, manages the Vanguard Total Stock Market ETF (VTI) index fund) charges you a percentage of your balance in that investment, which is known as the expense ratio. For the Vanguard Total Stock Market ETF (VTI) index fund, the expense ratio is 0.04 percent as of this writing, which means you have to pay 0.04 percent per year of the money you have invested in that ETF ($40 per year for every $10,000 invested). This is a really low expense ratio.

Finally, list any fees you pay for a financial advisor if you have one.

THE SEVEN-STEP FAST TRACK INVESTMENT STRATEGY

	Account	Investment	Company Fee	Investment Fee or Expense Ratio	Financial Advisor Fee
1					
2					
3					
4					
5					
6					
7					
8					
9					
10					
11					
12					
13					
14					
15					

Here's a hypothetical snapshot of someone's investments and their fees to show you what your chart could look like.

Remember even a small difference in fees can make a massive difference over time, so any fee over 0.30 percent should be reevaluated, since there are likely more affordable but similar investment options you could choose. In some cases, as with your 401(k), the fees are determined based on the company your employer chooses to administer the plan, so you likely won't be able to reduce them. But if the fees are high, definitely talk to the human resources department at your company to see what they can do.

	Account	Investment	Company Fee	Investment Fee or Expense Ratio	Financial Advisor Fee
1	401(k)	Vanguard VTSAX	$200/year	0.04%	
2	401(k)	Fidelity Magellan	$200/year	0.67%	
3	401(k)	T Rowe Price PREIX	$200/year	0.23%	
4	Roth IRA	Vanguard S&P 500	free	0.04%	
5	Roth IRA	Vanguard VTIAX	free	0.11%	
6	Roth IRA	WBI Tactical	free	1.10%	
7	Brokerage	AMZN	$7.95 per trade	N/A	
8	Brokerage	FACE	$7.95 per trade	N/A	
9	SEP IRA	Vanguard Target 2045	free	0.16%	
10					
11					
12					
13					
14					
15					

STEP 5: PICK THE RIGHT INVESTMENTS

Next, we are going to pick investments that have low fees, minimize the impact of taxes, and maximize your returns.

While you can pick any investment you want within your IRA accounts, your 401(k) (or 403(b) if you work for a nonprofit) investment options will depend on what your company plan offers.

While you could theoretically go out and buy a bunch of individual stocks and bonds to diversify your portfolio, the easiest way to diversify your investments is to buy mutual funds or ETFs (exchange traded funds). These are packages of investments that allow you to invest in multiple stocks or bonds at once without having to buy a bunch of different products.

Both mutual funds and ETFs are built for the purpose of simple diversification, and either type of fund holds a collection of stocks, a collection of bonds, or a mixture of stocks and bonds (known as blended funds). These funds are typically built around a theme or sector—meaning they hold a group of investments of a specific type or within a particular industry. Mutual funds and ETFs are very similar, but mutual funds are priced only once a day by the fund insurer, while ETFs behave like stocks and the value can fluctuate throughout the day. Fees for owning these funds are often similar, though ETFs tend to be easier to manage and have no investment minimums.

Most companies offer a selection of five to thirty mutual funds and/or ETFs that include U.S. and international stock funds, bond funds, blended funds (stocks and bonds together), target date funds (blended funds that include a stock/bond allocation that will typically get more conservative as you get closer to traditional retirement age), as well as funds for things like gold and cash.

In order to try to make investing easier, some 401(k)/403(b) providers will offer what are called *model portfolios,* which are designed around a certain level of risk—from conservative to aggressive—and allocate the included investments in a way that aligns with that risk level. But these model portfolios often have high fees and are overly complicated. You should question any of the "default" investment options or selections in the account, since some 401(k) providers recommend the ones that will make them the most money and aren't necessarily best for you.

Also remember that you get charged fees for all of the investments you hold within your 401(k) or 403(b). Each fund will have its own management fee/expense ratio, so when you are evaluating which mutual funds to invest in, look at the fees for each one. If the fees are over 0.25 percent, then they are expensive and you should consider other options.

THE CASE FOR INDEX FUNDS

When you buy stock, you are buying a share of ownership in a real company. This means you literally own a small part of the company. As the company makes money or as people believe the value of that company will go up, the price of the stock can go up. The greater the demand for the stock and the more people believe in it, the higher the price can go. It can also go down if the opposite is true and the demand for the stock goes down. Stocks are traded all over the world on many different exchanges (which are basically networks of stocks). This investing strategy splits stocks into two types: domestic (companies in the United States) and international.

If you look at the stock market over relatively short periods of time, you might start to think that investing in stocks resembles gambling more than a safe bet. But over the long term, stocks have proven an incredibly reliable investment. While the entire stock market can swing wildly from one day to the next, and there is certainly risk in investing in stocks, as the country grows, wealth grows and the value of companies—and therefore the value of their stock—continues to grow.

On October 19, 1987, the U.S. stock market dropped 22.61 percent (the biggest percentage daily loss) and on March 15, 1933, the stock market was up 15.34 percent (the biggest daily gain). These are huge daily swings. But over the past hundred years, the entire U.S. stock market has grown an average of 7.3 percent per year. You can see the daily ups and downs in the stock market in the chart below, but the trend has always been up over time.

Unfortunately, many investors don't think about the long term and instead try to get the highest return possible today. When their accounts are down, they sell, thereby guaranteeing that they lose money.

Individual stocks can swing wildly in value over both short and long periods of time, which can either make or lose you a lot of money in a relatively short period of time. If you had bought $5,000 in Amazon stock in 1997, it would be worth at least $2.5 million as of this writing, because during this period Amazon has gone from $18 a share to over $1,200. But since you are investing in a business when you buy stock, there is always the chance that the business could go under and you could lose all of your

ow Jones Industrial Average — tracks US stocks (1900–2017)

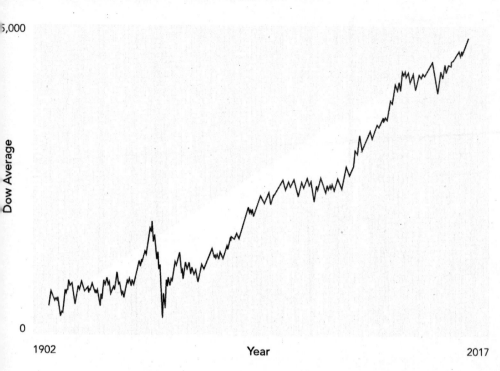

5,000

Dow Average

0

1902   Year   2017

money. Shares of Enron, an energy trading company, went from a high of $90.56 in the year 2000 to a low of $0.67 in January 2002. Stockholders ended up losing a collective $74 billion from investing in Enron stock.

While you might be an amazing stock picker, the odds are against you and the work required to research, analyze, and invest in a selection of companies that you hope will grow faster than the stock market just isn't worth your effort and time.

Research shows that, on average, 90 percent of active investing yields a disappointing performance compared to the stock market as a whole over a fifteen-year period. So instead of going out and trying to pick the next Amazon and investing in just one or a few stocks, you will beat 90 percent of all active stock investors by simply investing in a broad diversified group of U.S. stocks. When you invest in the entire stock market, you are much more likely to achieve the same long-term gains as the whole market, which, as I've already pointed out, has averaged 7.3 percent per year over the past hundred years.

Thankfully it's really simple to invest this way and you need to buy only one type of investment fund that you can buy in all of your investment accounts. To keep your investments as efficient and effective as possible, you should invest in a simple fund that owns a broad selection of the U.S. stock market (known as a total stock market fund) or a fund that owns a small piece of the biggest 500 companies in the United States (what are known as the S&P 500). A total market fund tracks (that is to say, tries to match) the performance of the U.S. stock market by investing in over 2,000 stocks in the United States. An S&P 500 fund is similar but tracks only shares of the top 500 largest companies in the United States.

Because they contain such a broad array of stocks, total stock market index funds allow you to easily invest in a diversified portfolio, and because they are passively managed, they typically have very low management fees and are tax efficient (both of which increase your future returns). Investing in index funds also gives you the opportunity to receive dividends (cash payments) from those stocks that issue them, which help to generate consistent investment gains.

While a total stock market fund offers more diversification, because it invests in more companies (small, medium, and large), the S&P 500 is also diversified, and the largest 500 companies in the United States generate a disproportionately high percentage of the profit and growth of and represent about 75 percent of the entire U.S. stock market. Many companies offer an index fund that tracks the U.S. stock market, and many companies actually offer two levels (investor and admiral/premium), where you pay a higher or lower fee based on how much you invest.

Some of the most popular index funds with the lowest fees are the Vanguard Total Stock Market Index Fund (VTSAX) or Vanguard Total Stock Market Index ETF (VTI), both of which hold the top 2,800 stocks in the United States; the Schwab Total Stock Market Index ETF (SWTSX); BlackRock's iShares Edge MSCI Min Vol USA ETF (USMV); and the Fidelity Total Market Index Fund Premium Class (FSTVX). There are also many companies that have an S&P 500 fund, like the Vanguard 500 Index Fund Investor Shares (VFINX); the Vanguard 500 Index Fund Admiral

THE SEVEN-STEP FAST TRACK INVESTMENT STRATEGY

	Vanguard 500 Index Fund (VFINX)	Vanguard Total Stock Market Index Fund (VTSAX)
1 year (as of 12/31/17)	21.79%	21.17%
3 year	11.38%	11.08%
5 year	15.75%	15.55%
10 year	8.49%	8.72%

Shares (VFIAX); Schwab S&P 500 Index Fund (SWPPX); and the Fidelity Spartan 500 Index Shares (FUSEX).

You might be wondering whether you should pick a total U.S. market fund or an S&P 500 fund. Depending on who runs your retirement accounts at work or the investment company you choose, you may have access only to either a total U.S. market or an S&P 500 fund and not both. Either would be a great choice, and the long-term investment returns will likely be similar between the two. Using the Vanguard 500 Index Fund (VFINX) and Vanguard Total Stock Market Index Fund (VTSAX) as examples, you can see the returns over the past one, three, five, and ten years were pretty similar.

If you are currently investing, how well do your portfolio returns compare to those of either a total stock market or S&P 500 fund? To update these comparison performance numbers, simply do a Google search or go to Vanguard's tool to compare the performance of any two funds.

Have you been one of the rare people to beat the stock market over the past one, three, five, or ten years? While it's definitely possible to "beat the market" over a one-year period, it's really hard to do over a period of five plus years and beat it consistently over the long term.

	Account	Investment	Performance			
			1 year	3 year	5 year	10 year
1						
2						
3						
4						
5						
6						
7						
8						
9						
10						
TOTAL						

Socially Responsible Index Investing

While the returns of a total stock index fund are tough to beat, they can come at a price. One problem I have with total stock index funds is that because they hold a collection of almost all stocks in the U.S. markets, they invest in some companies that have questionable labor, environmental, and health practices. For example, when you buy into an index fund, you are supporting big tobacco, Big Pharma, and companies that have previously been investigated for violating child labor laws.

The older I get, the more important socially responsible investing is becoming to me, so I've started to shift some of my own investments into funds designed for socially responsible investing, like Vanguard's FTSE Social Index Fund (VFTSX). A good ETF to take a look at is the iShares MSCI KLD 400 Social ETF (DSI).

While you are going to sacrifice some returns and the fees are a bit higher with these funds than they are with a total stock index or S&P 500 fund, it might help you sleep at night knowing that you are investing only in companies that are doing good in the world, or at least not doing bad.

> Socially responsible investing becoming easier as more funds are being launched regularly, but like any investment, make sure you do your homework and understand the return trade-offs you are making.

In addition to investing in a U.S. stock index fund if you think that the U.S. stock market is going to perform poorly in the future, you can consider investing a small portion of your portfolio in an international stock index fund for broader diversification. Investing outside of the United States is generally considered to be risker but is useful for diversification because international markets have historically behaved differently from the U.S. stock market. Adding an international stock index fund to your portfolio might give you greater growth potential over the long term, but I recommend you invest no more than 5 percent of your portfolio in an international stock index fund, which is far below the 30 percent that many investment advisors currently recommend.

To keep your investments as efficient and effective as possible you should invest in index funds whenever possible across all of your accounts. You should also set up all of your index fund dividends (the cash issued by the companies who have a dividend in the index fund) to automatically reinvest within the index fund. This means that whenever a company issues a dividend, you will automatically be using the dividend to buy new shares of the index fund to keep your money growing and compounding. If you withdraw your dividends, then the money will either sit in cash within your tax-advantaged account or your will be responsible for paying taxes on the withdrawals from a taxable account. If you do decide to withdraw your dividends for some reason, likely to spend the cash or invest it in something else, some dividends get taxed at a lower qualified dividend tax rate equal to the capital gains tax rates—so you can take the dividends as income and pay less tax than your income tax bracket.

If your target asset allocation is 80 percent stocks/20 percent bonds, you should have 80 percent of your money in stock index funds and 20 percent of your money in bond funds. You can often get all the diversification you need with one or two stock funds and one or two bond funds, in what's known as a simple "three fund" or "four fund" investment portfolio. Don't overcomplicate it. Keeping it simple will make it much easier to minimize fees, minimize taxes, monitor performance, keep diversified, and easily rebalance to maintain you your target asset allocation.

For your stock allocation, opt for a total stock market index fund, which tracks the performance of the entire U.S. stock market, whenever one is available. If you want to be a little more aggressive you can invest most of your money in a total U.S. stock market index fund and then a small percentage in an international stock market fund. My investment accounts have always been invested in a few simple index funds—a total stock market index fund and an international index fund. If you don't have a total stock market index fund, then the next best selection is an S&P 500 index fund.

BUILDING YOUR TOTAL STOCK MARKET FUND IF YOU DON'T HAVE ACCESS TO ONE

If you don't have access to either of these funds, then you can invest in funds to mirror the holdings of those types of funds. In other words, you can create your own diverse portfolio based on a mixture of stocks for different-sized companies that will approximate what you would get in a total market fund. While it will take you a little bit of time to design your own diverse portfolio, it's actually pretty easy and well worth your time to achieve optimal diversification.

All of the publicly traded stocks in the United States fit within one of three buckets: large-cap stock funds (companies with a market value over $10 billion), mid-cap stock funds (companies with a market value between $2 billion and $10 billion), and small-cap stock funds (companies with a market value between $300 million and $2 billion). You can invest in one fund for each of them to build a portfolio that is similar to a total stock market index fund. To do this I recommend investing 40 percent of your stock allocation in a large-cap fund, 30 percent in a mid-cap fund, and 30 percent in a small-cap fund. This will give you the right amount of diversity.

For your bond selection, most bond fund options you will have access to in your 401(k)/403(b) will likely be pretty similar, so you should pick the bond fund with the lowest fees and the most diverse selection of bonds. You can figure this out by looking at the prospectuses for each fund, which are available on either your 401(k) plan website or through a simple Google search. Look for a bond fund that has a collection of government and corporate bonds. Remember you are using bonds to mitigate the risks of your stock holdings, so you don't need to take a lot of risk. Typically, most bond funds will average a return of 2 to 4 percent compounding per year. Look at the one-, five-, and ten-year historical performance of the bond fund within the prospectus and pick one that generates a relatively high and steady return.

You can also consider investing in leveraged municipal (muni) bond funds, which are issued by local and state governments and are a good tax-efficient option and generate a consistent amount of income. You can invest in them easily through a municipal bond ETF. These are popular bond investments for early retirees that want to generate a fixed amount of income.

In the chart below, you will see a number of the popular types of funds and investment options in 401(k)/403(b) plans. Note that the ones your company offers may have different names depending on the company that offers them. I've also included recommendations for how you can achieve your target asset allocation using the funds typically available in these types of accounts. These can also be used to meet your target asset allocation in your IRA. Also note that where there is no percentage recommendation for a particular type of fund, it is because I don't recommend these investments (e.g., income equity funds and international bond funds) if the others are present. You can use this chart as a starting point to create your own diversified portfolio.

You can ignore all of the other options—things like gold and REITs (real estate investment trusts) in your 401(k)s, 403(b)s, or IRAs. While they can add diversification, they aren't really necessary and you are better off focusing just on stocks and bonds in your asset allocation. Keep it simple using total stock market, S&P 500, and total bond market index funds when you can.

Sample Portfolios Based on Target Asset Allocations

Risk (Stock/Bond Allocation)		Sample Portfolios/Asset Allocation by Risk (Left to Right) and Investment Options You Might Have						
		If you have total stock index fund	If you don't have total iwwndex, but have S&P Index	If you don't have total stock index fund you can create that diversity	If you only have target date funds			
		100%/0%	100%/0%	100%/0%	Depends on target fund	80/20%	70/30%	60/40%
Stock Funds								
Total Stock Market Index	Tracks the entire stock market. Huge benefits are instant diversification and low fees. If you have access to this type of passively managed index fund, it's a great option.	100%				80%		60%
S&P 500 Index	Tracks the S&P 500, so offers diversification but skewed to the large-cap stocks		100%					
Large-Cap Stocks	A fund of companies worth at least $10 billion. These are the biggest companies in the US, which makes the more stable and some issues cash payments (dividends)			40%			40%	
Mid-Cap Stocks	A fund of companies worth between $2 and $10, billion who offer higher potential returns, but with greater risk, since they have more growth potential			30%			20%	
Small-Cap Stocks	A fund of companies worth between $300 million and $2 million. Investing is risker, but has highest potential returns			30%			10%	
Growth	Funds, focused on growth that typically are actively managed, so they have higher management fees							
Income Equity Funds	A collection of stocks that pay dividends so the income is consistent. These can be helpful for balancing early retirement portfolios							
International/ Emerging Market	Historically international and emerging market stocks perform the opposite of the U.S. stock market, so they can help with diversification, but I don't recommend							
Bond Funds								
Domestic	A collection of short- and long-term U.S. bonds					20%	30%	40%
International	A collection of international bonds, riskier than the U.S.							
Blended Funds (Stocks/Bonds)								
Target Dates (ex: Target 2050)	These are funds of funds that auto-rebalance as you get closer to the target date. You can get cheaper fees picking the mix yourself, but if index funds aren't available, target date funds can be a good option.				100%			
Income/ Dividend Funds	A collection of governments and corporate debt, and stocks that pay dividends. Will generate consistent returns/income							
Other								
Gold	Tracks gold, too conservative, not worth investing in							
Cash/Money Market Funds	Fixed income, like holding your money in cash							
Real Estate Investment Trusts	Holds pieces of real estate investments, can be used for diversification							

STEP 6: MAX OUT YOUR TAX-ADVANTAGED ACCOUNTS

Taxes can take a massive chunk out of the future earnings of your investments, so it's important to minimize their impact as much as possible. If you're not currently a money nerd, this is how you become one. Learning about tax optimization might sound boring but it will save AND make you a ton of extra money in your investments. Here's how much.

Let's say you make $100,000 per year and plan to invest 10 percent ($10,000) of your salary per year and need to decide whether to invest it in a tax-advantaged or taxable account. You are in the hypothetical 30 percent tax bracket and your employer offers a 4 percent salary match for your 401(k) contributions.

Here's the performance difference of that single $10,000 per year investment over the next thirty years. When you invested in a tax-advantaged account like a 401(k), you can contribute that money without paying taxes on it, so if your contribution is $10,000, with your employer contribution of 4 percent ($4,000), your total contribution is $14,000. Growing at 7 percent per year over the next thirty years, that $14,000 would be worth $106,572. Let's say you contribute that same $14,000 every year over the thirty years; because of the impact of ongoing contributions and compounding, you'd have contributed $300,000 of your own money and your employer would have contributed $120,000. This $420,000 growing at 7 percent per year over the next thirty years would be worth $1,521,594! Because you contributed $300,000 of your own money, your investment return would be $1,221,594.

When you withdraw it in retirement, likely your income will be much lower, so let's say you are married and filing jointly and in the 12 percent tax bracket; you would have approximately $1,369,434, or a $1,069,434 return on your original investment.

Now, if you invested that same $10,000 in a taxable account, you would have to pay your 30 percent taxes on the money before investing it and you wouldn't get any employee match, so you would be able to invest only $7,000. That $7,000 growing at 7 percent per year would be worth $53,286 after thirty years, and if you contributed the same $7,000 in the taxable account each year, growing at 7 percent each year it would be worth $760,797 after 30 years. You would have contributed $210,000 over that thirty-year period, resulting in investment profits of $550,797. If you are in the same position and married and filing jointly, you would be subject to a capital gains tax, so if you kept your income under $77,200, then you would pay 0 percent tax on the gains.

The return of investing in a tax-advantaged account with an employer match was huge. Investing in a tax-advantaged account, you would have $760,797 more money in your account and $608,637 more to spend after paying taxes when you withdraw the money.

The key to getting the maximum tax benefits is to strategize:

1. when you put money into your investments
2. when you take the money out of the investment

When you contribute money to a tax-advantaged account, you are able to take a tax deduction when you invest new money into the account (thus reducing your annual tax bill) or when you withdraw money from the account (thus reducing your tax burden later). There are big advantages with both types of accounts. Optimizing for taxes will make a difference not only in how much money you have to live on today, but also in how much you have to invest for the future.

You can invest in three types of investment accounts:

	Taxable account	Tax-Advantaged 401(k) with match	Benefit of Tax-Advantaged Account
Total Value	$760,797	$1,521,594	$760,797
Total Return	$550,797	$1,221,594	$670,797
After-Tax Total Value	$760,797	$1,369,434	$608,637
After-Tax Total Return	$550,797	$1,069,434	$518,637

1. **Tax-free contributions: tax-advantaged accounts where you don't pay taxes when you invest the money, but you do pay taxes with you withdraw money.**
   - Types of accounts: 401(k) offered by employers, Solo 401(k) for individuals with self-employment income, 403(b) accounts, 457(b) accounts, Traditional IRA (individual retirement account), SEP IRA (simplified employee pension individual retirement account), HSA (health savings accounts)
   - Investment principal/contributions: Taxed on withdrawal
   - Investment gains: Taxed on withdrawal
   - Tax deduction: In most cases your contributions are tax deductible, so they reduce your amount of taxable income
   - Withdrawal policy: 10 percent early withdrawal penalty if you withdraw before age fifty-nine and a half, but there are strategies you'll learn to eliminate this penalty
   - Contributions limits: Yes
2. **Tax-free withdrawals: tax-advantaged accounts where you pay tax before you invest the money, but don't pay taxes when you withdraw money**
   - Types of accounts: Roth 401(k) offered by employers, Roth IRA (individual retirement account)
   - Investment principal/contributions: Taxed before contribution
   - Investment gains: Not taxed on withdrawal
   - Tax deduction: Your contributions are not tax deductible
   - Withdrawal policy: You can withdraw contributions anytime tax-free from a Roth IRA (there are restrictions on 401(k)), there is a 10 percent early withdrawal penalty on investment gains if you withdraw before age fifty-nine and a half, but there are strategies you'll learn to eliminate this penalty
3. **Taxable accounts where you pay tax before you invest the money and also when you withdraw it**
   - Types of accounts: Stock and mutual fund holding brokerage accounts

- Investment principal/contributions: Taxed before contribution
- Investment gains: Taxed at withdrawal
- Tax deduction: Your contributions are not tax deductible
- Withdrawal policy: No penalties

This doesn't mean you shouldn't pay your taxes—it means that you should use the tax law to your advantage and pay what you actually owe. Many people pay a lot more in taxes than they should be paying (perhaps one of the reasons the government makes the tax code so long and confusing?).

You can optimize your money by using the right accounts in the right way and to their maximum benefit. There are many types of investment accounts, some designed for retirement planning offered by an employer and others for individual investors. While many employers offer some form of a retirement account, there are often restrictions on what kind of investments you can make in them. Typically, investment options in employer-managed accounts are limited to a few funds, which limits the control you have. For example, you can't buy individual stocks within a 401(k) account offered by your company, but you can in your own IRA or brokerage (i.e., taxable) accounts.

There are also restrictions on which types of tax-advantaged accounts you can have at the same time and contribute to in each year, as well as how much money you can contribute within a given year. The most popular types of tax-advantaged accounts with their limits, advantages, and limitations are highlighted below:

Now that you know what to invest in, here's how you should maximize each account. You should always try to max out your tax-advantaged retirement accounts before investing your money anywhere else. There are two types of tax-advantaged accounts—those offered by most employers (401(k), 403(b), 457(b)) and those that you can buy on your own, which are known as IRAs (individual retirement accounts). While there are some restrictions that we will cover, you should maximize your contributions to both of these types of tax-advantaged accounts.

There are two types of both 401(k) and IRAs. There are the traditional plans, which allow you to contribute money tax-free until you withdraw it

Account	Employer or Individual	Tax Advantaged	Investment Holdings	Contribution Limits if you are under 50 (2018)	Contribution Limits if you are over 50 (2018)	Advantages	Other Restrictions
Traditional 401(k)	Employer	Upon Investment	Mutual Funds and ETFS	$18,500	$24,500		
Roth 401(k)	Employer	Upon Withdrawal					
Employer (non-profit)	Employer	Upon Investment	Mutual Funds and ETFS	$18,500	$24,500		
457(b)	Employer (Government)	Upon Investment	Mutual Funds and ETFS	$18,500	$24,500	You can take your money out penalty free before 59.5	
Roth IRA	Individual	Upon Withdrawal	Anything	$5,500	$6,500	You can get out your money and gains tax-free	Can only contribute to a Roth IRA or Traditional IRA each year
Traditional IRA	Individual	Upon Investment	Anything	$5,500	$6,500		
SEP IRA	Individual	Upon Investment	Anything	$55,000	N/A		Can't contribute to both SEP IRA and Solo 401(k)
Solo 401(k)	Individual	Upon Investment	Mutual Funds and ETFS	$55,000	$61,000	If you work for yourself you can contribute money as both an employer and employee up to $53,000!	Can't contribute if you have a 401(k) at your employer
HSA (Health Savings Account)	Individual	Upon Investment	Mutual Funds and ETFS	Individuals: $3,450 Families: $6,900	Over 55, $1,000 more		

at a later date. And then there are Roth accounts, which are taxable up front (meaning you pay taxes on any money you contribute) but not on withdrawal. In other words, you can withdraw money (including gains) tax-free. Not all companies offer Roth options, but they are getting more popular.

HOW TO INVEST IN EACH OF YOUR ACCOUNTS

A quick reminder that what follows below is the most tax-efficient order to invest in each of your tax-advantaged accounts. However, you might find a reason to diverge from it based on your specific situation or goals. There are also always going to be exceptions to these guidelines, since there are way too many nuances than can be covered in this book and there will likely be tax law changes in the future. As with all of these investment recommendations, please use this as a set of guidelines to adapt to your personal situation over time.

Max out your government 457(b) plan if you have one.

A government 457(b) plan is hands down the best tax-advantaged investment account available because you are allowed to withdrawal the money penalty free before you are fifty-nine and a half. This makes it a great early retirement investment option since you can use the money whenever you want in the future. While there is no early withdrawal penalty, you will be taxed on your withdrawals at your income tax rate. However, note that this benefit is typically only for government-offered 457(b) plans, not 457(b) plans offered by nongovernment agencies, which have more restrictions.

Another great benefit of the government 457(b) plan is that if you have one in addition to a 401(k) or 403(b), then you are in luck, because you can contribute $18,500 to each account pretax. If you want to retire early and have a government 457(b) plan, you should max it out before investing in any of your other tax-advantaged investment accounts. This allows you to invest a total of $37,000 of pretax dollars.

If you don't have a government 457(b), but you have access to a 401(k) or 403(b) plan, you should contribute enough to get your employer 401(k) or 403(b) match.

The next, and likely first, account you should take full advantage of is your 401(k) or 403(b) offered by your employer. If your employer offers a matching contribution on its 401(k) or 403(b), contribute as much money as you need to get the full employer match. For example, if your employer matches 100 percent of your contribution up to 4 percent of your salary, then contribute 4 percent of your salary. Some employers match only 50 percent of your contributions, but that's still like getting a 50 percent return on your money, so you want to max it out. This is completely free money!

401(k) accounts come in two forms—Traditional and Roth. Here are the guidelines for whether you should contribute to a Traditional 401(k) or Roth 410(k) account. Many employers don't offer a Roth 401(k), but if they do, then whether you should choose a Traditional 401(k) or Roth 401(K) depends on if you believe your tax bracket will be higher or lower in the future when you need withdraw the money.

Typically you would expect your income to be less when you retire, so taking the tax deduction today by contributing to a Traditional 401(k) pretax would be a wise choice, but if you anticipate that you might be making a lot more money in the future or that tax brackets will increase, then a Roth 401(k), which you contribute after-tax dollars to, would be the better choice.

However, if you plan to retire early and want to withdraw your money before you are fifty-nine and a half years old, the Roth 401(k) presents a few challenges, so I recommend you invest in a Traditional 401(k), because your tax bracket will likely be lower when you retire, so taking the tax break up-front makes the most sense. As we already mentioned, the Traditional 401(k) will give you more opportunities to eliminate early withdraw penalties through a Roth conversion ladder presented in chapter 12. In most cases, if you qualify for the tax deduction from a Traditional 401(k), then you should invest in a Traditional 401(k) over a Roth 401(k).

The benefits of investing in a 401(k) or 403(b) are that you are able to:

1. **Contribute the money without paying taxes on it.** The advantage is that you are able to invest at least 10 to 37 percent more money (depending on your tax bracket), which means more money that can grow and compound over time.

2. **You can deduct the contribution amounts from your taxable income, so you end up paying less income tax.** The advantage is that since you are able to deduct your contributions to your retirement accounts from your taxable income, you end up paying less tax now, and depending on your other tax deductions, your contributions might push you into a lower tax rate, thereby further reducing your entire tax bill.

3. **Many employers offer a contribution match, which is free money and will amplify your investment returns.** Many employers off to match your contributions based on percentage of your salary between 2 and 5 percent. Always contribute to get the match.

Next, max out your (Health Saving Account) HSA if you have one.

With healthcare costs continuing to rise, some employers are offering HSAs where you can contribute pretax money to help you cover your medical costs. Two of the biggest benefits of contribution to an HSA account, and why you should contribute to it before your IRA (Individual Retirement Account), is that you are able to both deduct your contributions from your taxable income and use the money you contribute (and the investment gains) tax-free anytime for medical expenses. This means you get double the tax benefits, because you get a tax deduction when you contribute the money and when you withdraw it tax-free to use for medical expenses! Huge benefit.

Your HSA is also just like having another retirement account because you get to keep any money you don't spend each year and your investments will continue to grow and compound each year you don't use the money, just as in a 401(k) or IRA. You can then withdraw from your HSA to cover your medical expenses at any time if you need the money, but if you let it keep growing after the age of sixty-five, you can then withdraw your investment and investment gains to use for any purpose, even if it's not medically related.

To take full advantage of the tax benefits of an HSA, you should maximize your contributions to it each year and pay for your medical expenses out of your cash account if you can afford it, leaving your HSA contributions invested to maximize its growth over time. You can contribute up to $3,450 per year if you are single and $6,900 if you are married. If you are over fifty, you can contribute an extra $1,000, so it's $4,450 per year if you are single, $7,900 if you are married. It's worth noting that you typically need to enroll in a higher-deductible healthcare insurance plan when you enroll in an HSA, so if you have medical issues or to go to the doctor a lot, you might end up spending more on medical bills using an HSA. Run the numbers to see if it makes sense for you.

Open and max out an IRA (Individual Retirement Account).

As of this writing, you can contribute up to $5,500 a year to your Traditional IRA or Roth IRA. Whether or not you should invest in a Traditional IRA or Roth IRA account depends on how much money you are currently making, what your tax bracket is after deductions and exemptions, and whether you believe your tax bracket will be higher or lower in the future. Here are some guidelines:

1. **If you are in a low tax bracket and qualify based on your income level, you should invest in a Roth account so you have the ability to withdraw the money tax-free when you might be in a higher tax bracket (either because you are making more money or tax brackets get increased in the future).**

2. **If you make too much money to contribute to a Roth, then you should contribute to a Traditional IRA because you can take the up-front tax deduction on your contribution, reducing the amount of taxes you pay today because your tax bracket is likely going to be higher today than when you choose to retire.**

   If you plan to retire early, then there are distinct advantages to investing in a Traditional IRA account over a Roth IRA account, since you can eliminate the 10 percent early withdrawal penalty by eventually converting your Traditional account to a Roth IRA account as you get closer to retirement. Because of a strategy known as a Roth IRA conversion ladder (which I'll explain in detail in chapter 12), you can withdraw the money you converted from your Traditional IRA to a Roth IRA, and paid tax on, five years later without paying the 10 percent withdrawal penalty and tax-free because you paid tax when you converted the money.

3. **If you make too much money to take the Traditional IRA deduction, then you should invest in a non-tax-deductible Traditional IRA and immediately do a backdoor Roth IRA conversion and convert the contribution to a Roth IRA.** Even though you make too much money to contribute to a Roth IRA, the IRS allows you to do a conversion and pay tax on any money you convert if you haven't paid tax on it already. But if your income was too high to take the Traditional IRA deduction, then you have already paid tax on your Traditional IRA contribution, so you have to pay taxes only on the gains (which if you convert quickly will be low or even none). If you already have a balance in a Traditional IRA that you previously took a deduction for, you could be subject to additional taxes when doing a Roth conversion. If that's the case, it's still worth doing a conversion, but you might need some help from your IRA company to do the conversion in the most tax-efficient way.

Most investment companies that manage IRAs have tools that let you do this conversion easily. If you do the conversion right away, you don't have to pay any taxes on the conversion as long as you don't have any other money in a Traditional IRA.

A quick recap, since we covered a lot: If you qualify for Roth IRA, then you should invest in one, but if you don't qualify for a Roth, then you should invest in a Traditional IRA and take advantage of the tax deduction, and if you don't qualify for a tax deduction, then you should invest in a Traditional IRA and do the backdoor Roth conversion. While this might sound a little complicated, you will pick it up quickly after doing it once, and then each year your contributions will just be a regular part of your routine.

Next max out your 401(k) or 403(b).

If you make more than $135,000 as a single person or $199,000 as a couple, then you can't contribute to a Roth IRA. If this is the case, then you should go ahead and max out your Traditional IRA to take advantage of those tax benefits. As of this writing, you can contribute up to $18,500 in your 401(k) or 403(b).

If you have a side hustle or work for yourself, set up an SEP IRA or Solo 401(k) and invest as much money as you can.

If you have a side hustle in addition to your full-time job, and you've already maxed out your 401(k) and IRA, then you should open either an SEP IRA (simplified employee pension) or a Solo 401(k) so you can invest some of your side-hustle money pretax. Here is how to choose between an SEP IRA and a Solo 401(k).

In a SEP IRA you can contribute up to 25 percent of your income, which ends up, after Social Security and Medicare taxes, being approximately 20 percent of your annual profit. If you make $100,000 side hustling, then you can put $20,000 into your SEP IRA, reducing your tax burden by $20,000 and increasing your investments. The maximum that you can contribute to a SEP IRA is $55,000, so you would need to make $230,000 in business profit to max it out. SEP IRAs are good for side-hustle income whether you have a 401(k) or not, but you can invest in both a 401(k) offered by your employer and a SEP IRA.

You can have a Solo 401(k), also known as an Individual 401(k), only if you don't have any employees, and depending on your personal situation, you can actually contribute more money to a Solo 401(k). For example, while both the SEP IRA and a Solo 401(k) have a $55,000 contribution limit and you can contribute up to 20 percent of your profit into either of them, but with a Solo 401(k), you can also contribute an additional $18,500 as an employee (of yourself!). It's like giving yourself a company match. And remember, you can deduct all of that money from your taxable income. So if you make $100,000 profit but put $38,500 in your Solo 401(k) ($20,000 in profit + $18,500 as an employee), you will be taxed on only $61,500 of your income. Because of this double contribution benefit, it makes more sense to open a Solo 401(k) instead of a SEP IRA if you work for yourself, since you get more flexibility and can potentially contribute more money.

Even if you have a full-time job that offers a 401(k), you can still open your own Solo 401(k), but the maximum employee contribution is $18,500 total across both accounts, meaning you can't contribute the additional $18,500 (in addition to 20 percent of your profit) to your Solo 401(k) if you've maxed out your employer 401(k). But you can still make the 20 percent profit contribution to a Solo 401(k) even if you have a 401(k) through your employer.

Contribute to your FSA (flexible spending account).

An FSA is like an HSA, where you can contribute pretax money to use for medical expenses, but unlike an HSA, you lose any money you don't spend by the end of the year so the benefits aren't as good. With an FSA you can contribute up to $2,650 to the account each year.

However, another benefit you should ask your employer about is a dependent care FSA, which many companies offer but few employees know about. With a dependent care FSA, you can contribute money pretax to an account you can use to cover care expenses for your dependents (children or disabled relatives), including summer camps, day care, preschool, and babysitting services. If you have access to a dependent care FSA and are married and file taxes jointly, then you can contribute up to $5,000 per year to your dependent care FSA. Hooray for tax-free day care!

Contribute to a 529 if you have kids.

If you have children, you can open a 529 plan that can grow tax-free to cover the cost of college for when your children are older. These plans are offered through each state, and while you can't deduct your contributions from your federal taxes, some states do offer tax deductions. However, you shouldn't invest in a 529 until you have maxed out your own tax-advantaged investment accounts because the tax benefits of a 529 aren't as valuable and you should be saving for your retirement (and own future security) before saving for your kid's college fund. Regardless, what you invest in a 529 can grow tax-free, and the withdrawals for eligible education expenses are also tax-free. While there are no contribution or income limits, some states do place restrictions on the total balance you can have in a 529 account, so check with your state guidelines.

STEP 7: INVEST IN TAXABLE ACCOUNTS

After you've maxed out your tax-advantaged accounts, if you still have money left over to invest, you will want to open a taxable (aka brokerage) account. If you want to reach financial independence as early as possible, then you need to be investing quite a bit of money into after-tax accounts, because the contribution limits on most tax-advantaged accounts won't allow you to retire as quickly as possible. Even in the best-case scenario with a Roth IRA ($5,500) a 401(k) ($18,500), and a SEP IRA ($55,000), you can contribute only $79,000 a year.

If you happen to be one of the super lucky ones who can also contribute another $18,500 to a 457(b), that will up your annual investment to $97,500, which is $975,000 in ten years (not including investment gains). You might be able to contribute another $3,450 to $6,900 into an HSA, but that only benefits your medical expenses until after you turn sixty-five. So, while contributing $79,000 to $97,500 into tax-advantaged accounts is a lot of money and will definitely help you fast-track your financial freedom, you also want to be investing as much as you can into taxable accounts as well.

Remember when you invest in a taxable account, you are investing the money after you've already paid income tax on it, so you don't get any tax advantages when you invest the money or when you withdraw it later. Except in one case, any investment you hold for over one year is subject to the capital gains tax rate, which is typically lower than income tax rates.

The most popular form of taxable investment account is known as a brokerage account, and you can open one at many companies that offer low fees. A few popular brokerages are Vanguard, Charles Schwab, and Fidelity. Look for a brokerage firm that charges you a simple low transaction fee (less than $5 per trade) to hold your investments, not one that takes a percentage of your investment gains.

Some investment gains in taxable accounts can get taxed at the end of the year. One example is dividends that companies pay out to you in cash. These are taxed whether or not you withdraw or reinvest them. However, tax treatment on dividends depends on the type of dividend, so you should check the tax treatment for each by simply looking at the end-of-year tax statement your investment company generates or by contacting your brokerage company. As long as you've held the stock long enough (length depends on the stock), then some of the dividends might be what are known as qualified dividends, which get taxed at the capital gains tax rate, which is often lower than your income tax rate.

Also, every time you sell anything in your taxable accounts you will be responsible for paying taxes on the investment gains that year. This is why you don't want to be buying and selling a bunch of stocks in your taxable account, because it can lead to a very large tax bill at the end of the year. If the stock loses money when you sell, you can deduct up to $3,000 in losses from your taxes each year. If you lose more than $3,000, then you can carry over the losses into as many years as needed. This is called a loss carry-over, and you can take it for as many years until you are able to deduct all of your losses on your taxes.

If you sell your investments in a taxable account after holding them for

US Federal Tax Brackets and Long-Term Capital Gains (2018)

Tax Bracket	Single Taxpayers	Married Filing Jointly	Head of Household
10%	$0–$9,525	$0–$19,050	$0–$13,600
12%	$9,526–$38,700	$19,051–$77,400	$13,600–$51,800
22%	$38,701–$82,500	$77,401–$165,000	$51,800–$82,500
24%	$82,501–$157,500	$165,001–$315,000	$82,500–$157,500
32%	$157,501–$200,000	$315,001–$400,000	$157,500–$200,000
35%	$200,000–$500,000	$400,001–$600,000	$200,000–$500,000
37%	over $500,000	over $600,000	over $500,000

Long-Term Capital Gains Rate	Single Taxpayers	Married Filing Jointly	Head of Household
0%	$0–$38,600	$0–$77,200	$0–$51,700
15%	$38,600–$425,800	$77,200–$479,000	$51,700–$452,400
20%	over $425,800	over $479,000	over $452,400

SOURCE: Internal Revenue Service

less than a year, you will get taxed at your current income tax rate. If you hold them for longer than a year before you sell them, then you will get taxed at the capital gains rate, which is typically lower than your income tax rate.

A quick note on selling versus withdrawing: In a taxable account, you get taxed when you sell even if you don't withdraw the money, but in a tax-advantaged account, you get taxed only after you sell and withdraw.

Yet another reason why you should be holding stocks for the long term: If you can keep your taxable income below $75,900 if you are married or $37,950 if you are single, then you won't pay any tax on your investment withdrawals from your taxable accounts. *No taxes.* This is one of the massive benefits of keeping your income low (or at least mastering your tax deductions). Tax-free withdrawals means you need less money saved to reach financial independence.

WHAT TO INVEST IN A TAXABLE ACCOUNT

You should largely keep the same investing strategy you are using in your tax-advantaged accounts within your taxable accounts. This means sticking with the same stock and bond allocation you have in your 401(k)/403(b), 457(b), and IRA accounts. So if you have 80 percent of your investments in stocks and 20 percent in bonds in those accounts, then you should invest the same amounts in your taxable accounts. You should also continue to invest in low-cost total stock market index and bond funds, which will have fewer tax implications each year because there is very little buying and selling within those types of funds.

Hold bonds/fixed income assets in your taxable accounts

While it's a bit tougher to do, as your investment balances grow, one strategy you should consider is holding all of your tax-efficient bond funds (across your target asset allocation) within your taxable accounts so you will pay no taxes at the end of each year. Say, for example, you have 100 percent of your investments in stocks/equities across your tax-advantaged accounts and you want to shift your target allocation to 90 percent stocks/10 percent bonds. You could start investing in bonds in your taxable account if you've maxed out your contributions to your tax-advantaged accounts.

Doing this means you don't have to touch your tax-advantaged account asset allocations. Plus you will keep your tax burden as low as possible at the end of each year, since bonds typically have lower returns than stocks.

BUYING INDIVIDUAL STOCKS

While total stock market index funds should form the core of your investing strategy, if you do decide to invest in individual stocks in either an IRA or taxable account, you should buy only stocks that you plan to hold for a long time. While it's not easy to make money picking individual stocks, your chances increase when you believe in the fundamentals of a company and hold the stock for a long period of time. Remember that when you are buying a stock, you are buying a small piece of an actual company, so you should invest only in companies in which you would be proud to be a part owner. If you do pick the right stocks, you can make a lot of money over a long period as the value of a company grows.

While there are tons of self-proclaimed stock-picking experts and individual stock-investing strategies, don't listen to the noise. The individual stock investing strategy that actually works is known as value investing—it's the strategy Warren Buffett, the world's most successful investor over the past fifty years, uses. The idea is that you wait until you find a company that is undervalued and then you invest in it. In other words, you are looking for a deal. If you are interested in investing in individual stocks, check out the book *The Intelligent Investor* by Benjamin Graham, the grandfather of value investing and Warren Buffett's teacher.

Another popular individual stock-investing strategy is known as dividend investing. As you've learned, some companies share some of their profits with their shareholders in the form of a regular cash payment or distribution known as a dividend. These dividends are one of the reasons why it's smart to invest in a total stock market index fund, because you get consistent dividend payments from a bunch of different stocks. There are many investors who build a portfolio of stocks that pay dividends, so they get the added benefit of stocks that can continue to go up in value and they generate consistent fixed income in the form of dividends. One of the risks with this type of strategy is that just because a company pays a dividend one time doesn't mean they always will, and building a collection of dividend stocks is more work than simply investing in an index fund. It is worth exploring, however, if you're interested.

If you decide to invest in individual stocks, then no matter what investing strategy you choose, I recommend you invest only up to 5 percent of your entire investment portfolio in all of your individual stocks combined. It's not worth the risk of betting more of your money on an individual stock when you can generate consistent returns investing in the entire stock market.

To help you visualize how this all fits together, when I was investing to reach financial independence, I invested 100 percent of my money in stocks, with 95 percent in stock index funds and 5 percent in individual equities that I plan to hold for the long haul, like Amazon and Apple. However, over time as the value of my individual stocks has grown, now a higher percentage of my portfolio is dedicated to individual stocks because I haven't sold them.

MY INVESTMENT PORTFOLIO

Below are most of my actual stock investment holdings between 2010 and 2015 and my savings rate when I went from $2.26 to over $1.25 million in five years. While I strongly recommend investing mostly in index funds, there are some individual company stocks that you might believe in so strongly in that you can't not invest in them. I started small, but during this period I ended up over investing in individual stocks because I believed in the long-term potential of Amazon, Facebook, and Apple.

I was one of the first 20,000 Facebook users while a student in college and couldn't not invest during their IPO (initial public offering). While I believe in these company's missions and believe their stock would increase in value, I could never have anticipated the growth over the past seven years. In order to re-diversify and mitigate the risk of owning individual stocks, I have recently been investing additional money into index funds. The key is to use a total stock market index fund as the foundation of your portfolio and build from it based on the level of risk/reward you are willing to take. This is all meant to say be cautious with your individual stock investments, and if you are just starting out don't invest more than 5 percent of your net worth into individual stocks.

What is not included in the chart below are a few stocks that I lost money on and sold during this period (these amounted to less than $5,000 in losses), my investment in the Bitcoin cryptocurrency (which is highly speculative and I don't recommend investing any more than 1 percent of your net worth in any cryptocurrency), or any of my real estate investments.

Investments	2010	2011	2012	2013	2014	2015
Index Funds						
Vanguard Total Stock Market Index Fund (shares)	520	4894	6903	9821	12552	14616
price per share (as of last day of year)	$31.57	$31.30	$35.65	$46.69	$51.60	$50.79
Total Value	$16,416	$153,182	$246,092	$458,542	$647,683	$742,347
Vanguard Total International Stock Index (shares)			1892	2785	3218	3449
price per share (as of last day of year)			$25.05	$28.01	$26.00	$24.24
Total Value			$47,395	$78,008	$83,668	$83,604
Individual Stocks						
Amazon (shares)	30	200	200	300	300	400
price per share (as of last day of year, adjusted for splits)	$180.00	$173.10	$250.87	$398.79	$310.35	$675.89
Total Value	$5,400	$34,620	$50,174	$119,637	$93,105	$270,356
Facebook (shares)			800	900	900	1070
price per share (as of last day of year, adjusted for splits)			$25.91	$54.65	$78.02	$104.66
Total Value			$20,728	$49,185	$70,218	$111,986
Apple (shares)	100	100	100	300	300	400
price per share (as of last day of year, adjusted for splits)	$41.46	$52.05	$69.00	$74.57	$104.86	$101.70
Total Value	$4,146.00	$5,205.00	$6,900.00	$22,371.00	$31,458.00	$40,680.00
Total Income	$43,000	$294,000	$233,000	$248,000	$239,000	$271,000
Savings Rate	53.49%	40.68%	55.97%	68.10%	57.45%	60.48%
Total Invested Each Year	$23,000	$119,610	$130,402	$168,895	$137,317	$163,901
Total invested in Portfolio	$23,000	$142,610	$273,012	$441,907	$579,224	$743,125
Total Percentage Growth	12.88%	35.34%	36.00%	64.68%	59.89%	68.07%
Portfolio Total	$25,962	$193,007	$371,289	$727,743	$926,132	$1,248,973

CONCLUSION

The more you invest, the more your money will grow. Keep at it. While your number might feel massive and unattainable right now, the only way to get there is to take it one day at a time and just get started. If you're sitting on the sidelines because you are afraid you don't know enough about investing, don't. Getting started early is more important than waiting and making the perfect investment. And if you are sitting on the sidelines waiting to "time the market," you're wasting your time. I can't do it. Experts can't do it. No one can do it. Timing the market is impossible. Play the long game.

You'll learn quickly and will figure things out as you go. You are going to make mistakes. I did. We all do. You'll learn from them. An easy way to get started is through automation. You can easily set up your 401(k), Roth IRA, and other investment accounts to automatically deduct money from your paycheck or bank account. Most companies who manage investment accounts make it easy to set up automated investments—so you can buy shares of mutual funds, ETFs, stocks, and bonds automatically on a set schedule. The nice thing about investing is ETFs is that you can buy them in most investment accounts, they have low fees, and most ETFs don't have any minimums (so you can open an account for $5 and invest small amounts every day).

But automation is not enough. As we've already discussed, when you automate your finances, because you are saving consistently, you might feel like you are saving enough, but you aren't saving as much as you can. Saving enough and saving as much as you can are very different.

Remember Travis? He has been automatically saving 5 percent of his salary in his 401(k) account for years, and he thinks that's enough, so he has never increased the amount he's saving each month. Keeping his savings rate at 5 percent will force him to keep working a lot longer than he realizes—likely an additional twenty to thirty years.

We all get busy. Life happens. Priorities change. But if you want to get the best investment returns you can, you need to combine automated and manual investment management. Here's how a hybrid automated and manual investing approach works:

THE SEVEN-STEP FAST TRACK INVESTMENT STRATEGY

1. Keep increasing the percentage you are automatically contributing into your investment accounts as high as you can.
2. Manually invest all additional money you make from side hustling and bonuses as quickly as you can.

For example, your 401(k) might be automated to contribute 10 percent of your salary with each paycheck. That 10 percent will be contributed without your doing anything. But I recommend increasing that contribution rate as high as you can over time. Try to increase your savings rate at least 1 percent or more every thirty to ninety days. Some months it will be easier than others. Push yourself. It's this manual pushing that will help you save as much as possible. When you get a raise or bonus, invest as much of it as you can. When you make $60 watching your neighbor's cat, invest it. It will take you a few minutes and you can do it from your phone.

You can also us microinvesting apps like Acorns or Digit, which deposit small amounts of money into an investment account by rounding up your purchases or taking small amounts of money out of your account to help you invest even more money as supplement to this strategy. But these types of apps should be used only *in addition* to your regular automated and manual strategy as a way to save even more money. They are not sufficient vehicles for investing by themselves as some people believe.

Don't get complacent. The more you invest every day, the faster you will reach financial independence. If it means that much to you, you'll make time for it. Every $10 you invest today could help you reach financial freedom days, weeks, or maybe even months sooner in the future. Imagine how much time making that extra investment is buying you in the future.

As with any strategy, use these recommendations as guidelines and customize them to align with your own financial situation, lifestyle, and goals. Just like you may need to adjust your number, you will want to monitor your progress and the performance of your investment strategy at least once a year. Tax rates and tax policies might change or other people might find new loopholes, so keep up with it.

There are many people who've traveled this path before you, including me. While I can't predict the future (specifically the stock market performance and tax policy and tax rate changes), based on my experience and years of research, I am confident this strategy will help you perform in the top 10 percent of all investors worldwide and hit your number as quickly as possible.

RECAP

1. **Investing is the ultimate form of passive income and the accelerator of financial freedom.** It's how you make money on your money without having to exchange any of your time.

2. **This strategy is built on five key concepts you can directly influence:**
   I. Minimizing risk
   II. Minimizing fees
   III. Minimizing taxes on your contributions
   IV. Maximizing returns
   V. Minimizing taxes on your withdrawals

3. **The core of your investment portfolio should be made up of stocks (shares of actual companies), bonds (money that you are loaning someone), and real estate (properties).** These are the easiest, most dependable investments, and can make you a lot of money.

4. **If you do need help investing, you can hire a fee-only financial advisor for a few hours to help you set up your accounts.** You should work only with advisors who charge on an hourly or project basis, not based on AUM (assets under management).

5. **Step 1: Separate your short-term and long-term investing goals.**
   a. You should be investing differently depending on whether you need the money in the short term (within the next five years) or the long term (after five years). Most of your money should be invested for the long term so you can live off it for the rest of your life.
   b. Short-term investments should be in cash, CDs, or bonds
   c. Long-term investments should be in stocks and bonds

6. **Step 2: Figure out how much you have to invest.**
   a. As you already know, the higher your savings rate, the more money you can invest and the faster you'll hit your number. Sit down and think about how much money you can invest each day, month, quarter, and year. Set a foundation—a baseline number that you are going to invest in each account over each period.

7. **Step 3: Determine your target asset allocation.**

THE SEVEN-STEP FAST TRACK INVESTMENT STRATEGY

a. Next you need to determine your target asset allocation, which is the percentage of each asset (e.g., stocks, bonds, and cash) you have in your investment accounts. Your target asset allocation determines the level of risk/reward of your investment portfolio and is one of the most important investment decisions you will need to make.

b. The best way to pick your target asset allocation is based on how long it will be before you need to use the money.

c. If you are ten or more years away from walking away, I recommend you invest 100 percent in stocks for now.

d. After you determine your target asset allocation, you should maintain it across all of your investment accounts. Readjusting your allocation rates so they align with your target allocation is known as rebalancing and should be done quarterly (four times a year).

8. Step 4: Evaluate your current fees (and try to keep them as low as possible!).

a.Investment fees can have an enormous impact on how quickly your money grows, how much money you'll have within a given time frame, and how many years it will take you to reach your number.

9. Step 5: Pick the right investments.

a. When you buy stock, you are buying a share of ownership in a real company.

b. Individual stocks can swing wildly in value over both short and long periods of time, which can either make or lose you a lot of money in a relatively short period of time.

c. Research shows that, on average, 90 percent of active investing yields a disappointing performance compared to the stock market as a whole over a fifteen-year period

d. To keep your investments as efficient and effective as possible, you should invest in a simple fund that owns a broad selection of the U.S. stock market (known as a total stock market fund) or a fund that owns a small piece of the biggest 500 companies in the United States (what are known as the S&P 500).

e. If you don't have access to either of these funds, then you can invest in funds to mirror the holdings of those types of funds.

f. You can ignore all of the other options—things like gold and REITs (real estate investment trusts) in your 401(k)s, 403(b)s, or IRAs.

While they can add more diversification, they aren't really necessary and you are better off focusing just on stocks and bonds in your asset allocation. Keep it simple using index funds when you can.

10. **Step 6: Max out your tax-advantaged accounts.**

a. Taxes can take a massive chunk out of the future earnings of your investments, so it's important to minimize their impact as much as possible.

b. The key to getting the maximum tax benefits is to strategize (1) when you put money into your investments and (2) when you take the money out of the investment.

c. You can invest in three types of investment accounts:

   i. Tax-free contributions: tax-advantaged accounts in which you don't pay taxes when you invest the money, but you do pay taxes with you withdraw money.

   ii. Tax-free withdrawals: tax-advantaged accounts in which you pay tax before you invest the money, but don't pay taxes when you withdraw money.

   iii. Taxable accounts in which you pay tax before you invest the money and also when you withdraw it.

11. **Step 7: Invest in taxable accounts.**

a. After you've maxed out your tax-advantaged accounts, if you still have money left over to invest, you should open a taxable (aka brokerage) account.

b. Every time you sell anything in your taxable accounts, you will be responsible for paying taxes on the investment gains that year

c. If you sell your investments in a taxable account after holding them for less than a year, you will get taxed at your current income tax rate. If you hold them for longer than a year before you sell them, then you will get taxed at the capital gains rate, which is typically lower than your income tax rate.

12. **Automation is not enough.** Here's how a hybrid automated and manual investing approach works: (1) keep increasing the percentage you are automatically contributing into your investment accounts as high as you can; and (2) manually invest all additional money you make from side hustling and bonuses as quickly as you can.

CHAPTER 11

REAL ESTATE INVESTING

How to Turn $10,000 into Millions Using Other People's
Money

nvesting in real estate is not just an exceptional way to diversify your
investment portfolio and risk; in many ways, real estate is a better investment than stocks because you can use mortgage loans (that is to say,
other people's money) to buy a property, and there are a ton of tax advantages, like the ability to keep $500,000 in tax-free profit from the sale of
your primary home (if you're a married couple filing joint taxes). There are
many other cash flow and tax advantages that we'll cover in this chapter
that make real estate such an amazing investment.

Real estate investing is seriously legit—incredible, actually. You've already learned how house-hacking can help you to significantly, if not completely, eliminate your biggest expense (housing), but you can actually go
a lot further than owning a home, getting free rent, and earning an extra
couple of thousand bucks per month. You can put a 3 percent down payment on your first home and turn it into a multimillion-dollar real estate
portfolio within a few years.

You can buy and flip properties for tax-free profits or you can buy and
hold properties, turning your rentals into a consistent cash flow that covers your living expenses and generates enough money to pay down your
mortgages or to invest in more properties. And you can use real estate to
generate enough consistent cash flow to cover your living expenses for the
rest of your life. Many investors have used real estate as their primary way
to achieve financial independence in five years or less. Here's the blueprint.

THE CASE FOR REAL ESTATE

It's important to remember that real estate investing carries risk and that real estate values, just like stock values, are never guaranteed to go up. In fact, in some cases the value of real estate can actually drop a lot. It wasn't that long ago we lived through a real estate crisis in which more than 10 million homeowners in the United States were left underwater, meaning they owed more on their mortgages than their homes were worth. But the main reason that happened was because banks were giving too many mortgages to people who couldn't afford them.

In fact, real estate investing is historically less volatile than stock market investing, and the housing market has recovered exceptionally well since its low in 2010. Home prices appreciated an average of 43 percent nationally between 2010 and 2016. Appreciation is typically created by a neighborhood's improving or increasing in demand, or through renovations done on a home, such as an addition or a kitchen remodel. Property appreciation is especially high in cities. Approximately 62.7 percent of the U.S. population live in cities, and that number is growing. Globally, 54 percent of the population live in cities, and this is projected to increase to 66 percent by 2050.

As you've already learned, historically the stock market has compounded, after being adjusted for inflation and dividends, at about 7 percent per year. Real estate, by contrast, appreciates between 3 and 5 percent on average per year. Upon first glance, therefore, real estate doesn't seem like a better strategy than plain old investing in stocks, but real estate has a few advantages that stocks don't. First, you can buy properties using someone else's (a bank's or a lender's) money. And as you learned earlier, you can also house-hack by getting renters to offset, completely cover, or even pay you more money than your mortgage.

You can also make a lot of money, sometimes quickly, buying and selling properties as a side hustle. This can put some quick money in your pocket, but the real value in flipping is that you can use the profits to invest in more properties without paying taxes, using what's known as a 1031 exchange. You can keep doing 1031 exchanges forever by keeping your real estate profits invested in property. You can't do that with stocks! And when you die, your tax liability from any 1031 exchanges disappears for your heirs.

This is a massive advantage for real estate investing over stock investing. When you invest in stocks, your portfolio grows only in proportion to the money you invested and any compounded gains. With real estate, your investment grows as the property increases in value, and since you don't have to put up all of the money up front, you can make your money grow much quicker. This is called leverage, and when you use it responsibility, you can make a lot of money using other people's money. Yes, you have to pay the bank back, but the point is, you don't need more money to make the same return; if you put $10,000 down up front, you'll actually make an even higher return on your investment than you would if you put down $100,000 up front.

For example, a $10,000 down payment on a $200,000 home that appreciates to $250,000 in value created a $50,000 or a 5 times or a 400 percent return on your original $10,000 down payment. If you put down $100,000 on the $200,000 property and it goes up to $250,000 in value, you would have returned only 50 percent of your $100,000 investment. A 50 percent return is a lot less than a 400 percent return. So in most cases, your ROI is actually higher the lower your down payment, because you are putting down less of your own money but capturing all of the gains.

This is one of the main reasons real estate investing can be so much more powerful than stock investing. Say you have $10,000 to invest. You can buy $10,000 in stock with that money, or you could put a $10,000 down payment on a home. Let's say you put $10,000 in the stock market that grows 30 percent over the next three years. That $10,000 in stock is now worth $13,000, and even after you factor in the 10 percent capital gains tax on the growth, you're still left with $12,700—an amazing return in only three years. But if you use that $10,000 to put a 5 percent down payment on a $200,000 home that appreciates $50,000 in value over three years (not unrealistic in cities or popular markets), then your $10,000 down payment has now generated at least $50,000 in profit. As a bonus, if the home is your primary residence (meaning you've lived there two out of the last five years), you won't pay any taxes on that $50,000 (up to $500,000 in profit for couples or $250,000 for individuals). You can then use that profit for a down payment on another property or even multiple properties, all tax-free!

Another huge benefit of buying real estate using a mortgage is that all of the interest on up to a $750,000 mortgage on your primary and secondary residence (if you have one) is tax deductible. In addition to the mortgage tax deduction, you can also deduct up to $10,000 in property and state taxes from your federal tax return. As the current tax bill stands, this deduction is expected to increase to cover the interest on a mortgage of up to $1 million by the year 2026.

Many people think they need a huge down payment or that they need to commit to stay in a home for at least five years for a real estate investment to be worth it. But neither of those is true. You can buy your first property with as little as 1 to 5 percent of a down payment, which for a $200,000 home is between $2,000 and $10,000. And in most cities in the United States, the rent-to-buy break-even point (i.e., the point at which it's equally expensive to buy and rent a home) is 2.1 years. This means if you plan to live in a home for at least 2.1 years, it often makes sense for you to buy it. While there are many decent rent-to-buy calculators, the best two I've found are by *The New York Times* and Zillow.

If you buy a home, you can rent out the extra rooms to cover some of the mortgage or even make more than the mortgage. As the rent you charge your roommates or tenants goes up and the property appreciates, you can invest the extra cash into a new property. Within a few years you could have five or more properties, all generating cash flow and appreciating in value, and your equity ownership will increase as you use your rental income to pay down the mortgages.

BUYING A PROPERTY CAN BE MORE FLEXIBLE THAN RENTING

You might feel like buying a property means you have to put down roots in a place, but that's an old-school mindset you need to get rid of. Investing in real estate is about being creative with how you use your home to both make money and live how you want. In this way, buying a multi-room or multi-unit property can actually give you more flexibility than renting. Since you own the property and you're the landlord, you can always adjust the arrangement over time to best suit your lifestyle.

If you want to save the most money and live for free, you can rent out all the rooms and sleep on a couch in the basement. I heard about one property owner who lived in a closet off the kitchen. Or you can stay in the smallest room (or apartment if you own multiple units) and rent out the bigger rooms or apartments. If you eventually want to upgrade, you can take the nicest room or the nicest unit.

And if you end up wanting to move to another property or another city, you can always keep the property for cash flow and let it continue to grow in value. If you get married or have kids and own a duplex or triplex, you can convert it into one large home. Or if you buy a property and don't like living in it after a year, just rent it out to cover the mortgage and find another place to live. Just because you buy a place doesn't mean you're stuck with it—it just means you have an asset that can grow.

There are also incredible tax benefits for real estate investors that help you keep more money in your pocket and make it easier to build a real estate portfolio. If you rent out your property, you can deduct tons of expenses, including property taxes (up to $10,000), mortgage insurance, repairs, management fees, and any other expenses associated with running and maintaining your rental properties. Not only do these deductions help you save money on taxes, but any improvements you make will help make the property more valuable. One note: If you live in a really expensive area where the property taxes are high, you can't deduct more than $10,000, which means owning a property could get expensive. But for most real estate owners and investors, these tax deductions really add up and make homeownership more affordable by decreasing your tax bill.

In addition to these benefits, even though your rental property is likely appreciating, you can actually deduct for depreciation, which allows you to deduct a certain percentage of the price you paid for the structure (not the land) over a long period for "wear and tear." The standard residential deduction is 27.5 years, so you can take the value of the structure (say, $200,000) and divide it by 27.5, which gives you $7,772, and then you multiply that by your marginal tax rate (for example, 25 percent), which would equal $1,818 that you could deduct every year from your taxes for depreciation. Check out IRS Publication 527 to learn more.

Another advantage to real estate investing is that properties are tangible assets, so you can take out loans secured by your properties. This gives you access to more cash if you want to refinance or take some of the equity out of your properties to invest in the market or buy more properties. One of the best benefits of cash-out refinancing is that you can take out the money *tax-free*! This is an amazing way to take cash out of properties that have appreciated without having to sell the property.

Then if you really want to make a lot of money, you could refinance that property to take out some of the appreciation and use the cash to buy a second property. Then you can do it again to buy your third, fourth, and fifth property and pretty quickly build a multimillion-dollar real estate portfolio.

HOW TO BUY A HOME WITH LITTLE MONEY DOWN

In order to buy your first property, you need to (1) save enough for a down payment on a mortgage and then (2) qualify for a mortgage. A mortgage is when a bank or lender lends you money to buy a home. As you've already learned, using other people's money to grow your net worth is one of the biggest advantages of real estate investing. And while it might seem daunting to take out a large loan from a bank or a lender, mortgages can actually be "good debt" because you are using them to buy a property that can generate cash flow and increase in value. You can also use a mortgage to buy a home that is undervalued, so you are immediately able to acquire more equity than you are paying for. If you have decent credit, you also don't need to put a lot of money down and can likely get away with a 1 to 5 percent down payment.

There are two popular types of mortgages—fixed rate mortgages (FRM), where the interest rate stays the same throughout the term of the loan, and adjustable rate mortgages (ARM), where the rate increases or decreases after a certain period based on certain market factors. The interest rate and the type of mortgage you are able to get from a lender is largely based on your credit score. The higher your credit score, the lower your interest rate will be. Interest rates go up and down based on a number of factors and can vary considerably by lender, so it's essential to get mortgage rate quotes from multiple lenders. When I was shopping for my first mortgage, rates varied by more than 2.0 percent, which over the period of a loan can mean paying up to hundreds of thousands of dollars in additional interest.

Shop around for the best mortgage rate you can get. I'd recommend getting quotes from at least five, if not more, lenders. But you do have to be careful when getting multiple mortgage quotes, because having a bunch of lenders pulling your credit score can lower it, effectively negating the opportunity of shopping for a better rate or even the ability to get a loan. As the first step, before selecting which lenders can pull your credit score, I recommend telling the lender your credit score without giving them your Social Security number and asking what the estimated mortgage rate would be. They can plug it into their system and give you a close enough range. Then when you find two or three who give you the lowest quotes, you can take the next step to get a formal quote. While this might sound like a lot of work, it should take only a few hours, and it's worth it to save even a small percentage on your mortgage interest rate. That few hours could save you tens of thousands of dollars in potential interest payments on your loan.

Fixed rate mortgages typically come in fifteen-year and thirty-year time horizons. The longer the time horizon, the lower your monthly payment, but the more interest you will pay. Interest rates are also typically higher for thirty-year mortgages, since the bank is lending you money for a longer period of time and therefore is taking on more risk of default.

Most Americans have a thirty-year mortgage and for the first few years end up paying a lot of interest—about 80 percent of their total payments. If you can afford the larger monthly payment, opt for a fifteen-year mortgage instead, since you will pay less money in up-front interest whether you plan to keep the property for just a few years or longer. You can still get a fifteen-year mortgage with as little as a 3 percent down payment in some markets, so you don't need to use a lot of your cash to get a better interest rate on a fifteen-year mortgage than a thirty-year mortgage.

Adjustable rate mortgages are riskier because your interest rate is fixed for only a defined period of time (typically five years), after which it could go up or down depending on the current interest rates in the market. While getting an ARM is more like a gamble since there is no way to predict where interest rates will be in five years, it can be a really smart decision if you can get a good rate and plan to sell your home in five years or less. This way you end up paying a lot less in interest during the short period you have the loan before you sell.

No matter what type of mortgage you select, you don't necessarily have to stay locked in for the entire period. You can always refinance the loan with either the same or a different lender in order to get a lower rate. If rates drop, you could reduce the amount you're paying in interest, or you could switch from a fifteen-year to a thirty-year loan and reduce your monthly payment.

Another benefit of refinancing is that if you have some equity in the property and want to keep building your real estate investments, you can often take cash out and use that money to buy another property. However, because it costs money to refinance, it really makes sense to refinance only if you can recoup the expense of refinancing by paying less in interest over the time you plan to live in the home. It likely doesn't make sense to refinance if you are going to live in the home for less than three to five years but could save you a lot in interest payments if you plan to live in the home or hold the mortgage while renting the property for five plus years. If you are considering refinancing, ask your potential lender to do a break-even calculation as a starting point to evaluate whether it's worth it.

HOW MUCH HOME CAN YOU ACTUALLY AFFORD?

The costs of homeownership can really add up, but they shouldn't scare you. One popular piece of advice is that your monthly mortgage payment, plus taxes and any assessments, shouldn't be more than 40 percent of your monthly take-home pay. While I am an aggressive investor, 40 percent in my opinion is too high a percentage. I think it should be 30 percent or less to be safe. You don't want to be what's known as *house poor,* when most of your take-home pay goes to your mortgage and you don't have any money left over to invest or spend on your life. No matter how much you love the home, it's not worth putting all of your money into it. If you do, you are taking a huge risk that can cost you not only a lot of money but also your home.

You should also make sure you have a secure job and/or other ways to make consistent income (outside of any rental income you plan to earn on the property). The way you do this is by buying a house you can *actually* afford, not one your bank or lender *says* you can afford. In most cases, if you have a decent credit score, you will be approved for a mortgage larger than you should take out. The bank wants to lend you as much money as they can so they can make as much as they can in interest on the debt, but that doesn't help you in the long run. Don't buy it. Take out as small a mortgage as you need to buy a property where the mortgage payment is less than 30 percent of your monthly income.

Also, keep in mind the other costs involved in home buying and ongoing homeownership. Your mortgage payment is just what you owe the bank and doesn't include property taxes (which can add a lot to your monthly bill if you live in an expensive area) and assessments (which are charged by condo and neighborhood associations to cover common expenses). The costs can really add up, so it's important to be very clear on exactly what you will be paying each month for your property. Here's an example of the cost breakdown for buying a $300,000 condo in Chicago.

No matter how much money you make, some cities or places just aren't very affordable, so you either need to make a lot of money or get creative. For example, you can put a low down payment (between 1 and 5 percent) on your home or get a few roommates to help you pay or fully cover your mortgage. In some cities like New York, Seattle, San Francisco, Los Angeles, Washington, D.C., and others, it's really expensive to buy properties. But once you start making more money or if you can get some of your friends together to buy a property or get some money from your parents, they can be great places to invest in real estate because property there tends to appreciate quickly.

If you find a property that you've determined is a great value in a growing real estate market and you don't have enough cash or you can get a mortgage rate below 4 or 5 percent and you believe you can get a higher return investing your money, then you don't need to put a 20 percent down

Onetime Costs	
Closing Costs	$1,000
Taxes and Fees	$2,400
Moving Expenses	$3,000
Total	$6,400
Recurring Costs/Monthly Payments	
Principal Payment (goes to your mortgage balance)	$1,256
Interest Payment	$721
Property Taxes	$420
Monthly Assessment (for common areas and neighborhood/building upkeep)	$600
Maintenance/Repairs	$200
Total	$3,197
Annual Expenses	$38,364

payment on the home. It's a common myth that you need to put 20 percent down, which you definitely don't, and if you wait too long, you might miss out on a great property and investment opportunity.

A guy I know (I'll call him Scott) lives in Los Angeles and has been saving for a 20 percent down payment for the past four years. During that time, real estate has skyrocketed in Los Angeles and he is no longer able to afford a home in the neighborhood he originally wanted to live in. But if he had put down 3 percent on a home in that neighborhood four years ago, he would have been able to buy into the market immediately, live in a home he wanted, and benefit from the appreciation. And based on the data I've seen, the appreciation is tremendous—any of the properties he was looking at could have easily gone up in value $400,000 to $500,000 in that time. So not only is he still renting, but he lost the opportunity to buy a home and make a ton of money. Now he's completely priced out of the market—all because he wanted to wait for a 20 percent down payment.

Note that you can put down less than a 20 percent down payment only on the home that is considered your primary residence (you can have only one primary residence). Any investment property that you don't live in will likely require a 20 to 25 percent down payment.

For your primary residence, if you can get a mortgage rate lower than 5 percent, you're likely better off keeping the cash you would typically use for a down payment (even if you have the money available) invested in stocks and using the bank's money to buy an appreciating property. If your mortgage rate is higher than 5 percent, then you are better off putting down as close to 20 percent as you can. But no matter what, don't put down a 20 percent down payment if you are going to be cash poor (not have enough money saved in an emergency fund) or you could get a much higher return in the market. Also, never use more than 30 percent of your net worth for any down payment on a property.

When you put down less than 20 percent, you have to pay something called private mortgage insurance (PMI), which is simply insurance for the mortgage lender if you default on your mortgage so the bank doesn't lose money on their investment. PMI is typically $75 to $150 per month for a loan up to $300,000, but it does fluctuate based on the size of your loan, your credit score, and your down payment.

But PMI is no big deal and worth it to buy a property with less than 20 percent down as long as you can afford it. You can get rid of PMI by having at least 20 percent equity ownership in the property (based on an assessment). You can achieve this four different ways:

1. The property can appreciate to the point where your current investment is worth 20 percent of the total value.
2. You can make repairs or upgrades on the property that increases its value so you now have 20 percent equity.
3. You can refinance to get a new mortgage and get an appraisal that shows you own 20 percent.
4. You can pay down the mortgage more quickly than necessary until you own 20 percent. Depending on your market, this might take a few years, but it might be worth paying a little

more each month to be able to put down less than 20 percent to buy into the market and/or get a higher return on your investment elsewhere.

If you are a first-time home buyer, you should definitely check with your city or county to see if they have any first-time home buyer credit programs. For example, Chicago offers several programs for first-time home buyers, including one that covers up to 2 percent of a down payment! Don't leave money on the table—always check to see if there are programs you can take advantage of.

When I bought my first home in Chicago, I put down 5 percent and got a small first-time home buyer grant. If I had waited until I had saved a 20 percent down payment, it would have taken me at least another year, and not only would I have missed out on the exact property I wanted, but the market would have been about 20 percent more expensive. While that type of rapid appreciation can be rare, it often makes a lot of sense to put down a low down payment, get into the market quickly, and use any extra cash you could have otherwise put toward your down payment to invest in something earning a higher return than your mortgage interest rate (like the stock market).

In the past five years, my property has appreciated over $350,000, so had I waited until I had the 20 percent down payment, I would have missed out on hundreds of thousands of dollars in potential gains. Did I know my property was going to appreciate so much? Of course not. In many ways, I got lucky, but I did know that the market was down in Chicago, so I knew I could find a good deal. I bought the property in the middle of winter when prices are typically lower in Chicago (who wants to go house hunting in a Chicago winter?), and I bought a unique property (a loft in an old printing building that's a national historic landmark). It has a good vibe.

If you get a good mortgage interest rate with good terms, it can be pretty easy to use a bank's money to buy and hold properties. For example, I have a 2.625 percent fifteen-year fixed mortgage, which is really low. I have been able to get a much higher return investing the cash I would have used to pay off my mortgage by putting it into the stock market. Since the stock market has been on a tear over the past year, that money has returned 23 percent. Since my mortgage rate is so low, I'm going to keep my extra cash invested instead of paying off my mortgage early. However, if I did decide to retire and live solely off my investment income, then I would likely pay off the mortgage entirely.

Once again, it comes down to making the right mathematical decision. One of the reasons this has been possible is because mortgage rates have been at historic lows and stocks have absolutely crushed it over the past eight years. Back in the 1980s, when mortgage rates were 10 to 12 percent, it would have made more sense to pay off a mortgage as quickly as possible, since other investments were unlikely to return that much. It can also make sense to try and pay off your mortgage quickly to hedge against the risk that the real estate market will decline.

TWO WAYS TO INVEST IN REAL ESTATE

There are two primary ways to invest in real estate: you can buy and sell (aka flip) properties or buy and hold them for the long term. While the primary focus of this chapter is buying and holding real estate, let's look at how both strategies can help you hit your number in different ways.

Buying and flipping properties means you buy a property and then try to sell it within a few years (or even a few weeks). Sometimes the homes need repairs and sometimes they don't, but the strategy is to look for values—homes that are worth more than you pay for them or could be worth a lot more with some repairs. Flipping can be a great side hustle, and there are deals to be found in almost any city or town. While in some cities deals are tougher to find because so many other flippers are looking for them, too, you just have to keep hunting and be ready to buy when you find one.

Buying and flipping homes can help you make some extra money that you can then use to either buy more properties or add to your stock investments. As you've already learned, because of the 1031 exchange rule, you can keep rolling over your profits tax-free by using them to buy new properties. Or you can flip your way into larger and larger homes so you can buy your dream home. You can also flip your way into buying a multi-unit property or apartment building that you can then hold and rent out.

Just like buying and holding stock for the long term, buying and holding real estate is a more effective strategy than flipping to help you reach financial independence faster, since you can build up a portfolio that generates consistent monthly cash flow through rental income that can cover your mortgage debt and monthly expenses, as well as have a portfolio of assets that will also appreciate over time. You can't get that with stocks. You can also deduct most of the interest and many of the expenses of owning rental properties, making things like upgrades, repairs, and management expenses tax deductible.

When it comes to hitting your number as soon as possible, cash flow is more important than appreciation (since monthly rental income can cover your monthly living expenses, allowing you to live while letting 100 percent of your investments grow). Also, cash flow is more reliable than appreciation, since either your tenants pay their rent or you evict them, but appreciation is based on many factors like supply and demand that you can't really control.

Depending on your number and monthly expenses, you probably don't have to own many properties to generate enough cash flow from rental payments to cover your monthly expenses. Say you need $60,000 to live each year, which is $5,000 per month. To figure out your monthly rental income target, you want to add at least 25 percent to your expected monthly expenses to account for the expenses required to manage a rental—like repairs and the cost of a management company if you use one. To meet your monthly expenses you would need enough properties to generate ($5,000 × 1.25 = $6,250) in rental income per month.

This might be one property that generates $6,250 per month or five properties that generate $1,250 each per month. You can also accomplish this as you increase the rent on your properties. Typically rents increase between 3 and 5 percent per year in most U.S. markets but can increase even more if the neighborhood is in demand. Realistically you can charge as much as someone is willing to pay.

Below is an example breakdown of how buying just five properties over ten years could generate $6,250 per month in cash flow and a ton of equity/appreciation that increases your net worth.

In this example, you've acquired five properties over the past ten years, and because your rental income on all the properties increases, so does your monthly cash flow. Also, as the value of the properties increase and your total debt decreases, then your equity/ownership increases. And this is in just ten years. If you keep holding the property, both your rental income and equity/ownership will continue to grow. If you decide you want to cash out in the future, you could sell your properties and cash in on the equity/ownership appreciation. But a better long-term strategy would be to keep your properties and let both your rental income and equity grow forever.

With this example, if you can buy more than five properties or buy homes that go up more in value, you can hit the monthly cash flow target and thus financial independence a lot faster. While five properties might sound like a lot, most people can easily manage five properties as a side hustle that requires less than five hours of their time per week, or you can outsource the work by finding a good management company and handyman pretty easily. Real estate investing is scalable and gives you a lot of flexibility, so you can buy as many properties as you want depending on how much money you want to make and how much time you want to spend managing them. While there are many real estate investors who end up turning their real estate side hustle into a full-time job, you can align your own investment strategy with your desired lifestyle.

If you don't want to put in the time, you can pretty easily find a management company who will charge 7 to 10 percent of the monthly rent to manage the property (including finding tenants, scheduling repairs, and so forth). With a good management company, you don't even have to live in the same city as your properties—many real estate investors don't. You could even live in Bali (where the cost of living is relatively low) and easily generate passive income from your real estate properties in the United States.

As you've already learned, no one can predict the stock or the housing market; anyone who tells you he or can is blowing smoke. But just like stocks, you can buy properties that are better values and have a better chance at appreciating. For example, properties by colleges are good investments, since students need places to live, as are unique or historic properties that have a lot of character in a desirable area or properties in a popular vacation destination. Typically, the more desirable a property is, the more it's going to go up in value, or at least hold its value when the market is soft.

Example of a Five-Property Real-Estate Portfolio That Generates $5,000 a Month in Cash Flow

Years	Properties	Debt/Mortgages	Monthly Debt, Tax, & Assessment Payments	Rental Income	Monthly Cash Flow	Value of Properties	Equity/Ownership
1	1	$200,000	$2,000	$2,000	$0	$250,000	$50,000
2	1	$190,000	$2,000	$2,100	$100	$260,000	$70,000
3	2	$380,000	$3,500	$4,200	$700	$475,000	$95,000
4	2	$365,000	$3,500	$4,500	$1,000	$500,000	$135,000
5	3	$565,000	$5,600	$7,000	$1,400	$700,000	$200,000
6	4	$780,000	$8,400	$10,400	$2,000	$1,100,000	$320,000
7	5	$980,000	$10,100	$12,900	$2,800	$1,450,000	$470,000
8	5	$940,000	$10,400	$13,700	$3,300	$1,480,000	$540,000
9	5	$880,000	$11,400	$16,700	$5,300	$1,520,000	$640,000
10	5	$840,000	$12,100	$18,350	$6,250	$1,550,000	$710,000

Your first home purchase is one of the most important investment decisions you will make in your life, and if you take just a little extra time to find the right property at the right price, you could make a lot of money quickly as the rent and property go up in value.

Whether you live in the city or the country, there are always deals to found. While it might seem daunting at first, real estate investing, like stock investing, isn't that complicated. But also, just like stock investing, you should invest only in what you understand and take only as much risk as you can tolerate. The more you know about the market and the neighborhoods, the better an investor you will be. You can either get this market knowledge yourself by keeping an eye on prices online and looking at properties in your target neighborhoods, or you can outsource it and work with a Realtor who knows the neighborhoods and scouts deals for you.

As you gain more experience, you can start branching out into buying two- and three-family homes, or even entire apartment buildings. While we won't get into buying entire apartment buildings in this chapter and that might sound crazy to you, it's actually a lot easier than you think. In Chicago, you can find six-unit apartment buildings (with the apartments already rented) for about $1 million, which you can buy with a down payment of between 15 and 30 percent. Note that any building with more than four units is considered a commercial building and will require a commercial property loan. But as long as the rental income can cover the mortgage, not only will the mortgage be easier to get, but you can start generating rental income and have an appreciating asset.

Scaling Your Real Estate Investing by Getting Investors

If you happen to really like investing in real estate, one of the fastest ways to scale your own real estate business is by taking on what are known as joint venture partners. These are other real estate investors who will invest in you and your properties. There are three big advantages to partnering up with another real estate investor. First you will often be able to get more favorable lending terms outside of banks. Second, an experienced real estate investor who invests is likely going to teach you a lot and be able to better respond to changes in the market.

If you are investing in real estate consistently, shifts in the market can change how you should be investing in properties. For example, if properties get too expensive in your market, then you might need to start looking for homes to rehab. Experienced real estate investors are going to have a good team around them and access to better resources—like repairmen, inspectors, property managers, lawyers, and other people to help with your own real estate investments. If they invest in you, they are going to bring their resources to the table so they can protect and get the best return on their investment.

While you can't predict or control property appreciation with real estate investing, you can control things like your costs and cash flow. Working with a experienced real estate partner makes it easier to do both and grow your business faster. If you do decide to look for a real estate investing partner, always look for someone who has been investing in real estate longer and has more properties than you. Try to work with the most experienced investor you can. But in order to get an investor, you'll need to have a proven track record of successfully investing in properties that are appreciating and generating increasing cash flow.

Hopefully you are convinced to go out and buy your first (or maybe second) property and start making money investing in real estate. As a wise investor once said, "You make money when you buy a property, not when you sell it." You want to try and find the best deal on a property you can. Here are some tips to increase your chances of finding a great investment property.

9 TIPS TO HELP FIND AN AMAZING INVESTMENT PROPERTY

1. Develop real estate investing criteria to follow.

What type of properties do you want to invest in and in what neighborhoods? Setting investment criteria will help you focus and become an expert in specific properties and neighborhoods, which will make it much easier to spot a deal. Most successful investors stick within their range and invest only in what they understand. Whether you invest in studios, single-family homes, apartment buildings, commercial real estate, or even parking spots, it's a lot easier if you have a niche and stick within your comfort zone.

2. Set a budget and get preapproved for a mortgage or loan.

I recommend you get preapproved for a mortgage before you start shopping for properties so you know how much you can spend. Plus preapproval signals to Realtors that you are serious about buying and will make it easy to buy a property quickly once you find one you love. Getting preapproved is simple to do by submitting some paperwork to lenders, who will approve you for a certain amount of money. Get quotes from at least four different lenders so you can find the best mortgage rate.

3. Look for properties that generate immediate positive cash flow and have high rent and appreciation potential.

You should buy only investment properties that immediately generate positive cash flow (meaning the tenant rents are high enough to at least cover the mortgage, taxes, and anticipated expenses for the property). It doesn't make any sense to buy an investment property that you are losing money on right after you buy it.

While it doesn't work in all markets (especially the expensive ones), one popular strategy real estate investors use to find properties that will immediately generate positive cash flow is what's known as the 1 percent rule. You want to look for properties where the anticipated monthly rent is at least 1 percent of the property sale price. For example, if a property is listed for $200,000 and you can get $2,000 a month in rent for the place, then it passes the 1 percent rule. If you can't get that much, then your rental income likely won't cover the mortgage payment and necessary expenses, which are typically less than 1 percent. To figure out what you can get in rent, look online to see what similar units in the neighborhood are renting for. If you want to be more conservative, you can shoot for 2 percent instead, but somewhere between 1 and 2 percent is a good place to start. You should also buy a rental that at least generates the cash required to cover the mortgage payments plus an additional 10 to 20 percent to cover the expenses and to provide an additional cushion if the apartment sits unrented for a few months.

You also want to try and buy a property that has the highest potential to increase in value and in a neighborhood where rents are likely to increase. Look for neighborhoods where rents are still affordable but because of their proximity to amenities, city centers, or universities have a higher chance of going up. Look for neighborhoods in transition or in which there are a lot of elderly sellers and the neighborhood is set for an influx of younger buyers and families. Follow the artists, musicians, hipsters, and students who often flock to cool neighborhoods and unique properties that in the next five years will appreciate the most. The cycle in many places is pretty predictable. Buy properties where others will want to live in five years or, if you can afford it, in neighborhoods that will likely always increase in demand—like Manhattan in New York, Venice in Los Angeles, or North Beach in San Francisco.

4. Find an amazing Realtor who does the hard work for you.

No matter how much time you spend hunting for real estate deals, a great Realtor is an invaluable asset. They'll know the market, understand your criteria, and know a deal when they see one. But while there are tons of Realtors, in my experience there are very few great ones. A great one is one who looks out for a deal for you, not just for themselves. Finding a great Realtor is like finding a great doctor—you want to find someone you vibe with and who has your best interests in mind. Start by looking at Realtor reviews on sites like Zillow and set up a few meetings. Most Realtors will be eager to meet with a potential buyer. Come prepared with a list of questions and ask them to tell you about two or three recent real estate investment deals they brokered for clients. Ask specifically about the investment deals they brokered and how well past client investments have done, not just sales.

5. Hunt when everyone else isn't.

A majority of homes are bought and sold during the spring months, but this is also when prices are the highest. One way to find a great deal is to look when no one else is looking, like the winter in a city where it's cold in that season. Homes that are bought in October through December appreciate more than homes bought at any other time of the year because there is less competition, which keeps the sale price relatively low. Also, sometimes when people are selling a property at a less desirable time of the year, they might be more desperate to sell and therefore more willing to give you a deal. Another great time to buy is at the end of the year, when both people and banks are interested in getting a home off their books.

6. Look for foreclosures or short sales.

Foreclosures are properties on which the owner can no longer pay the mortgage, so the bank is now selling it. You can find great foreclosure deals if you are patient, but also keep in mind that some foreclosures might be in rough shape. Sometimes if a property is super cheap there's a reason for it, so always invest in a thorough inspection. A short sale is when a lender (typically a bank) sells a property they own for a loss to get it off their books. Since the bank owns it, a property can take a long time to close, but it can be worth the effort. It doesn't hurt to make an offer. You can find foreclosures and short sales listed on websites like Zillow or Trulia or through a real estate agent. Just be ready to move quickly, since the good deals go fast.

7. Test-drive the neighborhood.

An easy way to test-drive a neighborhood is to rent a nearby apartment or home on a home-sharing website like Airbnb or VRBO. What's the neighborhood like on the weekends? In the evenings? How easy is it to walk to things? Taking a look at the property a few times won't give you these answers. Whether you are buying your primary residence or a rental property, you should always test-drive the neighborhood. If you like living there, then other people will, too. Always try to bring a friend, family member, or partner with you for a second or third opinion.

8. Find an experienced home inspector.

No matter how amazing a home looks, there is always going to be something wrong with it and sellers aren't required to let you know. This is why it's critical to get an inspection of any property you want to buy. Not all home inspectors are created equal—in fact anyone can market themselves as a home inspector without any credentials. You should do more due diligence than a simple Google search when looking for a home inspector.

Find a home inspector who has been at it for a long time and ask to see a sample report of a recent inspection they did. Not all home inspectors look at everything that should be inspected before you buy a home. For example, many don't typically look for bugs, but they should. Also make sure that you can go along for the inspection and have the inspector specifically point out what's wrong. Ask as many questions as you can because the last thing you want is to discover an expensive repair that needs to be done after you buy a home.

You should even go so far as to make your offer contingent on inspection, so you can back out if you find something that you don't like. Or at least be prepared to make a reduced offer based on any problems you'll need to fix. Many sellers will be willing to negotiate, especially if you find some big repairs that are required.

9. Be prepared to walk away from a deal.

There are more bad real estate deals than good ones, so just as with buying and selling stocks, you need to control your emotions. Far too many people get emotional when buying real estate, but you need to be prepared to look for the best investment property you can and always be ready to walk away from a deal if it doesn't meet your investing property criteria: if it's too expensive, it needs to many repairs, or you just feel that it's not right. A deal isn't closed until you sign on the dotted line, so don't be afraid to walk away if you feel it's the best thing to do.

Just like any type of investing, real estate investing certainly has its risks. But if you follow these principles, use a down payment you can afford, and use house-hacking to reduce the cost of owning a home, you can minimize the risk. No matter how large you want to build your real estate portfolio, real estate investing will give you a ton of flexibility, help you make a lot more money, and fast-track your financial independence.

RECAP

1. **Investing in real estate is more than an exceptional way to diversify your investment portfolio and risk.** In many ways real estate is a better investment than stocks because it appreciates more quickly and therefore so will your money.

2. **When you invest in stocks, your portfolio grows only in proportion to the money you invested and any compounded gains.** With real estate, your investment grows as the property increases in value, and since you don't have to put up all of the money up front, you can make your money grow much quicker.

3. **In order to buy your first property, you need to (1) save enough for a down payment on a mortgage and then (2) qualify for a mortgage.** A mortgage is when a bank or lender lends you money to buy a home.

4. **One popular piece of advice is that your monthly mortgage payment, plus taxes and any assessments, shouldn't be more than 40 percent of your monthly take-home pay.** While I am an aggressive

investor, 40 percent in my opinion is too high a percentage. I think it should be 30 percent or less to be safe.

5. There are two primary ways to invest in real estate: you can buy and sell (aka flip) property or buy and hold it for the long term.

6. If you happen to really like investing in real estate, one of the fastest ways to scale your own real estate business is by taking on what are known as joint venture partners.

7. Here are nine tips to help find an amazing investment property:

- Develop real estate investing criteria to follow.
- Set a budget and get preapproved for a mortgage or loan.
- Look for properties that generate immediate positive cash flow and have high rent and appreciation potential.
- Find an amazing Realtor who does the hard work for you.
- Hunt when everyone else isn't.
- Look for foreclosures or short sales.
- Test-drive the neighborhood.
- Find an experienced home inspector.
- Be prepared to walk away from a deal.

CHAPTER 12

MORE THAN ENOUGH

How to Live Off Your Investments for the Rest of Your Life

F ast-forward a few years and imagine you're on the final glide path to retire early, meaning you are close to making work optional. By now you've mastered what's in this book and more, and your finances are on point. You've been diligently saving 50 percent or more of your income for the past four years and investing it wisely. Based on your calculations, if the stock market doesn't drop the next three years by double digits, you're going to be on track to be able to retire in five years or less.

As you get closer to early retirement you'll have a much better handle on your monthly expenses, which by now you'll have worked hard to optimize so you're spending enough money to be happy and have everything you need. You'll have used your optimized expense projections to update your number and you'll be on track to reach it. At this point you'll start crafting your exit strategy and seriously planning three things:

1. Your cash flow strategy (aka how you will cover your monthly expenses), using any income streams, investment withdrawals, and cash
2. How to ensure you can live off your investments for the rest of your life
3. What you're going to do next (aka whatever you want!)

The number one goal with your investment withdrawal strategy is this: you want your money to last for the rest of your life. If you end up making a mistake, you may need to go back to work, which is easier to do when you are forty-five than when you are seventy-five. Just like calculating your number, living off your investments for the rest of your life is by no means an exact science, and your strategy will evolve over time. But there are a number of principles and strategies that can significantly increase the odds your money will last for the rest of your life. The key is to get as close as you can. This is not a process you go through once. Remember that you should be recalculating your number quarterly (four times per year) as part of your regular routine (don't worry—it takes only about five minutes).

It's never too early to start planning your investment withdrawal strategy so you can minimize any early withdrawal penalties (for withdrawing your money from your tax-advantaged accounts before you are fifty-nine and a half) and the impact of taxes from your taxable accounts. Knowing how to best withdraw your money in the future will undoubtedly make you a better investor today.

While I haven't retired yet, I've been planning how I could for the past few years. Here are the best withdrawal strategies being used today, but as you get closer to early retirement or the necessity to live off your investments, it will be worth some time to research new early retirement withdrawal strategies that are likely to develop as tax laws change, as well as loopholes identified by the financial independence community (if there is a new one, it will be found!). This chapter is by no means the definitive early retirement withdrawal strategy, but it will introduce you to the framework you will need to customize to your needs as you get closer to actually walking away from work forever.

PLAN YOUR CASH FLOW STRATEGY AND ADJUST YOUR ASSET ALLOCATION

As you get closer to walking away, you'll want to start planning how you're going to cover your monthly expenses. Your strategy should depend largely on how much money you need and whether you need to immediately start withdrawing your investments, or if you can rely on a dependable income stream, like rental income. If you are going to need to withdraw money from your investments to cover your expenses, you'll likely want to shift your investments to a more conservative stock/bond allocation so you can rely on bonds or some other type of fixed-income asset.

A common asset allocation for early retirees is 60 percent stocks/40 percent bonds or 40 percent stocks/60 percent bonds. These allocations both allow you to participate in stock market growth over time but have fixed income from bonds that you can withdraw and live on. With a more conservative allocation, if you are living off fixed-income assets you can leave your stock investments alone and let them keep growing and compounding. Although other early retirees who can withdraw less than 3 to 4 percent of their portfolio to cover their monthly expenses leave their money in 100 percent stocks to maximize its long-term growth potential, it's up to you to determine the level of risk you are willing to take and if you would prefer to live off fixed guaranteed income. One nice feature of bonds is that you know exactly how your bond investments will grow each year, so the income is guaranteed.

LIVE OFF YOUR SIDE OR PASSIVE INCOME AS LONG AS YOU CAN

If possible, use money you make from real estate rental income, side-hustle income, or sources of passive income to cover your monthly expenses before dipping into your investment gains. Once you do start withdrawing money, withdraw only what you need for the month at the beginning of the month and withdraw as little as possible.

While we covered this when you calculated your number, it's worth revisiting, because any income will reduce the amount of money you need to withdraw from your investments. For example, if you make an extra $2,000 a month off rental income and need $5,000 a month to cover your living expenses, that $2,000 a month in relatively passive income reduces the amount you need to withdraw from your investments to $3,000, a 40 percent decrease. Because of just $2,000 a month in rental income, you can leave an additional $24,000 a year in your investment accounts to continue to grow. And if you can get your side income to cover your monthly expenses, you could live off that income for the rest of your life and never have to touch your investments. This is easily one of the biggest benefits of building income streams outside of your full-time job.

ADJUST YOUR WITHDRAWAL PERCENTAGE BASED ON YOUR INVESTMENT PERFORMANCE AND THE PERFORMANCE OF THE STOCK MARKET

As you learned earlier in the book, if you have at least 25 to 30 times of your expected annual expenses invested, then based on the existing research, a safe withdrawal rate of between 3 and 4 percent (with annual adjustments for inflation) is going to significantly increase the odds your money is going to last for the rest of your life. Now, it's important to mention that what constitutes safe withdrawal rates is a hotly contested debate within early retirement circles, so it's worth reading up more as you get closer to wanting to retire. By the time you are ready to live off your investments for the rest of your life there might be new research and withdrawal recommendations, but based on all of the research released I've reviewed, the 3 to 4 percent range is a conservative estimate for not only preserving your principal, but ensuring future growth.

No matter what, you should plan to take out as little money as you need to live on and keep as much of your money invested and compounding as possible. Due to what's known as a *sequence-of-returns risk,* your investment performance of the first five to ten years has an impact on how long your money could potentially last. For example, if you retire right before a 30 percent stock market drop and all of your investments are in stocks, you'll be starting retirement with 30 percent less money and potentially less than your target number. The goal is to make it through the first five to ten years with your investment principal intact.

If the stock market drops that much in the first few years that you retire, it is extremely likely you will recover the losses over the next ten-year period, and research shows that even after the worst stock market declines in history, the 3 to 4 percent (plus adjustments for inflation) withdrawal rate led to a successful outcome (money lasting for the rest of your life) a vast majority of the time. If the stock market has dropped significantly over the past year, it might also be worth delaying retirement a year or two or growing your side-hustle income to offset the money you would need to withdraw. However, you always want to withdraw as little money from your investments as you can to support as much compounding growth as possible. Even if the stock market is up 23 percent one year, you should still stick to as little money as you need and leave the rest in to grow.

You can also minimize the sequence-of-returns risk with the right withdrawal strategy, which might include moving some of your investments into fixed income (bonds) that you can live off during your first five to ten years of retirement, while leaving the rest of your money in stocks to continue growing. This way you would guarantee income that's not impacted by the performance of the stock market.

You should try to live off cash and your fixed-income investments and supplement them with your stock market withdrawals; this way you are always keeping as much money growing in the stock market during both down and up years. During the years when the stock market is down, you should live off your fixed income and cash, and then the years it's up, you can live off your stock returns.

A 3 to 4 percent withdrawal rate is an extremely conservative withdrawal strategy, and as long as you are reasonable during your first five to ten years of retirement, after that period your investment portfolio could easily double, triple, or quadruple in size over the subsequent years, making it possible for you to easily increase your expenses and spend more money if you want. For example, if your expected annual expenses are $50,000 and you have $1,250,000 invested before you retired and you live off 3 to 4 percent withdrawals, your portfolio could very realistically grow to $5,000,000 or more over the next thirty plus years, making it possible as your money grows for you to take much larger withdrawals than $50,000 and start spending more as you get older. After all, 4 percent of $5,000,000 is a $200,000 withdrawal! But since you want your money to last for the rest of your life, withdraw only what you need.

WITHDRAW FROM TAXABLE ACCOUNTS FIRST

While this can vary depending on your personal financial situation, based on the current tax laws if you need to live off your investment gains before you are fifty-nine and a half, then it is better to withdraw from your accounts in the following order. First, take withdrawals from accounts that have no early withdrawal penalties. Also, you should withdraw only a percentage of your investment gains, not your principal, because you want to keep as much of your gains and your original investments growing.

The three big benefits of withdrawing from your taxable accounts are that there are no early withdrawal penalties so you can withdraw the money whenever you want, you pay taxes only on your investment gains, and your investment gains on investments you've held for at least one year are taxed at the capital gains tax rates, which are significantly lower than regular income tax rates. Using your gains in your taxable accounts first will let your tax-advantaged accounts keep growing, which ultimately gives you more tax benefits.

Here are the current capital gains tax rates compared to income tax rates.

If you're married, you and your spouse could withdraw any money you have in taxable accounts tax-free up to $77,200! Even if you withdraw more than $77,200, you are taxed at only a 15 percent capital gains rate up to $479,000 for a married couple filing jointly. Many early retirees have annual expenses that are less than $77,200, and they take advantage of the 0 percent capital gains rate to pay no taxes.

One caveat with your taxable account is if you've built a portfolio specifically to generate consistent stock dividend income that you plan to withdraw to live on. If you've built a dividend portfolio that completely covers your monthly expenses, then you can easily keep the portfolio intact and live off it forever!

After completely exhausting the gains on your taxable accounts, you can start withdrawing your principal before touching your tax-advantaged accounts. After you've exhausted your taxable investments, then you can start withdrawing from your tax-advantaged accounts using the following withdrawal strategy.

U.S. Federal Tax Brackets and Long-Term Capital Gains (2018)

Tax Bracket	Single Taxpayers	Married Filing Jointly	Head of Household
10%	$0 - $9,525	$0 - $19,050	$0 - $13,600
12%	$9,526 - $38,700	$19,051 - $77,400	$13,600 - $51,800
22%	$38,701 - $82,500	$77,401-$165,000	$51,800 - $82,500
24%	$82,501 - $157,500	$165,001 - $315,000	$82,500 - $157,500
32%	$157,501 - $200,000	$315,001 - $400,000	$157,500 - $200,000
35%	$200,000 - $500,000	$400,001 - $600,000	$200,000 - $500,000
37%	over $500,000	over $600,000	over $500,000

Long Term Capital Gains Rate	Single Taxpayers	Married Filing Jointly	Head of Household
0%	$0 - $38,600	$0 - $77,200	$0 - $51,700
15%	$38,600-$425,800	$77,200-$479,000	$51,700 - $452,400
20%	over $425,800	over $479,000	over $452,400

ata source: Internal Revenue Service

TAX-ADVANTAGED ACCOUNT WITHDRAWAL STRATEGY

Here's the order you should start withdrawing from your tax-advantaged accounts:

1. Traditional 401(k) or 403(b)
2. Traditional IRA
3. HSA
4. 457(b)

5. Roth IRA
6. Roth 401(k)

No matter what, you should take withdraws from your Roth accounts last because the investment gains are growing tax-free. If you need the money before you are fifty-nine and a half, the nice thing about a Roth IRA is that you can withdraw your contributions anytime without penalty and you can withdraw them first, letting your investment gains continue to grow. If you can hold out on your Roth IRA until you are fifty-nine and a half, when you can withdraw from it penalty-free, you will be able to maximize its remarkable tax benefits. Even if you have to withdraw from it earlier than that, you should withdraw from it only as a last resort.

If you invested in a Roth 401(k), then you should convert your Roth 401(k) to a Roth IRA before taking any withdrawals, because with a Roth 401(k) you have to withdraw a percentage of your contributions and gains, so you are taxed if you take early withdrawals and get subjected to a 10 percent early withdrawal penalty.

When you withdraw money from a tax-advantaged non-Roth account, you pay taxes on your principal investment as well as on any gains you've earned based on your tax bracket at the time of withdrawal. Since your tax bracket is based on your level of income, the lower your income when you retire, the less in taxes you will pay on these withdrawals.

If your only income is from your investments and you withdraw less than $77,400 after your deductions (remember you can still get the standard tax deductions even as an early retiree!) and you are married filing jointly, then your 401(k) withdrawals would be taxed at 12 percent. However, if you withdraw just one dollar more, $77,401, you would need to pay 22 percent. If you withdraw this money before you are fifty-nine and a half, you will also be subject to the 10 percent early withdrawal penalty on top of any taxes, all of which reduces the amount of money you can leave to grow in your investment accounts.

There is an amazing way to avoid the 10 percent early withdrawal penalty on your tax-advantaged accounts, but you have to get a little creative.

THE ROTH IRA CONVERSION LADDER

Let me introduce you to one of most valuable early retirement withdrawal strategies, the Roth IRA conversion ladder. Here's how it works. Because of a specific bit of magic hidden within the U.S. tax code, any money that been converted from a 401(k) to Traditional IRA to a Roth IRA can be withdrawn without the 10 percent early withdrawal penalty exactly five years after the conversion. Note: As is true with all tax strategies, the Roth IRA conversion ladder could change with a future tax law update. So definitely check if it's still possible when you are reading this in the future.

This is how the Roth IRA conversion ladder works:

1. First convert the money in your 401(k) or 403(b) into a Traditional IRA.
2. Next convert your Traditional IRA into a Roth IRA. You'll need to pay taxes here, so convert only as much as you'll need. It will be easier for you to determine how much you might need to withdraw to cover your living expenses as you get closer to retirement.
3. In five years you can withdraw the money you converted from your Roth IRA penalty-free.

The reason it's called a *ladder* is because every year you will want to convert another portion of your Traditional IRA to a Roth IRA so that you are building a ladder: at each step you have five years after the conversion to withdraw the money tax-free. A popular strategy is to live off your taxable investments for the first five years of early retirement, during which time you start building your Roth IRA conversion ladder so you can minimize the taxes you pay on the conversions.

By the time you retire or you need to live off your tax-advantaged money, you will have already staggered your annual Traditional IRA to Roth IRA conversions over the past five years so you can start withdrawing the money tax-free right away.

With any conversion of a Traditional IRA to a Roth IRA, you will be paying taxes at your income tax level on that portion of the converted amount you previously did not pay taxes on as well as on the investment gains included in the conversion. While you can set up your ladder whenever you want, in order to minimize the taxes, you should start building the ladder after you've already retired or when you income is low, so you can minimize the taxes you pay on the conversions. This is why it's important to live off your taxable investments first.

You will owe the taxes on the conversion when you do your taxes for the year the conversion happened, so the earlier in the year you convert, the longer you can delay paying taxes on the conversion. For example, if you do the conversion on January 2, you don't have to pay taxes on the conversion until the following April, when your taxes for the previous year are due. Always pay your Roth IRA conversion taxes with money from outside your Roth IRA, so you can leave more money invested and compounding tax-free! Money growing money!

While this might sound like a lot of work to eliminate the 10 percent withdrawal penalty, it's like a getting a 10 percent return on your money! You don't want to lose that 10 percent, especially since the more money you can keep invested, the longer it can continue to compound. You can also convert *any* amount of money (there are no limits). For example, if you convert $100,000 from your Traditional IRA to a Roth IRA in 2018, then exactly five years and one day later in 2023, you can withdraw the money completely free with no penalty.

While this is pretty easy to set up on your own, if you need help, you can call the company that holds your investments or hire a fee-only tax or financial advisor who specializes in early retirement to help you. Some financial advisors will have no clue what a Roth IRA conversion ladder even is, but it's important you do it correctly so you don't get stuck with a huge tax bill. This is why it's always best to build your ladder after you've retired when your income, and thus your tax rate, is low.

KEEP YOUR INCOME AS LOW AS POSSIBLE AND OPTIMIZE TAX DEDUCTIONS

The lower your income, the less tax you'll pay on your investment gains, and you might even be able to pay $0 in taxes if you manage your income so as to stay below the minimum income tax and capital gains tax thresholds. Once you do decide to live off your investments, it's essential that you limit your income from all sources to only what you need in order to keep your taxes as low as possible. While this might sound like a lot of work, it's not, and by the time you've determined you're close to reaching financial independence, you can learn more about how to pace your investment withdrawals monthly to keep your annual taxes as low as possible. The lower your expenses, the lower your tax burden will be and the further your money will go—yet another benefit of trying to live on less!

Tax deductions can also significantly reduce (and in some cases completely eliminate) the taxes you have to pay on your investment withdrawals. As of this writing the standard tax deduction for a married couple filing jointly is $24,000, and you can also take deductions for many other things like children, qualified stock dividends, medical expenses, business expenses, and more. It's worth learning as much as you can about tax optimization and/or hiring an accountant by the hour who knows about early retirement strategies to teach you the ins and outs of tax optimization. While tax optimization might sound boring, the better you are (or your accountant is) at doing your taxes, the more you can reduce your tax bill, the more money you can keep invested, so the more it can grow and the longer it can last. Just like the rest of money management, tax optimization also gets easier over time.

WHAT'S NEXT?

If you do plan to retire early, you'll want to have a plan for how you are going to spend your time. Definitely take some time to chill out, but it's healthy for humans to work in some capacity. However, the definition of "work" is completely open and can mean taking a part-time job doing something you love; pursuing a passion project or new business venture; engaging in a personal mission or community service; traveling the world; getting in shape; or anything you've always wanted to do. Remember "retirement" can mean whatever you want it to mean. That's freedom.

There are many stories of early retirees who worked hard and strategically to retire early only to be met with an "okay, what do I do now?" on the other side. When you've spent your whole working life trying to attain this goal, you'll need somewhere to put that energy once you reach it. Whether or not your identity was wrapped up in your job title, salary, and professional status or not, you should prepare for the transition.

A bunch of factors—for example, your personality, how you make money, how you reached financial independence, and whether you liked your job or not—will likely determine how easy the transition actually is for you. Once you do decide to make the transition, you can either ease into it or jump right in. Plan the best you can and do what feels right to you. Do what you've always wanted to do and take the time to discover new things. Let yourself grow and change. I can't even imagine where I'll be in five, ten, twenty, or thirty years.

Freedom is immense and uncertain. But life is infinitely rich when you open to it.

RECAP

1. Once you are ready to retire, you'll need to develop the right investment withdrawal strategy to ensure your money will last as long as possible.

2. It's never too early to start planning your investment withdrawal strategy so you can minimize any early withdrawal penalties (for withdrawing money before you are fifty-nine and a half from your tax-advantaged accounts) and the impact of taxes from your taxable accounts.

3. Live off your side or passive income as long as you can.

4. Make the most of your tax deductions.

5. Withdraw money from your taxable accounts first.

6. Tax-advantaged withdrawal strategy: Here's the order in which you should start withdrawing from your tax-advantaged accounts: (1) Traditional 401(k) or 403(b); (2) Traditional IRA; (3) HSA; (4) 457(b); (5) Roth IRA; (6) Roth 401(k).

7. Roth Conversion Ladder: Because of a specific bit of magic hidden within the U.S. tax code, you can withdraw funds that have been converted from a 401(k) to a Traditional IRA to a Roth IRA any time five calendar years after the conversion event with no 10 percent early

withdrawal penalty. Note that you will need to pay tax on the conversion from the Traditional IRA to the Roth IRA.

8. **If you do plan to really retire early, you'll want to have ways to fill your time and enough interests to keep you busy.** Ideally you should be retiring to something, like a passion project, a deep mission, worldwide travel, or something you've always wanted to do. Freedom is immense and uncertain. And life is infinitely rich when you open up to it.

CHAPTER 13

THE FUTURE OPTIMIZATION FRAMEWORK

Daily, Weekly, Monthly, Quarterly, and Annual Habits

Throughout this book you've learned the mindset and framework that can help you make as much money as possible. You've learned how to track your net worth, calculate *your number* and break it down into smaller goals, calculate your savings rate, see money for its future potential, get a raise and use your full-time job as a launching pad, find and grow a profitable side hustle, invest in real estate, minimize your investment taxes and fees, and maximize your investing returns.

While everyone wants to get rich quick and you might be able to do it, more realistically this book won't help you get rich quick, but it *will* help you get rich *quicker*. For some it will be harder than others, but whether it takes you five more or twenty more years to hit your number, the rules of the game are the same for everyone: spend less money, make more money, minimize your taxes, and invest as much as you can.

As you'll remember from earlier in the book, adopting an enterprise mindset is all about finding ways to make as much money as you can for your time. When I started taking money seriously in 2010, I was focused on making a million dollars as quickly as possible so I wouldn't have to work at a job I didn't like for the next forty years. A few years in, I realized I had a shot at making it happen in five years. But it took more than having a good plan.

While you've learned the strategies to make financial independence possible, they are worthless unless you put them into practice. In this chapter you'll learn the future optimization framework, which is designed to help you use everything you've learned in your daily life.

THE FUTURE OPTIMIZATION FRAMEWORK

The following four principles are the foundation of this framework and will significantly increase your chances of success in both money and other areas of your life.

JUST GET STARTED

Remember this book is about maximizing both your money and your time, so you need to start implementing the strategies you've learned as soon as possible. Don't waste time. Do something right now, today. Whether it's increasing the amount you are saving in your 401(k), planning how to get a raise, starting a side hustle, or just saving an extra $5. Do it right now.

Getting started is more important than making the perfect decision. Choosing "good enough" right now is more important than waiting for the perfect time or the perfect job or the perfect idea. Don't overanalyze it. While you might be the only one of your friends or family who is following this path (until you convert them!), don't wait until you've learned everything. You'll learn by doing. You're also not the first one to walk this path. You can learn from others. You can learn from me. You'll learn as you go. You'll always be learning.

No matter how many books you read or classes you take, there is absolutely no substitute for actually getting out and doing it. Trust me, the more experience you get, the easier it is to make decisions based on predictable outcomes. Seeing moneymaking opportunities becomes easier. Investing becomes easier. Being comfortable with risk gets easier. Knowing when to take risks get easier. Knowing when to say yes or no becomes easier.

I made a ton of mistakes, and you will, too. The key is to not let them derail you. Just keep at it. Do me a favor: put this book down and log into your bank account right now and take a screenshot of your bank account balances today; print one out and hang it in your bathroom or closet—somewhere you will see it every day. Now go to futureme.org, which is a free tool that allows you to send an email today to yourself at a specified data in the future. Write an email to yourself one year and five years into the future answering these three questions:

1. What does financial freedom mean to you?
2. What makes you happy?
3. Where do you want to be in one year and in five years?

Hit me up!

What does financial freedom mean to you? Use the hashtag #financial-freedombook or hit me up on Twitter @sabatier or @millennialmoney, Instagram @millennialmoneycom, email me at grant@millennialmoney.com, or share at financialfreedombook.com. I'd love to hear from you.

This is exactly what Anita, who retired at thirty-three, did. She sent emails to her future self to stay motivated throughout her financial independence journey. With each email she opened in the future, she realized how far she had come and how much she had grown. Remember, who you are in five years will likely be a lot different from who you are today—your goals and priorities and dreams will change as you do.

This is your starting point. You'll look back on this in one year and be amazed at how far you've come. Eight years ago, I was completely broke and knew nothing about anything in this book. Just one year later I had increased my savings rate from 0 percent to almost 60 percent, had diversified my income streams from one to seven, and had saved up over $100,000.

Here are ten things you can do get started today:

1. Increase your 401(k) contribution rate by at least 1 percent. Try for 5 percent or more.
2. Open a Roth IRA if you don't have one, or if you do, contribute at least $5 to it. If you don't qualify for Roth IRA, open a Traditional IRA and contribute at least $5.
3. Set up a daily or weekly automatic deposit of at least $5 to your Roth IRA or another account.
4. Review your job benefits and make sure you are taking full advantage of them.

5. Analyze your current market value and start building your case for a raise.
6. Write down five new side-hustle ideas.
7. Reach out to three new interesting people to schedule a lunch or coffee with them.
8. If you're renting your home, calculate if it makes sense to buy a home and figure out how much money you will need to do so.
9. If you own a home, start looking for a rental property.
10. Set up a savings rate tracking spreadsheet or start using an online tool.

FOCUS INTENSELY AND LEARN TO SAY NO

Just as it's never been easier to make money, it's also never been easier to waste time.

We surf the web mindlessly for hours or binge-watch TV shows for entire weekends at a time. People are good at wasting time. But remember your time is the most valuable thing you have. Make the most of it.

It doesn't matter how much time you spend at your desk or how many emails you send or how many meetings you have or how busy you are or how hard you work or how many things you get done, if you aren't working on the right things, you'll never accomplish anything of value.

If you want to get ahead with money (and other areas of your life), you've got to learn to say yes to yourself and no to almost everything else. No one cares about your time or money as much as you. Give both generously when you want and protect them dearly when you don't. If you just let life happen to you, then it's going to eat up both your money and your time. That's just the way the world works. If you don't push against the current, you're more likely to get carried away. Learning to say no was one of the hardest and most important lessons I've learned. And I'm still learning how to do it.

The more time you spend focusing on the things that actually help you make money and the less time you spend on things that don't, the more effective you will be. When your friends ask you to grab drinks after work, but you know you should be putting in extra time on your side hustle, saying no will put you one step closer toward reaching your goal. When your partner asks you to snuggle up and watch Netflix on a Tuesday night but you haven't completed what you wanted to that day, say no and realize that, in the long run, you're doing both of you a favor.

Of course, you can't say no all the time (nor would you want to), but investing more of your time today to reclaim 5 to 10 times the time tomorrow is an opportunity, not a sacrifice. Remember $1 today is $10 in twenty years, and one hour hustling today is worth twenty to thirty hours (or more) of freedom in the future.

Be relentless with your time and focus. You'll quickly learn to differentiate between the things that matter and the things that don't and will become more mindful of the trade-off. Here are ten ways you can start saying no and start focusing right now:

1. **Look at your to-do list.** What is one thing that isn't a priority and doesn't align with your goals that you can say no to today?

2. **Look at your calendar.** What meetings can you cancel?

3. **Now look at your calendar and block off at least five minutes a day to spend time with your money.** I recommend doing it first thing in the morning and making it a part of your morning routine.

4. **Look at your calendar and schedule in time for things that you really love and make you happy that have nothing to do with making money.** This is different from absent-mindedly wasting precious minutes (or hours) of your life on Facebook or Instagram. Whether it's reading a book, playing pickup basketball, or whatever, schedule time to do it. Life often has a way of getting in the way.

5. **If you get a ton of emails, set up a new personal email address that only your closest friends and family know about.** Create strong boundaries with email, which is most people's biggest time waster.

6. **Turn your phone on airplane mode and disconnect your computer from Wi-Fi to focus.**

7. **Limit your meetings and calls to specific times during the week.** I often block off one day and one evening for calls. Remember to block off time for yourself before anything else.

8. **Cancel any subscriptions, classes, or commitments that you've determined are a distraction to your achieving your goal and that don't serve you in some other way.**

9. **If you have a partner, schedule a time with him or her to discuss your new path and get him or her on board.** This might take some time. Don't push. Be patient. Talk about life goals as a bridge to the money conversation. Check out the Money Talk Cards at *https://financialfreedombook.com/tools* to guide the conversations.

10. **The next time that someone asks you to do something, think about how it fits into your larger personal and professional goals.** Say no when it's unclear.

EXECUTE CONSISTENTLY

The strategies in this book are not going to help get you rich overnight, but they will help you get rich over time if you stick with them. This is why consistent execution is so important.

Success is built on daily habits. Spending a few minutes each day monitoring your finances, trying to make more money, increasing your savings rate, and optimizing will not only add up but will actually compound over time. If you take a few minutes every day to focus on your money, you'll become more mindful and managing your money will become easier. It takes only about thirty days to build a habit, so put in the effort up front to build good habits and you'll find that making good money decisions becomes not only easier but second nature.

Balance your micro (daily) and macro (yearly and beyond) goals.

You've already broken down your number into daily, weekly, monthly, and annual goals. Try your best to hit your target numbers and then push beyond them. If you miss them one day, pick up the next.

Below is a blueprint of what I did daily, weekly, monthly, quarterly, and annually as I pursued financial freedom. It's pretty much the exact schedule I used to optimize my own money. Use this as a starting point and customize it based on where you are on your own financial freedom journey.

To keep track of your progress you should use both an online net worth tracker and a manual spreadsheet to regularly record your progress (as noted below). The exact spreadsheet template that I use and you can download, as well as the net worth tracker, is at https://financialfreedombook. com/tools

Daily (five minutes)

- Check your net worth using a net worth tracking app.
- Invest at least an extra $5 each day in one account.
- Strategize how to make an extra $50 today.

Weekly (ten minutes)

- Check secondary and passive income performance (for example, investment performance, website revenue, rental income, side-hustle income, and so forth).
- Check credit card charges from the past week to look for discrepancies.
- Look for missing payments owed to you.

Monthly (one hour)

- Review monthly saving performance (in dollars and percentages).
- Increase savings percentage at least 1 percent.
- Check passive and secondary income performance.
- Pay monthly bills. I actually recommend doing so manually instead of setting up automatic payments because paying the bill yourself every month will make you feel it more and force

you to reevaluate your expenses and identify ways to save money.

- Analyze personal and business cash flow (aka how much money is coming in and going out).
- Adjust your cash flow projection spreadsheet for the next month and rest of year. Especially if your income is variable, it's essential to project how much cash will be coming into your life over the next three to six months to ensure you are able to cover your expenses and invest. Cash flow management is an art, and you'll get better at balancing how much money you need over time.

Quarterly (one hour)

- Check *your number* progress and reanalyze the target.
- Check your target asset allocation and rebalance if necessary.
- Recalculate your real hourly rate for each of your income streams and combined income and record it on your spreadsheet.
- Check your credit score using a free service—look for anything weird, like debt that you didn't take out or payments that you made that are posted as late or delinquent.
- Check passive and secondary income performance.
- Analyze personal and business cash flow.
- Adjust cash flow projections.

Annually (three hours)

- Review automated investments and payments.
- Prepare for tax optimization and minimization.
- Project cash flow for the following year and analyze your estimates over the past year.
- Review investment account fees to ensure they haven't increased.
- Review annual subscriptions to magazines, streaming services, memberships.
- Review annual giving strategy.

Now that I have reached financial independence, my daily routines have shifted a bit. I spend less time tracking my individual expenses and more time adjusting my investment performance in order to ensure my money is working as hard as possible for me, optimizing my taxes to make sure I am being as tax efficient as possible, and analyzing the performance of my websites and online income streams. Over time as your investments grow, you should also start adding in regular tasks to optimize how you are spending, making, and investing money.

Now that J.P. has retired at twenty-eight, she tracks a mixture of permanent and rotating metrics. She permanently tracks her net worth and monthly expenses by category over a two-year period, and also rotates out other metrics that for specific period of time get her intense scrutiny, like how much money she is spending going out with friends.

SHARE AND KNOW WHEN TO ASK FOR HELP

No matter how much you know about something, there's always going to be someone out there who knows more. Money is too taboo in this world. We don't talk about it enough with the people around us, with our families, friends, romantic partners, and coworkers. We are embarrassed or unhappy with our salaries or we are scared of our boss, so we don't talk about our salaries with coworkers—possibly leaving money on the table. We are afraid to ask for help when we don't know the right answer or when we're deep in debt. We hide our debts or purchases from our partners because we're afraid of what they'll think.

The more you talk about money, the more you and those around you will learn. Share this book with your partner, a few of your friends, family members, or coworkers. Set up a monthly hangout to share your challenges and strategies for making more money. Pick up a deck of the Money Talk Cards to help facilitate your money conversations. They're available at *https://financialfreedombook.com/tools*. Join a local financial independence group or the financial freedom community at *https://millennialmoney.com*.

One of the fastest ways to accelerate financial freedom is to keep learning from others. Stay curious. Never stop. Read books. Download podcasts. Take courses. Everything you learn will compound throughout your life. The more you surround yourself with money ideas, the more you'll learn and the more money you'll make.

When I recently had a complex question about LLC equity structures, I reached out to one of the world's top experts on the topic and paid him $300 for fifteen minutes of his time. He usually charges $1,200 per hour but agreed to chat with me for fifteen minutes one day over lunch. I was able to get access (and learn from) a global expert, and now I have access to information that you can't even find online. I've done this many times for legal and tax questions.

You can also do it for financial questions or when you run into a complex issue. Many financial advisors can even chat with you over Skype on your own time. Ideally use financial advisors to fill your knowledge gaps, not manage your money. If you want to work with a financial advisor, work with fee-only financial advisors who charge per hour, not based on a percentage of your assets.

CHILL AS HARD AS YOU HUSTLE

Making money can be addictive, and it's easy to spend all of your time and energy pursuing financial independence. Between 2010 and 2015 I was at an all-out sprint the entire time. I didn't sleep much and made a lot of sacrifices, including losing some friendships and occasionally my health. I cycled between working super hard and crashing for entire weeks. There were weeks when I was so burnt out I couldn't get off the couch. It definitely wasn't healthy.

Looking back, I see a lot that I would have done differently, but the biggest mistake I made was actually working too much. I never set any boundaries, which is a huge risk for so many of us in the digital economy. There are many benefits to being able to work anywhere anytime, but it also makes it harder for us turn off. I was working about eighty hours a week for five straight years.

Now it's easy for me to see how I could have been more effective and maybe made even more money if I had simply rested more. I wasted a lot of time working on projects when I was too tired to be effective or lost weeks recovering. While it's totally worth putting in an extra twenty to thirty hours a week for a few years to buy an extra twenty to thirty years in the future, be mindful about how you are using your own time. Taking a break might be just what you need.

If you're feeling burned out, the best strategy is to stop immediately and rest—like, not keep working rest, actually get in bed and sleep rest. If you keep pushing, you'll likely get sick. Slow way down, get out into nature, do walking meditation, eat healthy, drink green juice, sleep, get exercise, do some yoga, and don't forget to breathe. Breath is the best medicine. Remember: life > money.

RECAP

1. **While you've learned the strategies to make early retirement possible, they are worthless unless you put them into practice.**

2. **Just get started.** Remember this book is about maximizing both your money and your time, so you need to start implementing the strategies you've learned as soon as possible. Don't waste time.

3. **This is your starting point.** You'll look back on this in one year and be amazed at how far you've come.

4. **Focus intensely and learn to say no.** Just as it's never been easier to make money, it's also never been easier to waste time. We surf the web mindlessly for hours or binge-watch TV shows for entire weekends at a time. People are good at wasting time. But remember your time is the most valuable resource you have. Make the most of it.

5. **Execute consistently: The strategies in this book are not going to help get you rich overnight, but they will help you get rich over time if you stick with them.** This is why consistent execution is important.

6. **Know when to ask to help: No matter how much you know about something, there's always going to be someone out there who knows more.**

7. **Chill as hard as you hustle.** While it's totally worth putting in an extra twenty hours a week for a few years to buy an extra twenty to thirty years in the future, be mindful about how you are using your own time. Taking a break might be just what you need. Breathing is the best medicine. Life > Money.

CHAPTER 14

LIVING A RICHER LIFE

A Path to Financial Independence

> Everything is connected to everything else.
>
> —THE BUDDHA

It's a warm early summer Monday morning and the air smells like flowers. The light pulls the color out of everything—the greens are greener; the pinks and blues from the hydrangea bushes are exploding, producing an almost psychedelic effect. The freshly squeezed orange juice just tastes sweeter, richer, fuller. Today feels open and free like those days when you were a kid with nothing but time to exist, explore, and be curious.

I am writing this on a balcony with grape vines spilling over the sides. I'm staying at the Castel Fragsburg, tucked high in the Dolomites in Northern Italy. I'm high above the road, looking down into the valley. The traffic is building on the highway below, as workers rush to their jobs on another Monday morning.

Just a few years ago, a scene like this would have played out only in my daydreams, but now that I've reached financial independence, it has become my reality. Money made it all possible, but strangely enough, money is now one of the last things on my mind. When I was broke, money meant anxiety, missed opportunities, and stress. I always felt like I wouldn't be able to live the life I truly wanted to live. When I didn't have any money, money was all I thought about.

But a radical shift happened. The moment I had $10,000 in the bank and realized that I had escaped living paycheck to paycheck, the stress started to disappear. Then when I had $50,000 (a full year of expenses) saved, I started worrying less about money. The more money I made and at level of financial freedom I reached, the more in control I felt. Once I reached financial independence at thirty, I felt free.

You can have this freedom, too. As long as you have a decent middle-class income and live in a place with a reasonable cost of living and you can save 40 to 50 percent of your income, you should be able to hit your number in ten to fifteen years. If you really hit the accelerator, you might be able to do it in five years or less. If you live in an expensive place or make less than $25,000 per year, it could take you longer, but no matter where you live, the more money you make and save, the faster you can make work optional. I know you can make it happen.

Once I reached financial independence at thirty and came up for air, I started searching for other people who'd also reached financial independence before the age of thirty-five. I was delighted to find a small but growing group of people I'm now happy to call my friends. Here are some of their stories and how they felt after reaching financial independence.

Steve spent his twelve-year career working in IT at a job he just never really liked. But his aha moment came when he got married and realized how much money he and his wife, Courtney, could save with two incomes. After getting married, they committed to saving 70 percent of their incomes, simply so they could have more options in life and do what made them happy—which was traveling around the country in their Airstream camper, taking life as it comes. Once they increased their savings rate and automated most of their investments, their net worth grew quickly. When they hit their goal of $890,000 at age thirty-five, they both walked away with the plan to live on $25,000 to $30,000 for the rest of their lives. Less than a year later, because they are able to live off less than their investment growth, their net worth is now over $1 million (and growing).

To Steve, financial independence means the freedom to say no and not to have to make decisions because of money. "Instead, I can think free and clear and make choices that directly affect my happiness rather than my pocketbook. I wouldn't trade this kind of freedom for all the money in the world. After all, we tend to remember the happiness we experienced, rather than the money we earned or things we owned, at the end of our lives. Happiness and freedom are the keys to life, and money is nothing more than the means to get there." Steve now blogs about his life after working at thinksaveretire.com.

Michelle used to work as a financial analyst but quit in 2013 to become a full-time blogger after two years of blogging at makingsenseofcents.com. After making a bit of money blogging and paying off her student loans early, she realized she could reach financial independence by increasing her savings rate (which at its peak was 90 percent) and earning enough income from her blog to cover her monthly living expenses. Michelle also realized she didn't need to spend a lot of money to be happy. "Many people think they need a huge house, car payments, and more in order to be happy in life, but that's just not the case."

Michelle reached financial independence at the age of twenty-eight after making over $1.5 million through her blog. Even though she never put her number in stone, she knows she has enough money because her investment gains easily cover the amount of money she spends each month and she has no plans to retire. Michelle really loves what she does: "Life is great, I work less than ten hours a week, and I can do what I love most—travel full time with my husband and our two dogs."

Anita used to suffer from depression, which has subsided now that she no longer has to work seventy hours a week and can flow with the rhythms of a much less stressful life. Her first job out of college, she worked in insurance making between $40,000 and $55,000 per year, but she eventually realized she would need to make more money if she wanted to make work optional as quickly as possible.

So Anita went to law school and took out $100,000 in student loans with the goal of getting a really high-paying job so she could save a lot of money. Shortly after graduating from law school, she landed a job at a big law firm as a corporate attorney specializing in mergers and acquisitions. During her five years she made between $160,000 and $310,000 and saved about 85 percent of her salary by living in a modest apartment and only buying stuff used. She paid off her low interest student loans in four years.

Anita hit her number at thirty-three and walked away from her high-paying legal career shortly after. Her coworkers and boss just couldn't believe she was actually walking away, but that was her plan all along. "To have control of your time and your life goes such a long way. If you are living the life you design, how can you not be happy?" Anita also blogs about her adventurous life at thepowerofthrift.com.

Justin worked as a civil engineer for ten years in Raleigh, North Carolina, with a starting salary of $48,000 in 2004 and an ending salary of $69,000 in 2013. After getting his job in college, Justin ended up with extra money at the end of the month, so he started investing it. He then ran the numbers and realized he would have enough money to live off for the rest of his life long before he turned sixty-five.

While Justin and his wife never had a target savings rate, they just tried to live a frugal life and save the rest. Their savings rate ended up fluctuating between 50 and 70 percent most years. While their original goal was to save $2.5 million, the longer they saved, the less they realized they needed, settling on between $1.3 million and $1.4 million as their goal. At the age of thirty-three, Justin was let go from his job, but after running the numbers he realized he never had to work again. "I still get a smile on my face every time I think about how fortunate I am to be in this position. It's eleven A.M. in the middle of the week and I'm lying in the hammock reading a book—every day if I want. That makes me happy." Justin blogs about his life and money at rootofgood.com.

Kristy and Bryce worked in IT in Canada and were able to save a ton of money quickly by not buying into the idea of needing to buy a home. They just really wanted to get out of the corporate world. Back when they were working, they felt like every day was a grind, and all they could think about was hoarding money so they could get out. They said they spent all of their time surviving, just keeping their head above water; they didn't have time to think about anything else.

Their savings grew quickly and they reached financial independence at thirty-one and thirty-two, with a little over $1 million saved. Now that they are financially independent, "when we wake up in the morning, we think about what can we do to help the world rather than what can we can do to help ourselves." This means spending their time giving back, including volunteering for We Need Diverse Books, a nonprofit dedicated to bringing diversity to children's books, and teaching people about investing on their blog millennial-revolution.com.

J.P. retired at the age of twenty-eight with over $2 million after making a ton of money working in financial services. While she has always wanted to be a writer and was a liberal arts major in college, after an on-campus interview with a financial services company, she realized she could use her job as a means to retire as quickly as possible. She didn't buy into the hype that just because you make more money, you need to spend more. By keeping her expenses as low as possible in New York, which included living in a 300-square-foot apartment, J.P. saved at least 80 percent of her income and walked away in five years. Now she spends her time writing, walking her dog, hanging with her family, and blogging at themoneyhabit.org.

Brandon worked in web development and focused on saving as much money as possible as soon as he got his first job. During a ten-year period he was able to get 15 to 25 percent salary raises from each company and the opportunity to work remotely. Brandon and his wife, Jill, keep their living expenses low, and while it took them some time to figure out the exact spending level that made them happy, they realized it was somewhere between $38,000 and $45,000 per year.

By focusing on investing in tax-advantaged accounts, they were able to keep their taxes as low as possible, save more money, and reach financial independence at the age of thirty-two. Having lived in both Europe and the United States, Brandon believes the United States is the "perfect place for financial independence to happen as quickly as possible" due to higher wages, the opportunity to control your expenses, and all of the tax loopholes you can find. Now Brandon spends his time making music and teaching others how to optimize their finances on his blog madfientist .com, and Jill continues working because she loves her job.

> I was out late the other night and I was, like, I'm going to be really tired in the morning. Then I remembered there's nothing on my schedule that needs to get done. Even though I want to be productive every day, I don't have to be. It's just an amazing feeling to know that my day is my own. I recommend it to anyone. It's totally worth any sacrifice it takes to get there.

Money has the potential to change your life. To give you more opportunities. To allow you to help your family, community, and causes you care about. Money is a reflection of who you are. How you save, invest, and what you buy, the charities your support, are all a reflection of you. How you spend your money is how you value the world. Money is a way we can turn what's inside us and around us into personal power to make a difference in the world.

One of the most profound lessons I've learned about money is you can either control it or let it control you. If you let it stress you out, if you make it your god, it wins. But when you are conscious of money's power and know how it works, you can win. Mastering your money is about mastering yourself. We all have emotions about money, but the more you talk about money and spend just a few minutes on it each day, the more aware and mindful you'll become and the easier it will be to understand and control.

Money is no longer some abstract confusing thing that you want, it's something you have and know how to get. Once you know how money works, you can let it go and come to it on your own terms. Instead of a worry, it becomes an opportunity. As you start saving and making more money, other changes will start happening in your life. You will worry less, feel more in control, and have more opportunities. As you master money, you gain freedom through it.

But remember, money is not the goal, time is. Time to do what brings you joy. Time to spend time with those you love. Time to take care of yourself. Time to live the life you want. Whether it takes you five years or twenty years to hit your number, you might be a very different person by the time you get there. So don't put your dreams on hold for the vague promise of retirement. Don't be afraid to change. Search for meaning. Let yourself grow.

Family and friends are more important than money. Money doesn't matter if you don't have anyone to enjoy it with. Spend time with your kids, siblings, parents, grandparents, and friends. Health is more important than money. Try not to burn yourself out. Take time to recover and recharge. No matter how hard you hustle, remember that a pendulum swings both ways. You need to chill as hard as you hustle.

LIVING A RICHER LIFE

I encourage you to think hard about what you want in life and how much money it will actually take to get it. Be honest with yourself about how much you actually need. Define what success means to you. To me, success isn't about money, it's about peace. It's about freedom.

Live your own life, not the one your neighbor or your coworker or the people on social media are living. Too many people get caught up in living a life they feel like they need to live, the life others think they should live. But it's your life, not theirs. It's your time, not theirs. We all get only one life, so live your own. You don't need a nice car or a big house to live an insanely amazing life; in fact, you don't even need a house or car at all. Don't be one of those people who look back on their lives and wish they would have been their true selves. The world needs you to be you.

The world is changing and the systems and jobs that our parents relied on are falling apart. But this is a new path. If you truly commit to the strategy in this book, you will master the capacity to make money and do it on your own terms.

Life, like investing, is about taking calculated risks. It's easy to sit back and play it safe. It's wired into our DNA: don't touch the fire, don't peek over that cliff. Fear keeps us safe, it keeps us alive. But it also keeps us from truly living, from growing, and from getting ahead. The more money you have, the more risks you can take. When you take risks, it will lead to bigger opportunities, experiences, stories, and a richer life.

Another thing I've learned about life and money the past few years—the more calculated risks you take, the happier you'll become. Find ways around the fire and over the cliff. Whether it's asking for a raise, starting a new side hustle, pushing your savings rate to 50 percent, quitting your job to pursue a better opportunity—whatever it is, taking calculated risks will fast-track your financial freedom.

Keep testing and optimizing. Don't be afraid to recalibrate. Life is about learning, balancing, adapting, spending and saving, risk and reward. The strategies you've learned work. Put them into practice and keep at it. And help others. Talk about money. Share your stories. Be open. Be kind. We are all on the same journey around the sun.

Now stop and take a deep breath. Look around you. Take in the moment. The light. The sounds. The people. And be grateful for what you do have—it's already so much more than most people have. The median income globally is only $1,225 a year. If you make $34,000 per year, you are in the top 1 percent of the entire world.

Financial independence is about having the freedom to do whatever *you* want. You can have it. Making a lot of money quickly is possible. Having more time is possible. Living life on your own terms is possible. You have a unique opportunity that many don't. You really can have all the money you'll ever need.

Thank you for spending your precious time with me. I wish you much luck, money, freedom, and happiness. I'd love to hear from you. Use the hashtag #financialfreedombook or hit me up on Twitter @sabatier or @millennialmoney, Instagram @millennialmoneycom, or you can email me at grant@millennialmoney.com. Yes, that's my actual email. For bonus content and more, check out *https://financialfreedombook.com/bonus*.

ACKNOWLEDGMENTS

2 Pages TK

ACKNOWLEDGMENTS

GLOSSARY

Asset allocation—Your asset allocation is the percentage of each asset (for example, stocks, bonds, and cash) you have in your investment accounts. Your target asset allocation determines the level of risk/reward of your investment portfolio. Typically, stocks are riskier investments than bonds, so the more stocks you hold in your portfolio, the risker it is—meaning the more it could go up or down. To pick your target asset allocation, figure out how long it will be before you need to use the money. The more time you have before you need to withdraw your investments, the risker your target asset allocation should be, because you have more time to weather short-term ups and downs and participate in the long-term potential gains.

Assets—These are things you own that have value and could be sold. Your assets are worth the amount you can sell them for, not what you paid. Examples include investments, your business, real estate, cars, cash, jewelry, and anything that you own that has value. When calculating your net worth, you subtract your liabilities from your assets.

Assets under management (AUM)—Some financial advisors and investment managers charge you a percentage of your assets under their management as a fee to manage your investments. This is typically in the 1 to 2 percent range, and you still get charged it even if your investments are down. These fees cut into your returns and your losses and can add up substantially over time, significantly reducing the amount of money you have in the future. I recommend working with fee-only financial advisors, not those who charge you based on AUM.

Backdoor Roth IRA conversion—If your income is too high to contribute to a Roth IRA, you can still make a contribution through a backdoor Roth IRA conversions. To do this, you contribute money to a non-tax-deductible Traditional IRA (meaning you can't deduct your contribution from your taxes) and then convert it by selling it and buying a Roth IRA. You have to pay tax on the money you contributed to your Traditional IRA before doing the conversion, but you have to pay tax only on the investment gains from your Traditional IRA contribution, so if you convert quickly and minimize any gains, you might not have to pay any taxes at all. However, if you already have a Traditional IRA with previous deductible contributions and investment gains in it, there might be tax consequences for making the conversion, so I always recommend consulting with the company that manages your IRA to understand the impact of a backdoor conversion on your taxes.

Bonds—A bond is a form of debt issued when a company, government, or municipality needs money. It's a loan with a guaranteed interest rate attached. When you buy the bond, you are lending money to whoever issued it for a certain period of time at a fixed interest rate. Because the interest rate is fixed (meaning it's set by the bond issuer and doesn't change over time), bonds are known as fixed-income investments, so you can count on the returns as long as the issuer doesn't default on the loan. High-quality bonds (where the borrower, such as the U.S. government, is likely to pay it back) are traditionally viewed as less risky investments than stocks because their interest doesn't change the way a stock price does.

Cash flow—This is the amount of money flowing in and out of your accounts over a given period of time. Managing cash flow is important so you have enough cash on hand to pay your bills and make investments.

Certificate of deposit (CD)—A CD is a certificate issued by a bank for a guaranteed rate of interest on the money you invest over the defined period. It's a common low-cost way to invest money that often will generate a higher investment return than a traditional savings account. However, there are sometimes penalties for taking out the money before the end of the period.

Compounding—Compounding exponentially increases the value of your money or the money you owe over time because the future growth of your money is on your original contribution plus the investment growth, which accelerates over time. For example, if you invest $100 and it grows by 10 percent, you will have $110 at the end of the year (10 percent of $100 = $10; $100 + $10 = $110). If the market grows by another 10 percent the following year, you will earn 10 percent not only on your original $100 investment but also on the $10 return you earned the previous year. This means that at the end of the second year, you would have earned an additional $11 (10 percent of $110 = $11), for a total of $121. This cycle will continue over time, generating increasingly larger growth each year.

Cost of living—This is how much it costs to live in a particular city or country. Common food staples, housing, and entertainment are factored into the cost of living and can vary widely by location. For example, the cost of living in New York City is much higher than it is in Chicago. You can compare the cost of living in two cities by looking at the cost-of-living index or by using a cost-of-living comparison calculator. Check out https://store.coli.org/compare.asp or Bankrate for good calculators.

Dividends—Some companies share some of their profits with their shareholders in the form of a regular cash payment or distribution known as a dividend. It is often best to automatically reinvest dividends back into your investment unless you need the cash.

Emergency fund—An account with money you can easily access in which you save six months of living expenses in either cash or a low-risk investment. In any type of emergency where you need extra money, you should be able to access the emergency fund without incurring any withdrawal penalties or disturbing your long-term investments.

Enterprise mindset—Take advantage of every opportunity to make more money and build wealth in as many ways as possible—by cutting expenses, optimizing fees/prices, minimizing taxes, building multiple income streams, and utilizing whatever other ways present themselves. Focus on making as much money as possible per minute and hour of your time.

Exchange traded funds (ETFs)—ETFs are designed for the purpose of simple diversification and hold either a collection of stocks, a collection of bonds, or a mixture of stocks and bonds (known as blended funds). These funds are typically built around a theme or sector—meaning they hold a group of investments of a specific type or within a particular industry. ETFs behave like stocks and the value can fluctuate throughout the day, making them more flexible investments than mutual funds. They also tend to have very low investment minimums.

Expenses—This is the money you spend living your life. The lower your expenses, the less money you need to save for the future.

Flexible spending account (FSA)—An FSA is a benefit offered by some employers where you can contribute pretax money to help you cover your medical costs. You can use this money only to cover medical costs. While an FSA (if offered by your company) can be used in conjunction with any insurance plan, you lose any money that you don't spend at the end of the year. Plus the contribution limits for FSAs are typically lower than they are for HSAs. Another benefit you should ask your employer about is a dependent care FSA, which many companies offer but few employees know about. With a dependent care FSA, you can contribute money pretax to an account you can use to cover care expenses for your dependents (children or disabled relatives) including summer camps, day care, preschool, and babysitting services.

GLOSSARY

Fiduciary—This is a financial advisor or company required to act in your own best interests. You should always ask whether a financial advisor is a fiduciary.

457(b)–The 457(b) is a type of retirement plan offered by private employers and the U.S. government. If your employer has a 457(b) plan in addition to a 401(k) or 403(b), then you are in luck, because you can often contribute the maximum to both! Another big benefit of the 457(b) account is that you can withdraw the money at any time without any penalties. However, there are some nuances between government and nongovernment 457(b) plans that I can't cover here, but you should check out.

401(k) and 403(b)—401(k)s and 403(b)s are very similar, with the biggest difference being that costs are typically lower that 403(b) plans because they are offered by nonprofits. These are retirement plans offered by employers that allows you to make pretax contributions so the money you contribute isn't taxed and you can deduct your contributions from your taxable income. However, a 401(k) or 403(b) is not an investment; it holds investments, so you need to select how to invest your money within your 401(k). Some employers offer a 401(k) contribution match: they match a percentage of the money you contribute, typically between 2 and 6 percent. Employer contributions are free money and are always worth contributing to get. The government restricts how much you can contribute to a 401(k) or 403(b) each year.

Geographic arbitrage—This is the strategy of minimizing or eliminating the impact of inflation and taxes in your home country by moving to another one with lower or no inflation or taxes so your money goes further. Depending on where you live and the strength of your currency, you may be able to get a lot more for your money living in another country or utilizing cheaper services outside of your country, like healthcare, which is significantly cheaper outside the United States.

Health savings account (HSA)—An HSA is an employee benefit offered by some employees where you can contribute pretax money to help you cover your medical costs. While you can use this money only to cover medical costs, it will allow you to reduce your tax burden, thereby giving you more money to invest. An HSA is a better benefit than a standard FSA because it gives you the ability to contribute more money, you can invest it, and you don't have to spend it each year. It's worth noting that you typically need to enroll in a high-deductible healthcare insurance plan when you enroll in an HSA, so if you have serious medical issues or to go to the doctor a lot, you might end up spending more on medical bills using an HSA. Run the numbers to see if it makes sense for you. However, your HSA is just like having another retirement account because you get to keep any money you don't spend each year and your investments will continue to grow and compound each year you don't use the money, just as in a 401(k) or IRA. You can then withdraw from your HSA to cover your medical expenses at any time if you need the money, but if you let it keep growing, after the age of sixty-five, you can then withdraw your investment and investment gains to use for any purpose, even if it's not medical related.

House-hacking—House-hacking is an incredible way to invest in real estate and live for free. House-hacking is when you buy a two- or three-bedroom home and rent out the additional rooms to offset, completely cover, or even make money on your mortgage. You can also house-hack by buying multiple units in the same building and renting them out to cover the cost of your own.

Individual retirement account (IRA)—An individual retirement account is a retirement account that you can open on your own outside of an employer. There are three primary types of IRAs—a Traditional IRA, a Roth IRA, and a SEP IRA. There are many nuances to IRA accounts, including when you can and can't deduct your contributions from your taxes, as well as contribution limits, so check on the guidelines in this book and online.

Inflation—Inflation causes price to go up every year for most staples like housing, transportation, and food, but there are ways to minimize the impact of inflation so you will need less money and you can let your investments keep growing. Inflation is generally caused by supply, demand, production costs, and tax policies. It is country specific, so it can vary dramatically by the strength of a country's currency and its purchasing power. This is why it's more affordable to live in certain countries if you currently live in the United States, where is the dollar is strong compared to other currencies.

Investing—When you invest in something, you expect it to go up in value. While you can invest in anything, I've found stock, bond, and real estate investing to be the most manageable and dependable investments. Investing isn't gambling, and there are ways to minimize the risks, as you'll see in the investing section of this book.

Liabilities—The amount of money you owe, including credit card debt, student loan debt, mortgages, and any other debt you owe. You use your liabilities when calculating your net worth by subtracting your liabilities from our assets.

Mortgage—You can use mortgage loans (i.e., the bank's money) to buy a property, and then the interest on the mortgage is tax deductible, as well as up to $10,000 of your property taxes, both of which add to your real estate investment returns by reducing your taxes.

Mutual funds—Mutual funds are designed for the purpose of simple diversification and hold either a collection of stocks, a collection of bonds, or a mixture of stocks and bonds (known as blended funds). These funds are typically built around a theme or sector—meaning they hold a group of investments of a specific type or within a particular industry. Mutual funds are priced only once a day by the fund insurer and typically have investment minimums.

Net worth—Your net worth is the difference between your assets (that is, things that have value like cash, your home if you own it, and investments) minus your liabilities (that is, any kind of debt). Your net worth is the most important personal finance number for you to track on a regular basis. I track mine daily, and you should, too. Or at least once a week.

Passive income—The holy grail of moneymaking, passive income sources make money that requires little to none of your time. While passive income can take a lot of time to set up, the long-term return is often worth it. Examples of passive income include rental income, blogging income, online course income, and drop-ship income. But stock investing income is the ultimate passive income, since it requires very little setup, and due to compounding, generates increasingly large returns over time. This is the main strategy the wealthy use to both get and stay rich.

Real hourly rate—The amount of money you are actually paid after factoring in the impact of taxes and the additional time (and money) required to do the job, such as getting ready, commuting, and buying clothes for work.

Roth IRA conversion ladder—The Roth IRA conversion ladder is a strategy to eliminate the 10 percent early withdrawal penalty. Any money that been converted from a 401(k) to Traditional IRA to a Roth IRA can be withdrawn without the 10 percent early withdrawal penalty exactly five years after the conversion. If possible, it's best to build your conversion ladder after you retire to minimize the tax implications.

Rule of 72—Divide 72 by your expected compounding rate (7 percent) to determine how many years it would take for your money to double. At 7 percent compounding, 72/7 percent = 10.2 years, so at that compounding rate, your money will double every ten years. Thus if you invest $60,000 instead of spending it on a new car, your money would be worth $120,000 in ten years, $240,000 in twenty years, and so on.

Savings rate—To calculate your savings rate, you want to add up all of the dollars that you save, both in pretax accounts (for example, 401(k)s and IRAs) and after-tax accounts (brokerage) and divide it by your income. Your savings rate is directly correlated to the amount of time it will take you to hit your number. Even a 1 percent or $1 per day increase can make a difference.

Sequence of return risk—After you retire, the first ten years of your investment returns will impact how much your money grows and how long it might last. If you retire and the stock market is down over the next five years, you might want to go back to work to supplement your withdrawals or adjust your living expenses. The goal is to make it through the first five to ten years with your investment principal intact.

Side hustles—Anything you do to make money outside of your full-time job. They often require little time and money to launch and are incredible ways to both make more money to invest and learn new skills. One key to fast tracking financial freedom is side hustling to invest.

Social Security—Social Security provides benefits you can take from the U.S. government starting when you turn sixty-two, but the longer you wait, the more money you get. Even though whenever you get paid through a paycheck, you are contributing to Social Security, it's unclear whether Social Security will still be around or available in thirty plus years.

Stocks—When you buy stock, you are buying a share of ownership in a real company. This means you own a small part of the company. As the company makes money or as people believe the value of that company will go up, the price of the stock can go up. The greater the demand for the stock and the more people believe in it, the higher the price can go. It can also go down if the opposite is true and demand for the stock goes down. Stocks are traded all over the world on many different exchanges (which are basically networks of stocks). Stock values are based on investors' perception of the value of the stock; the price is set based on how much people are willing to buy and sell the stock for.

Taxable account—A taxable investment account is one that doesn't have tax advantages, so you are required to pay taxes on money before you invest it and when you withdraw it. However, if you hold investments for a least one year, they are often taxed at the capital gains tax rate, which tends to be lower than income tax rates.

Tax-advantaged account—A tax-advantaged account is an investment account that helps you to minimize the taxes you pay either when you invest the money, when you withdraw it, or in some limited cases both. Examples include 401(k)s, IRAs, and 403(b)s.

Travel-hacking—Travel-hacking is all about finding the loopholes and using timing, strategic searching, airline reward points, credit card bonuses, and other promotions to reduce or eliminate the cost of travel.

Withdrawal rate—The percentage of your investment portfolio that you withdraw to cover your monthly living expenses. To increase the probability that your money lasts for the rest of your life, a withdrawal rate in the 3 to 4 percent range is typically recommended, although you should always withdraw as little as possible and only when you need the money.

NOTES

000 **70 percent of employees in the United States:** Gallup, Inc., "State of the American Workplace," http://www.gallup.com/services/178514/state-american-workplace .aspx?.

000 **69 percent of Americans:** Cameron Huddleston, "69 percent of Americans Have Less Than $1,000 in Savings," https://www.gobankingrates.com/personal-finance /data-americans-savings/.

000 **Among the 83 million millennials in the United States:** Amelia Josephson, "The Average Salary of a Millennial," https://smartasset.com/retirement/the-average -salary-of-a-millennial.

000 **With an average of $36,000 in student loan debt:** "A Look at the Shocking Student Loan Debt Statistics for 2018," Student Loan Hero, https://studentloanhero.com /student-loan-debt-statistics/.

000 **Millennials under twenty-five are saving:** "How America Saves 2017," Vanguard Group, https://pressroom.vanguard.com/nonindexed/How-America-Saves-2017.pdf.

000 **As of 2016, the median household income:** U.S. Census Bureau, "Median Household Income in the United States," https://www.census.gov/library/visualizations /2017/comm/income-map.html.

000 **48 percent of Americans over fifty-five:** 2017 Retirement Confidence Survey, Employee Benefit Research Institute, https://www.ebri.org/surveys/rcs/2017/.

000 **average American watches 5.4 hours of TV a day:** John Koblin, "How Much Do We Love TV? Let Us Count the Ways," https://www.nytimes.com/2016/07/01/business /media/nielsen-survey-media-viewing.html.

000 **the stock market tends to experience average annual gains:** Bill Barker, "How Have Stocks Fared the Past 50 Years? You'll Be Surprised," https://www.fool.com /investing/general/2016/04/22/how-have-stocks-fared-the-last-50-years-youll-be-s .aspx.

000 **Thirty-two percent of credit card holders:** Jamie Gonzalez and Tamara Holmes, "Credit Card Debt Statistics," https://www.creditcards.com/credit-card-news /credit-card-debt-statistics-1276.php.

000 **Warren Buffett, the world's most successful investor:** Peter Walker, "Multibillionaire Warren Buffett Made $32.2m a Day in 2016 (the Year of Populism)," https://www.independent.co.uk/news/world/americas/warren-buffett-billions-millions-makes-per-day-2016-berkshire-hathaway-donald-trump-gates-foundation -a7500126.html.

NOTES

000 **Americans on average spend roughly 53 minutes:** Christopher Ingraham, "The American Commute Is Worse Today Than It's Ever Been," https://www.washington post.com/news/wonk/wp/2017/02/22/the-american-commute-is-worse-today-than -its-ever-been/.

000 **In 2016 the average American family's before-tax income:** U.S. Bureau of Labor Statistics, Consumer Expenditures 2016, https://www.bls.gov/news.release/cesan .nr0.htm.

000 **the average American household:** Nerdwallet's Americn 2017 Household Credit Card Debt Study, https://www.nerdwallet.com/blog/average-credit-card-debt -household/.

000 **The cost of housing accounts for about 33 percent:** U.S. Bureau of Labor Statistics, Consumer Expenditures 2016, https://www.bls.gov/news.release/cesan.nr0.htm.

000 **over $96 billion in car loans:** Federal Reserve Bank of New York, "Household Debt Surpasses Its Peak Reached During the Recession in 2008," https://www.newyork fed.org/newsevents/news/research/2017/rp170517.

000 **The average monthly new car loan payment:** Peter Gareffa, "Auto Loan Lengths Soar to Record High, Edmunds Finds," https://www.edmunds.com/car-news/auto -industry/auto-loan-lengths-soar-to-record-high-edmunds-finds.html.

000 **the average cost of owning a car:** AAA NewsRoom, "Your Driving Costs," http:// newsroom.aaa.com/auto/your-driving-costs/.

000 **Only about 34 percent of Americans:** Stephen Miller, "Employees Dazed and Con-fused by Benefit Choices," https://www.shrm.org/resourcesandtools/hr-topics/ben efits/pages/open-enroll-benefits-confusion.aspx.

000 **In 2016, 43 percent of the American workforce:** Niraj Chokshi, "Out Of the Office: More People Are Working Remotely, Survey Finds," https://www.nytimes.com /2017/02/15/us/remote-workers-work-from-home.html.

000 **Eighty-nine percent of Americans:** Stephen Miller, "Many Would Rather Find a New Job Than Ask for a Raise," https://www.shrm.org/resourcesandtools/hr-topics /compensation/pages/hesitant-to-request-raise.aspx.

000 **Companies typically use either:** Julie Kantor, "High Turnover Costs Way More Than You Think," https://www.huffingtonpost.com/julie-kantor/high-turnover -costs-way-more-than-you-think_b_9197238.html.

000 **But research shows that self-employed workers:** Olivia Petter, "Self-Employed People Are Happiest Types of Workers, Study Claims," https://www.independent .co.uk/life-style/self-employed-happiest-workers-job-freedom-employees-study -sheffield-a8259206.html.

000 **On October 19, 1987, the U.S. stock market:** http://www.wsj.com/mdc/public/page /2_3024-djia_alltime.html.

000 **90 percent of active investing:** Burton Malkiel, "Index Funds Still Beat 'Active' Port-folio Management," https://www.wsj.com/articles/index-funds-still-beat-active -portfolio-management-1496701157.

000 **appreciated an average of 43 percent:** "Stock Market vs. Real Estate: Which Has Rebounded Better Since the Recession?" Redfin Real-Time, https://www.redfin .com/blog/2016/11/stock-market-vs-real-estate-which-has-rebounded-better-since -the-recession.html.

000 **Some 62.7 percent of the U.S. population:** U.S. Census Bureau, "U.S. Cities Are Home to 62.7 Percent of the U.S. Population but Comprise Just 3.5 Percent of Land Area," https://www.census.gov/newsroom/press-releases/2015/cb15–33.html.

NOTES

000 **Globally 54 percent of the population:** UN Department of Economic and Social Affairs, "World's Population Increasingly Urban with More Than Half Living in Urban Areas," http://www.un.org/en/development/desa/news/population/world -urbanization-prospects-2014.html.

000 **Real estate, by contrast, appreciates between 3 and 5 percent:** Meredith Miller, "What Does 'Normal' Home Value Appreciation Look Like?" Zillow Research, https://www.zillow.com/research/zillow-home-value-appreciation-5235/.

000 **sale price relatively low:** "Stock Market vs. Real Estate: Which Has Rebounded Better Since the Recession?"

000 **Redfin Real-Time,** https://www.redfin.com/blog/2016/11/stock-market-vs-real -estate-which-has-rebounded-better-since-the-recession.html.

000 **If you make $34,000 per year:** Hugo Gye, "America Is the 1 Percent: You Need Just $34,000 Annual Income to Be in the Global Elite . . . and Half the World's Richest People Live in the U.S.," *http://www.dailymail.co.uk/news/article-2082385/We-1— You-need-34k-income-global-elite—half-worlds-richest-live-U-S.html.*

INDEX

TK (hold 8–10pgs)

INDEX

INDEX

INDEX

INDEX

INDEX

INDEX

INDEX

INDEX

INDEX